WILLIAMS-SONOMA

Savoring

Soups & Salads

Best Recipes from the Award-Winning International Cookbooks

GENERAL EDITOR

Chuck Williams

AUTHORS

Georgeanne Brennan · Kerri Conan · Lori de Mori · Abigail Johnson Dodge

Janet Fletcher · Joyce Goldstein · Diane Holuigue · Joyce Jue

Michael McLaughlin · Cynthia Nims · Ray Overton · Jacki Passmore

Julie Sahni · Michele Scicolone · Marilyn Tausend

Oxmoor House ®

CONTENTS

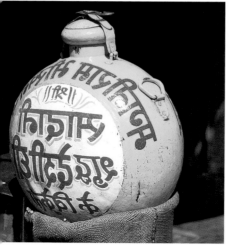

A steaming bowl of soup, a crisp plate of salad—is there any other combination that can suit such a wide range of tastes? Soup can be comforting or festive, a luxurious indulgence or a thrifty way of stretching a handful of the most basic ingredients. Cilantro-scented broths in Mexico and Vietnam, garlicky stews in Portugal and Provence, creamy chowders in America: soup lies at the heart of much of the world's home cooking. Salads, far from being limited to the typical toss of crisp green leaves, are interpreted in hundreds of ways across the globe.

From the warm disk of goat cheese nestled atop baby greens—a French tradition made into a California classic by Berkeley's iconic Chez Panisse restaurant—to the tart, dill-feathered pickled cucumbers brought to the Midwest by generations of German and Scandinavian immigrants, American salads mix bountiful produce with a world of culinary influences. Caesar salad, with its salty-rich dressing of egg yolk, anchovies, and olive oil bathing romaine lettuce under a shower of Parmesan, was invented in Tijuana; it's now on American menus (often with chicken or salmon) from coast to coast. What were once regional soups—New England's clam chowder, Texas's chili—are now found on tables across the country. Whether paired with tiny oyster crackers, a basket of warm rolls, or simply thick slices of homemade bread and butter, a bowl of soup and a salad remain an American favorite for an easy lunch or casual supper.

To the south, a rich chicken broth is the basis for many of Mexico's soups. The best cooks simmer the chicken in water for a very long time with just a few pieces of onion, parsley, or garlic to lend flavor that doesn't overpower the taste of the chicken. But the geographic, historic, and climatic diversity of Mexico's provinces has translated into a wide-ranging culinary repertoire of soups. Chilled avocado soup will cool a sweltering afternoon in Michoacán, while residents of Veracruz often start the day with a bowl of invigorating, chile-rich crab soup. In the highlands, a black bean soup is flavored with smoky chiles and an unusual herb, *xonequi*, that is used nowhere else.

Vegetables, while used widely in the Mexican kitchen, are rarely served as a salad, though an increasing array are now being offered in many restaurants and resorts.

Raw vegetable salads are also rare in China. In Southeast Asia, however, tossed combinations of vegetables, seafood, and meat or chicken are daily staples, dressed with lime juice, sugar, fiery chile, and pungent fish sauce. Asian soups often begin with a meat broth aromatic with star anise, ginger, or cinnamon. Soup is regarded as part of the main meal: a hearty offering like Sichuan hot-and-sour soup or noodle soup might be joined by grilled pork chops over rice. During a Chinese banquet, soup comes to the table between courses to provide textural and flavor contrast. In India, soups often accompany *chat*, the delicious samosas, kabobs, fritters, chips, and crackers that form the repertory of the *chatwalas*, snack vendors found throughout the region.

From shellfish or vegetable-based bisques served to start an elegant meal to crocks of bubbling onion soup brought to the table in a boisterous late-night bistro, soup is an integral part of French cuisine. Shimmering consommés, winey stews, and garlic-laced seafood soups appear again and again on French tables, from urban dining rooms to seaside cafés.

Likewise, no discussion of Provençal cooking is complete without a mention of bouillabaisse, the grand fish soup that can trace its history back twenty-five hundred years to the arrival of the Phocaean Greeks. Its evolution depended on the tastes and provisions of the inhabitants of Marseilles, as sea expeditions brought saffron, fennel, orange peel, and tomatoes to the dish.

Garlic and olive oil add their fragrance to the Italian *zuppe di pesce*, a briny steam of fish and seafood plucked fresh from the Adriatic or the Mediterranean seas. Further inland, a variety of beans, grains, and flours are used to thicken soups flavored with greens, mushrooms, and vegetables. Bread is the backbone of many Italian soups, from summer's *pappa al pomodoro* to winter's hearty *ribollita*. Italian salads rely on tossing whatever is freshest in the market quickly together with olive oil, salt, and a splash of vinegar. The many combinations—fennel and oranges, celery with olives, tomatoes with onion and basil—mix sharp and sweet, crunchy and smooth, salty and mild.

Salads in Spain and Portugal are equally simple, serving as a means to refresh the palate and pique the appetite. Iberian soups range from the sublimely cooling gazpacho to the warming *caldo verde* of Minho, in the far north of Portugal, to the sturdy *cocidos*, or stews, of central Spain.

The recipes on the following pages, drawn from a rich cultural array of culinary traditions from around the world, offer delectable soups and salads to suit every palate and every occasion.

Left: Centuries-old Hacienda Tomozón is now an elegant hotel with stately landscaped grounds and rooms opening onto inviting courtyards. **Above, left:** Sturdy turnips and other vegetables are essential components of the rustic Provençal pantry. **Above, right:** This cabbage is a staple of the nothern Chinese winter diet. It is a common sight to see a household's winter stock of cabbages lining hallways or entrances.

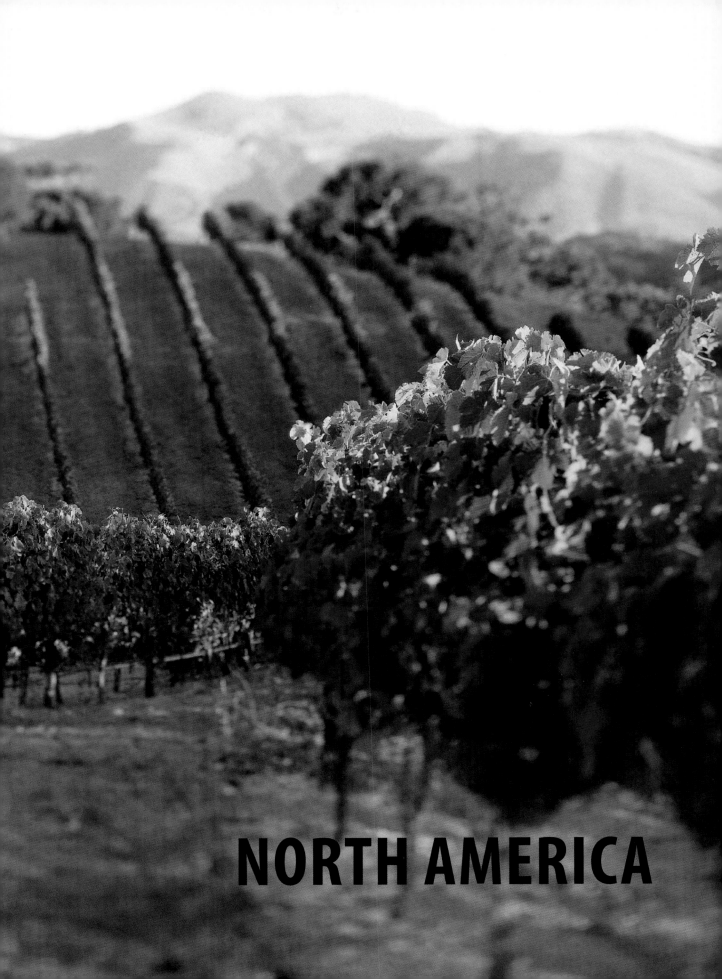

NORTH AMERICA

The crisp, mild wedge of iceberg lettuce that once reigned supreme as the archetypical American salad now has flavorful competition from a host of other greens, from mesclun—the delicate mixed baby lettuces sold in bulk in many markets—to frisée, arugula, escarole, baby spinach, leaf lettuces, cresses, and myriad other salad-bowl choices. For time-pressed shoppers, lettuce packers have developed precut salads—washed, dried, and specially bagged to extend their shelf life. Some of these salads are even packed with a dressing. In better supermarkets, beautifully trimmed romaine hearts tempt many shoppers to prepare their own Caesar salad, certainly one of the most popular restaurant starters across the country.

Preceding pages: Many California wineries offer tours and tastings every day. Top: This seventeenth-century Mexican cathedral at Morelia is a visual feast of pink stone walls, baroque twin towers, and cupolas. Above: Some American farmers specialize in growing heirloom tomatoes. Right: A bountiful selection of greens draws eager shoppers at San Francisco's Ferry Plaza Farmer's Market.

In California, meals often begin with a salad, as befits the residents of a state known as the nation's salad bowl. Creative salad makers top baby leaf lettuces with goat cheese, add crunch with shaved fennel and walnuts, or toss juicy slices of California-grown oranges with farmers' market beets and buttery avocados. Many easterners, with stronger ties to Europe, shrug their shoulders at this behavior; like the French, they generally prefer their greens lightly dressed and served after the main course, to cleanse the palate and pave the way for dessert.

Soups also enhance meals, telling stories of America's immigrant past, reflecting local resources along with the efforts of cooks to transform or stretch what was readily available. Consider the myriad clam chowder recipes, found on menus from coast to coast today but originally associated with New England fishing villages. Challenged to find ways to keep fish palatable to fishermen facing a steady diet of it, coastal cooks made soup, layering fish or shellfish with salt pork, onion, potatoes, milk, black pepper, and sometimes crackers for thickening—the predecessor of today's cream-and-butter-enriched New England clam chowder. The soup then traveled to Washington and Oregon with migrating New Englanders, who adapted the recipe to the local razor clams. Storing well over the winter, New England's hard squashes could be roasted and puréed into delicious soups throughout

the autumn and winter, often sweetened with the addition of a few ripe apples from the orchard.

In the Southwest border states of Texas, Arizona, and New Mexico, cooks make a tortilla soup in the Mexican tradition, a clear broth with shredded chicken and tortillas. In casual Texas restaurants, the opening role that soup often plays elsewhere might go to a cup of thick, meaty chili topped with onion and grated cheese.

In Mexico, soup always seems to be on the table for at least one meal of the day. It may be just a tiny cup of intensely flavored shrimp (prawn) broth to intrigue the appetite, a ladleful of tomato-enriched *caldo* with carrots, rice, and slivers of chicken at the start of dinner, or a bowl so satisfying and nourishing that it is the complete meal. It was the Spaniards who first brought to Mexico the traditional robust soups that utilized the easily obtainable ingredients from different regions of Spain. And while they were able to bring or raise some familiar ingredients with them, to re-create these dishes, native cooks had to improvise. The local chiles, corn, beans, and tomatoes were put to good use, and instead of the much-beloved *cocido* of boiled beef and chickpeas (garbanzo beans), there was *menudo* of hominy and tripe, or *caldo de res*, a rich beef broth with chunks of beef and local vegetables. Pork, a staple of Spanish cuisine, became the basis for Mexican stews studded

with hominy or spiced with smoky chipotle peppers. Tropical plants, like plantains and pineapples, found their way into dishes such as the lentil soup of San Luis Potosí.

A rich chicken broth is the basis for many Mexican soups. Nearly every market has one section given over to chickens, with the biggest and fattest birds hung by their feet over the counter, the plucked bodies golden from a diet of brightly colored marigold petals. Prospective buyers select the right chicken to provide the best soup stock. An old hen is usually preferred, especially if it is complete with eggs. The best cooks simmer the chicken for a very long time with onion, parsley, or garlic before using it as a base for a staggeringly wide range of recipes. One classic, tortilla soup, can be found on the menu of almost every eating place in Mexico. Enlivened with tomatoes and chiles, then poured over tortilla strips and adorned with chiles, cheese, and avocado. A spoonful of *crema* on top is the crowning touch.

Green salads are a fairly recent addition to Mexican cuisine but are rapidly gaining in popularity, especially in restaurants in cosmopolitan areas like Mexico City and the coastal resorts. Often, a Mexican touch is added with a dice of sweet mango or crunchy jicama. Cool combinations of lightly cooked vegetables—tender cactus paddles known as *nopales* or cucumber-like squash called *chayote*—are served both as salads and as accompaniments to grilled meat or fish.

Left: A *rebozo*, or shawl, is perfect for hauling home goods from a Mexican market—or even to carry a young child while shopping. **Above, left:** The paddles of the nopal cactus lend a pleasing texture to salads and salsas throughout Mexico and the American Southwest. **Above, right:** In Mexico, locally raised lettuce is most frequently used as a refreshing garnish, though it is also found in increasingly popular green salads.

Beet, Orange, and Avocado Salad

California • America

In late winter, when California's navel oranges are at their sweetest, Hass avocados are also at their peak. Take advantage of nature's good timing to make a tricolored salad of navel oranges, avocados, and beets.

3 tablespoons extra-virgin olive oil

1 tablespoon sherry vinegar

1 large shallot, very finely minced

1 large clove garlic, very finely minced

Salt and freshly ground pepper to taste

3 red beets, about ¾ lb (375 g) total weight

2 navel oranges or blood oranges

1 ripe but firm avocado

Chopped fresh cilantro (fresh coriander)

Serves 4

1 In a bowl, whisk together the olive oil, vinegar, shallot, garlic, salt, and pepper to make a vinaigrette.

2 Preheat the oven to 400°F (200°C). Remove the beet tops, if attached, leaving ½ inch (12 mm) of the stem. Put the beets in a baking dish and add water to a depth of ¼ inch (6 mm). Cover and bake until a knife pierces the beets easily, about 50 minutes. When they are cool enough to handle, peel and slice into thin wedges. Place in a bowl and add enough of the vinaigrette to coat. Toss gently, then adjust the seasoning. The beets may need additional vinegar.

3 Cut a slice off both ends of each orange so it will stand upright. Stand it on a cutting board and, using a large, sharp knife, cut away the peel and white pith by slicing from top to bottom, following the contour of the fruit. Using a small knife, cut along either side of each segment to free it from the membrane. Put the segments in a bowl and drain off any juice. Add enough vinaigrette to coat the oranges and toss gently. Halve and pit the avocado. Using a large spoon, scoop the flesh from each half in one piece. Put each half cut side down on the cutting board and slice thinly crosswise. Add the slices to the remaining vinaigrette and toss gently with your hands to coat.

4 Choose a rectangular platter. Arrange the avocado slices, orange segments, and beet wedges in separate rows. Garnish with cilantro and serve.

Wild Mushroom Soup

Sopa de Hongos • Puebla • Mexico

During the summer rainy season, wild mushrooms appear in the hills surrounding Anáhuac, the central plateau of Mexico, and can be found in markets at Cholula, a university town.

¼ cup (2 fl oz/60 ml) safflower or canola oil

1 white onion, finely diced

8 cloves garlic, finely diced

4 serrano chiles, seeded and finely diced

3 ripe plum (Roma) tomatoes, peeled and finely diced

2 tablespoons olive oil, or as needed

2 lb (1 kg) fresh wild mushrooms, brushed clean and sliced

2 teaspoons sea salt, plus salt and freshly ground pepper to taste

9 cups (72 fl oz/2.25 l) chicken stock

4 fresh epazote leaves, finely chopped (optional)

Serves 8

1 In a Dutch oven or other large, heavy pot over medium-high heat, warm the safflower or canola oil. Add the onion and sauté until deep gold, about 6 minutes. Add the garlic and chiles and sauté for 1 minute longer. Stir in the tomatoes and simmer, uncovered, until very soft, about 15 minutes.

2 Meanwhile, warm the 2 tablespoons olive oil in a large frying pan over medium-high heat. Add the mushrooms and stir with a wooden spoon to coat evenly with the oil, adding more oil if the pan seems dry. Season with the 2 teaspoons sea salt and cook, stirring occasionally, until the mushrooms release their liquid, about 5 minutes.

3 Add the mushrooms to the onion mixture, pour in the stock, and bring to a simmer over medium-low heat. Add the epazote, if using, and stir well. Adjust the seasoning with salt and pepper and simmer for at least 15–20 minutes to blend the flavors.

4 Ladle the soup into warmed individual bowls and serve at once.

Watercress Salad with Mushrooms

Ensalada de Berros · Guerrero · Mexico

Salads are a recent addition to Mexican cuisine and, with restaurants in Mexico City and resort areas leading the way, are becoming extremely popular. Items such as extra-virgin olive oil and balsamic vinegar from Italy are standard in city supermarkets. A version of this recipe is served at a restaurant high on the cliffside overlooking Zihuatanejo's Playa La Ropa.

2 bunches watercress, about ½ lb (250 g) total weight, tough stems removed

8 fresh white mushrooms, brushed clean, stems removed, and caps thinly sliced

6 slices lean bacon, cut into 1-inch (2.5-cm) pieces

2 tablespoons balsamic vinegar

2 tablespoons extra-virgin olive oil

1 tablespoon corn or canola oil

½ teaspoon Dijon mustard

½ teaspoon sea salt

⅛ teaspoon freshly ground pepper

3 tablespoons sesame seeds, toasted

1 tomato, thinly sliced

Serves 4

1 Tear the watercress into small sprigs and place in a salad bowl. Add the mushrooms and toss lightly to combine. Set aside.

2 In a frying pan over medium heat, fry the bacon until crisp, 3–5 minutes. Using a slotted spoon, transfer the bacon to paper towels to drain. Reserve 1 tablespoon of the bacon fat.

3 In a small bowl, whisk together the vinegar, oils, reserved bacon fat, mustard, salt, and pepper. Taste and adjust the seasoning.

4 When ready to serve, sprinkle the bacon and sesame seeds over the watercress and mushrooms. Toss the salad with just enough dressing to coat the leaves and mushrooms. Scatter the tomato slices over the top and serve.

INGREDIENTS OF MAYAN CUISINE

Many dishes from Campeche, Yucatán, and Quintana Roo, the states that make up the Yucatán Peninsula, are unique. In fact, diners from other parts of the country consider the food an almost foreign cuisine. What makes it so different—some unusual ingredients—will be apparent to anyone who meanders through a local market.

Large stalls display bewildering mounds of seasoning pastes called *recados*. The most common is the brick red *recado rojo*, which includes ground achiote, the hard, red seeds from annatto trees, which is rubbed over pork, chicken, or even fish before pit-roasting and grilling. Each *recado* is made with different spices, and each is used to flavor specific dishes. Although citrus fruits are not indigenous to Mexico, precarious-looking pyramids of squat, aromatic *naranjas agrias* are constructed by Maya vendors. The juice of these bitter, or Seville, oranges is used to dilute the *recados* and is often substituted for

vinegar when pickling chiles and onions. The odd-shaped *lima agria* will be here, too. Its most distinguishing characteristic is the protruding nipple on the blossom end of the green fruit, and its most popular use is in the distinctively flavored soup named for it, *sopa de lima*.

The cooking of this region does not rely on numerous varieties of chile, but the ones used are unfamiliar to most outsiders. Among them are the rather mild, pale yellow or blond chile *x-cat-ik*; a very hot one called, simply, *chile seco*, the dried form of the local *chile verde*; and *chile dulce*, a sweet fresh chile. Finally, there is the habanero, a flavor-rich chile so incendiary that local cooks often just "walk it through the sauce." In recent years, these small green, yellow, and orange lanternlike chiles have become available almost year-round in well-stocked grocery stores outside Mexico, but here they are used only in Yucatecan cooking.

Chicken in Lime-Flavored Broth

Pollo en Lima Agria • Yucatán • Mexico

This dish is typical of the hybrid stews of Yucatán in which grilled meats are served in a seasoned broth enriched with mint, sweet and mild chiles, tomatoes, and bitter lime slices.

8 chicken thighs and half breasts, about 3 lb (1.5 kg) total weight

9 cups (72 fl oz/2.25 l) water

3 fresh oregano sprigs or 1 teaspoon dried oregano, preferably Mexican

Sea salt to taste, plus ½ teaspoon

½ cup (4 oz/125 g) *achiote* paste (page 221)

¾ cup (6 fl oz/180 ml) fresh bitter orange juice (page 226)

2 tablespoons safflower or canola oil

½ white onion, finely chopped

2 red or green bell peppers (capsicums), seeded and finely chopped

1 güero chile or any pale yellow chile, finely diced

4 ripe tomatoes, coarsely chopped

6 limes, sliced

½ cup (¾ oz/20 g) chopped fresh cilantro (fresh coriander)

⅓ cup (½ oz/15 g) chopped fresh mint

¼ teaspoon freshly ground pepper

Pickled red onions (optional)

Serves 8

1 Place the chicken in a large pot, add the water, and bring to a boil over high heat, skimming off any foam that forms on the surface. Add the oregano and salt to taste, reduce the heat to medium-low, and simmer, uncovered, for 20 minutes. Using a slotted spoon, transfer the chicken to a plate and let cool. Let the broth cool, then cover and refrigerate.

2 In a bowl, mix the *achiote* paste with the ½ teaspoon salt. Thin with the orange juice. Place the chicken in a shallow dish and pour the juice mixture over it. Turn the chicken to coat evenly. Cover and refrigerate for at least 6 hours or as long as 12 hours.

3 About 30 minutes before serving time, prepare a medium-hot fire in a charcoal grill. Alternatively, preheat the oven to 400°F (200°C).

4 Meanwhile, remove the chicken from the marinade and blot with paper towels. Lift off and discard the congealed fat from the broth and reheat in a saucepan to a simmer.

5 While the broth is heating, in a frying pan over medium-high heat, warm the oil. Add the onion, bell peppers, and chile and sauté until soft, about 10 minutes. Add the tomatoes and simmer until they break down, about 10 more minutes. Remove from the heat and let cool slightly, then pour the mixture into a blender or food processor and blend until smooth. Pass the purée through a medium-mesh sieve placed over the simmering broth, pressing on the purée with the back of a spoon. Add the lime slices, cilantro, mint, and pepper. Taste and adjust the seasoning. Simmer 10 minutes to blend the flavors.

6 When the coals are ready, place the chicken pieces on the grill rack and grill, turning once, until toasty brown, 5–10 minutes on each side. If cooking in the oven, place on a rack in a large roasting pan and bake, turning once, for about the same amount of time.

7 To serve, place a piece of chicken in each bowl, add some of the broth, and top with pickled onions, if using.

Black Bean and Corn Soup

Caldo Guadiana · Mexico, D.F. · Mexico

Corn, beans, and chiles, the triad of ingredients essential to the Mexican diet, are combined imaginatively in this soup. Consider serving it with crumbled *queso fresco* or *queso añejo* or Parmesan cheese, croutons, chopped serrano chiles or *chiles chipotles en adobo*, diced avocado, white onion, or minced fresh cilantro.

2 tablespoons safflower or canola oil

1 white onion, coarsely chopped

1 clove garlic, coarsely chopped

4 cans (14 oz/440 kg each) black beans

3 cups (24 fl oz/750 ml) chicken stock

1 fresh epazote sprig (optional)

1 cup (6 oz/185 g) fresh or frozen corn kernels

2 scant teaspoons chicken bouillon granules

Sea salt and freshly ground pepper to taste

Serves 6

1 In a large, heavy pot over medium heat, warm the oil. Add the onion and sauté until softened, about 5 minutes. Add the garlic and sauté for 1 minute. Transfer to a food processor or blender and set the pan aside. Rinse and drain the black beans, then add them to the processor and purée until smooth, adding the chicken stock as needed. Pass the puréed beans through a medium-mesh sieve to remove any remaining bits of skin.

2 Warm the oil remaining in the pot over medium heat. Pour the beans into the hot oil and simmer, uncovered, for 2 minutes. Add the epazote, if using, and the corn kernels and season with the bouillon granules, salt, and pepper. Simmer, stirring occasionally until the corn is tender, about 4 minutes. Add a bit more stock, if necessary. Ladle into heated bowls and set out small bowls of condiments (see note) for guests to garnish the soup as desired.

Chilled Avocado Soup

Sopa Fría de Aguacate · Michoacán · Mexico

On hot days, this quickly prepared cold soup, pale green and with the rich but delicate flavor of avocado, is a perfect way to start a meal. Top it with tomato salsa, if you like.

4 cups (32 fl oz/1 l) chicken stock

1 small white onion, quartered

3 peppercorns

4 avocados, preferably Haas

¼ cup (2 fl oz/60 ml) fresh lime juice

1 clove garlic, minced

1 cup (8 fl oz/250 ml) *crema* (page 223)

1 cup (1½ oz/45 g) chopped fresh cilantro (fresh coriander)

½ cup (1 oz/30 g) chopped fresh spinach

2 serrano chiles, chopped

Sea salt to taste

Serves 6

1 Pour the stock into a saucepan and place over medium-high heat. Coarsely chop the onion, reserving about 3 tablespoons. Add the onion and peppercorns to the stock, bring to a boil, and boil until the stock is reduced to 3 cups (24 fl oz/750 ml), about 5 minutes. Strain, discard the solids, and let the stock cool.

2 Cut the avocados in half, remove the pits, and scoop out the pulp into a blender or food processor. Add half of the reduced chicken stock and the lime juice and process until smooth. Pour into a bowl and stir in the remaining stock. Do not rinse the blender.

3 Put the garlic, reserved 3 tablespoons chopped onion, *crema*, cilantro, spinach, and chiles into the unrinsed blender and process until smooth. Stir into the avocado mixture until thoroughly blended. Taste for seasoning and add salt as needed. Cover and refrigerate in the coldest part of the refrigerator. Chill the soup bowls at the same time.

4 Taste the soup and add more salt if necessary. Pour into the bowls, garnish with salsa, if desired, and serve.

Hominy and Tripe Soup

Menudo · Nuevo León · Mexico

Throughout northern and parts of central Mexico, pieces of tripe are simmered in a rich pork broth to become that popular restorative soup called *menudo*. With all of the condiments that are heaped on top, it usually serves as a full meal, traditionally on Sunday, after a night of carousing. In Nuevo León, home cooks season the broth with chiles and then add *pozole* (hominy) for more texture. Serve the soup with lots of hot flour tortillas.

1 Wash the tripe under running cold water and cut into ½-inch (12-mm) squares. Put them into a large pot and add the vinegar and water to cover. Bring to a slow boil over medium-high heat and simmer, uncovered, for 10 minutes. Drain, rinse the tripe, and return to the pot. Add the pig's feet or calf's foot and the 2½ qt (2.5 l) water. If using the freshly prepared *pozole*, add it to the pot. Bring to a boil over medium-high heat, skimming off any foam from the surface. Add the onion, bay leaves, garlic, oregano, and salt. Reduce the heat, cover, and simmer until both the tripe and the pozole are tender, 2–4 hours.

2 While the meat is cooking, drain the ancho chiles, reserving the soaking liquid. Tear the chiles into small pieces and put into a blender along with ½ cup (4 fl oz/125 ml) of the soaking liquid. Blend until smooth, adding more liquid if necessary.

3 In a frying pan over medium-high heat, warm the oil. Pour in the puréed chiles and cook, stirring constantly, for several minutes. Ladle in 1 cup (8 fl oz/250 ml) broth from the simmering meat, reduce the heat, and simmer for 5 minutes. Add the chile sauce to the tripe. If using canned hominy, add it at this time as well.

4 Remove the pig's feet or calf's foot and skim off any excess fat from the surface of the *menudo*. When the pig's feet or calf's foot is cool enough to handle, cut off any meaty pieces and return them to the pot, discarding the bone and cartilage. Continue simmering for another 10–15 minutes to heat through and blend the flavors. The *menudo* is even tastier if prepared several days in advance and refrigerated in a tightly sealed container. When ready to finish, remove any congealed fat and reheat.

5 Ladle the soup into warmed deep bowls. Set out small bowls of the limes, pequín chiles, chopped onions, and 3 tablespoons oregano to pass at the table.

2 lb (1 kg) honeycomb tripe

1 tablespoon cider vinegar

2 pig's feet or 1 calf's foot, split lengthwise

2½ qt (2.5 l) water

1 lb (500 g) packaged freshly prepared *pozole* or 2 cans (14 oz/440 g each) white hominy, rinsed and drained

½ white onion, finely diced

4 bay leaves

3 cloves garlic

1 tablespoon dried oregano, preferably Mexican

1 teaspoon sea salt, or more to taste

3 ancho chiles, seeded and toasted (pages 222–223), then soaked in very hot water for 30 minutes

2 tablespoons safflower or canola oil

CONDIMENTS

6 limes, quartered

¼ cup (¾ oz/20 g) ground pequín chile or 3 serrano chiles, chopped

½ white onion, chopped

3 tablespoons dried oregano, preferably Mexican

Serves 8 generously

GASTRONOMIC TRADITIONS OF MEXICO

Despite the demands of today's world, the traditional sequence of eating meals still predominates throughout Mexico. To break the long night's fast, many Mexicans enjoy a freshly baked sweet roll and a cup of coffee or chocolate for *desayuno*. Many shoppers will make their way to a nearby church, where shawl-wrapped women sell homemade tamales and *atole*, a nourishing corn *masa* gruel.

This sparse meal may come as early as sunup, followed hours later by *almuerzo*, a much heartier breakfast, brunch, or lunch. On Sunday morning, especially in northern Mexico, *menudo*, a comforting tripe soup consumed after a night of alcoholic indulgence, is a staple. In other regions, a different soup may take its place. Yes, eggs are eaten, but however they are cooked, they will have a sauce of chiles, onions, and tomatoes. Juice, fruit, maybe meat, usually beans, and almost always tortillas will be part of an *almuerzo*.

Sensibly, the main, sustaining meal, or *comida*, is served in midafternoon, usually about two-thirty. If possible, the entire family gathers at home to eat. Sunday, especially, is a time when the family assembles for a relaxed midday meal, often at home, but sometimes in a favorite restaurant.

It is best to come to the table hungry. Plates of *antojitos* are served, accompanied with pungent salsas and with beer or tequila to wash them all down. Then a light but tasty soup is presented, often followed by a "dry soup" of rice or pasta. The main course may be fish, stuffed chiles, meat, or, on special occasions, a mole. If beans have not been part of this plate, they will be served on the side in broth. The dessert, a traditional flan, rice pudding, or fruit ice, is followed by coffee and maybe a brandy or an aged tequila. *Merienda*, a snack of *antojitos*, soup, tamales, or leftovers, is eaten before bed. For special occasions, an elaborate *cena*, or late supper, is enjoyed.

Caesar Salad

California · America

Legend has it that the Caesar salad was invented by Caesar Cardini at his restaurant in Tijuana, Mexico, just across the California border. Decades later, it still reigns as one of the most popular restaurant salads, a delightful marriage of crunchy romaine and creamy anchovy dressing. This straightforward version of the original uses hearts of romaine and croutons that are sautéed briefly in olive oil, then baked until crisp. If you are unable to find romaine hearts, buy whole heads and strip away the outer leaves to reach the pale hearts.

1 To make the dressing, in a small bowl, whisk the egg yolk with the warm water to thin it, then whisk in the olive oil, drop by drop. Once an emulsion has formed, gradually add the oil a little faster until all of it has been incorporated and a thick sauce has formed. In a mortar, combine the anchovies, garlic, and salt and pound to a paste. (Alternatively, on a cutting board, mince the anchovies, garlic, and salt to a paste.) Whisk the paste into the dressing. Whisk in the 2 tablespoons lemon juice and season with cracked pepper. Set aside.

2 To make the croutons, preheat the oven to 400°F (200°C). Warm a frying pan over medium-high heat. Add the olive oil and swirl to coat. When the oil is hot, add the bread cubes. Toss quickly to coat the cubes evenly with the oil. Season with salt, then transfer to a baking sheet.

3 Bake the cubes, stirring once or twice, until they are crisp and lightly browned, about 10 minutes. Set aside to cool.

4 Cut the romaine hearts in half lengthwise, then cut crosswise into bite-sized pieces. Transfer them to a salad bowl. Add the dressing and toss to coat the leaves evenly.

5 Add the Parmesan and croutons and toss again. Taste and adjust the seasoning, adding more lemon juice if desired. Serve at once.

DRESSING

1 egg yolk, at room temperature
(see page 223)

1 teaspoon warm water

½ cup (4 fl oz/125 ml) extra-virgin
olive oil

4 anchovy fillets

1 large clove garlic

Large pinch of salt

2 tablespoons fresh lemon juice,
or to taste

Freshly cracked pepper to taste

CROUTONS

1 tablespoon extra-virgin olive oil

2 cups (4 oz/125 g) bread cubes from
day-old coarse country bread
(½-inch/12-mm cubes)

Salt to taste

1 lb (500 g) romaine (cos) hearts

¼ cup (1 oz/30 g) grated
Parmesan cheese

Serves 4

Apple-Butternut Soup

New England · America

Hardy apples and winter squashes are common staples of New England larders. Apple varieties that stored well, like Baldwin and Northern Spy, date back to the 1750s and remain popular today. In the Northeast, the butternut is one of the most favored of the hard-shelled squashes available. It not only has rich, dense, string-free flesh, but it is also one of the easiest winter squashes to handle. Its smooth, thin skin peels with little effort.

6 tablespoons (3 oz/90 g) unsalted butter

1½ lb (750 g) apples (about 4 large), peeled, cored, and chopped

2 yellow onions, chopped

Leaves from 10 fresh thyme sprigs

1 butternut squash, 1¼ lb (625 g), halved, seeded, peeled, and cut into 1-inch (2.5-cm) chunks

6 cups (48 fl oz/1.5 l) chicken stock

Salt and freshly ground pepper to taste

Serves 8

1 In a large saucepan over medium-low heat, melt the butter. Add the apples, onions, and thyme and cook, stirring frequently, until soft and golden brown, about 15 minutes. Add the squash chunks and stir until fragrant, about 2 minutes. Pour in the stock, raise the heat to high, and bring to a boil. Reduce the heat to low and simmer until the squash and apples are very soft, about 25 minutes.

2 Remove from the heat and let cool slightly. Working in batches if necessary, purée the soup in a blender until smooth.

3 Transfer the puréed soup to a clean saucepan and place over medium-low heat. Season generously with salt and pepper and heat to serving temperature. Ladle into warmed bowls and serve at once.

Mushroom and Hominy Soup

Pozole Verde con Hongos • Mexico, D.F. • Mexico

Every region has its own version of *pozole*, but one thing they usually have in common is the use of pork for flavoring. This quick-and-easy alternative uses mushrooms instead.

3 tablespoons canola or peanut oil, or more if needed

1 lb (500 g) fresh white mushrooms, brushed clean and sliced

1 corn tortilla, left out overnight to dry

2 thin slices baguette, left out overnight to dry

7 cups (56 fl oz/1.75 l) water

5 teaspoons chicken bouillon granules

1 lb (500 g) tomatillos, husked, rinsed, and chopped

1 cup (1 oz/30 g) fresh cilantro (fresh coriander) sprigs, loosely packed

3 tablespoons finely chopped white onion

2 cloves garlic, finely chopped

1 serrano chile, finely chopped

3 tablespoons sesame seeds, toasted

3 tablespoons pumpkin seeds, toasted (page 226)

1-inch (2.5-cm) piece true cinnamon bark (page 223)

2 whole cloves

1 fresh epazote sprig (optional)

2 cups (12 oz/375 g) packaged freshly prepared *pozole* or drained canned white hominy, rinsed

Sea salt to taste

CONDIMENTS

1 cup (5 oz/155 g) finely chopped radishes

1 cup (5 oz/155 g) finely chopped white onions

1 cup (3 oz/90 g) shredded cabbage

½ cup (¼ oz/7 g) dried oregano, preferably Mexican

2 serrano chiles, finely chopped (optional)

Serves 6

1 In a cast-iron frying pan over high heat, warm the 3 tablespoons oil. Add the mushrooms and toss and stir until you can smell their earthy aroma, 1–2 minutes. Remove immediately with a slotted spoon. Reduce the heat to medium and fry the tortilla, turning once, until browned, just a few seconds on each side. Using the slotted spoon, transfer the tortilla to paper towels to drain. Pat off any excess oil. If needed, add a little more oil to the pan and reheat, then lay the bread slices in the pan and brown on both sides in the same way. Transfer the bread slices to paper towels. When the tortilla and bread are cool, break into pieces. Set the pan aside.

2 Pour the water into a large pot and bring to a boil over high heat. Add the bouillon granules and, when they have dissolved, add the mushrooms, reduce the heat to medium-low, and simmer, uncovered, until soft, about 5 minutes. Drain the mushrooms, reserving the broth.

3 Working in batches, put the tortilla and bread pieces, tomatillos, cilantro, onion, garlic, serrano chile, and ½ cup (4 fl oz/125 ml) of the broth into a blender or food processor and blend until smooth. Set the pan aside.

4 Reheat the oil in the frying pan over medium-high heat until just starting to smoke, adding more if necessary. Pour in the purée all at once and fry, stirring occasionally, for about 2 minutes. Reduce the heat to medium and simmer, uncovered, until the mixture thickens, about 10 minutes.

5 Meanwhile, put the sesame and pumpkin seeds into a spice grinder and grind very finely. Put the seeds and 2 cups (16 fl oz/500 ml) of the reserved broth into the blender and blend until smooth. Stir into the tomatillo sauce.

6 Return the remaining broth to the pot and bring to a simmer. Place the cinnamon bark, cloves, and epazote (if using) on a piece of cheesecloth (muslin). Bring the corners together, tie with kitchen string, and drop the pouch into the broth. Add the tomatillo-seed sauce and stir in the mushrooms and *pozole* or hominy. Simmer the soup, uncovered, for 10–15 minutes. Season with salt. Remove and discard the pouch before serving.

7 Ladle the soup into warmed bowls. Set out small bowls of the radishes, chopped onions, cabbage, oregano, and serrano chiles to pass at the table.

CHRISTMAS IN MICHOACÁN

On cold, clear December nights in Pátzcuaro, Michoacán, laughter can be heard down many a narrow passageway lined on both sides with *rebozo*-clad men and women cheering on a swarm of children swatting a fruit- and candy-filled piñata. Passersby are welcome to meet the host and his family, who will then immediately offer small earthenware cups of steaming hot chocolate and make room for guests to warm their hands over a squat charcoal-burning stove.

Soon, candles aloft, the celebration becomes part of a *posada*, a procession following a teenage boy and girl reenacting the roles of Joseph and Mary searching for lodging in Bethlehem before the birth of the baby Jesus. At each door along the way, the actors will knock, singing a request for lodging, always to be refused. Finally, when they reach the host's home, the couple will be admitted, and all of the participants are then invited to enjoy warm bowls of delicious *pozole*. This tradition has been held many times over the years and is forever to be associated with Christmas in Michoacán.

Onion Soup with Maytag Croutons

The Midwest • America

For decades, the Maytag family has been based in the small town of Newton, Iowa where they now run a multinational kitchen appliance empire. But at Maytag Dairy Farms, Inc., cheese making has changed little since Fred Maytag II started the business in 1941. The company's cow's milk blue cheese is still aged for six months, twice as long as most other American blues, which deepens the flavor and results in a creamy texture. If Maytag is unavailable, look for another artisanal blue cheese, especially one local to your region.

SOUP

Bouquet garni (page 222)

6–8 red, yellow, white, and sweet onions, in any combination, about 3 lb (1.5 kg) total weight

8 green (spring) onions

3 tablespoons unsalted butter

1 tablespoon olive oil, or as needed

1 large shallot, thinly sliced

1 tablespoon all-purpose (plain) flour

2 teaspoons sugar

1 teaspoon kosher salt or coarse sea salt, plus salt to taste

¼ cup (2 fl oz/60 ml) Cognac

8 cups (64 fl oz/2 l) beef stock or vegetable stock

Freshly ground white pepper to taste

CROUTONS

1 baguette

½ lb (250 g) Maytag Blue cheese, at room temperature

Serves 6–8

1 To make the soup, place the bouquet garni ingredients on a small square of cheesecloth (muslin), bring the corners together, and tie securely with kitchen string. (Alternatively, place the ingredients inside a large tea ball.) Set aside.

2 Cut the bulb onions in half through the stem end and slice crosswise paper-thin. Trim off the green tops from the green onions and reserve. Thinly slice the white portions.

3 In a large, heavy saucepan over medium-high heat, melt the butter with the 1 tablespoon olive oil until almost smoking. Add the sliced onions and shallot and cook, stirring constantly, until they start to wilt, 3–5 minutes. Continue to cook the onions until they begin to color, stirring frequently to loosen any caramelized bits, about 10 minutes. If the onions start to stick, add a drizzle of olive oil.

4 Reduce the heat to medium-low, cover, and sweat the onions, stirring occasionally, until they begin to turn golden, about 30 minutes. Uncover, raise the heat to medium-high, and add the flour, sugar, and 1 teaspoon salt. Cook, stirring constantly, until the onions darken, about 5 minutes. Carefully pour in the Cognac and stir to scrape up any browned bits on the pan bottom. Add the stock and the bouquet garni and bring to a boil. Reduce the heat to low, cover partially, and cook, stirring occasionally, until the soup thickens and the onions break down, about 30 minutes. Season with salt and white pepper. (The soup can be made up to this point and refrigerated for up to 2 days before continuing.)

5 Meanwhile, make the croutons: Preheat an oven to 375°F (190°C). Slice the baguette on the diagonal into ½-inch (12-mm) slices. You should have about 32. Spread on a large baking sheet and toast in the oven for 10 minutes. Turn the slices over and toast until golden on both sides, about 5 minutes longer. Remove from the oven and let the slices cool on the baking sheet until they can be handled. Using about ¼ lb (125 g) of the blue cheese, smear a little on one side of each crouton. Trim away any tough portions of the reserved green onion tops, then thinly slice.

6 When ready to serve the soup, preheat a broiler (grill). Remove the bouquet garni from the soup and discard. Crumble the remaining cheese evenly over the croutons on the baking sheet. Slip the baking sheet under the broiler about 4 inches (10 cm) from the heat source and broil (grill) until the cheese starts to melt and the croutons turn brown around the edges, about 1 minute. Remove the sheet from the broiler, transfer the croutons to a serving plate, and sprinkle with the green onion tops.

7 Ladle the soup into warmed bowls. Top with the croutons and serve.

Ingredients

1 chicken, about 3½ lb (1.75 kg)

3 tablespoons corn oil, plus more for deep-frying

2 tablespoons olive oil

2 large yellow onions, finely chopped

2 carrots, peeled and finely chopped

2 celery stalks, finely chopped

8 cloves garlic, finely chopped

2 teaspoons dried Mexican oregano

3 qt (3 l) water

1 can (14 oz/440 g) whole plum (Roma) tomatoes, drained and chopped

1 teaspoon salt, plus salt to taste

½ teaspoon freshly ground black pepper

6 blue or yellow corn tortillas, or a combination, each 6 inches (15 cm) in diameter

½ lb (250 g) Monterey jack cheese, diced

1 avocado, halved, pitted, peeled, and sliced

4 green (spring) onions, including tender green tops, sliced

½ cup (¾ oz/20 g) finely chopped fresh cilantro (fresh coriander)

2 limes, quartered

Red pepper flakes

Serves 6

Tortilla Soup

The Southwest • America

Easy to make, tortilla soup consists of little more than a rich broth embellished with various garnishes as the diner sees fit. Serve it as the main course for a lunch or light supper, following cheese crisps or guacamole and preceding flan or fresh fruit.

1 Cut the chicken into 5 pieces: 2 breast halves with wings, 2 whole legs, and the back. In a soup pot over medium heat, warm the 3 tablespoons corn oil. Working in batches, fry the chicken pieces until well browned on both sides, 12–14 minutes total. Transfer to a plate. Discard the oil.

2 Return the pot to medium-low heat and add the olive oil. Add the yellow onions, carrots, celery, garlic, and oregano. Cover and cook, stirring occasionally and scraping up any browned bits on the pan bottom, until the vegetables begin to soften, 10–12 minutes. Return the chicken to the pan. Add the water, tomatoes, the 1 teaspoon salt, and the black pepper and bring to a simmer. Cover partially and cook for 20 minutes. Remove the white-meat pieces and reserve. Re-cover partially and simmer for another 20 minutes. Remove the dark-meat pieces and reserve. Re-cover partially and simmer for another 20 minutes. Remove from the heat and strain the broth, discarding the solids. Skim off as much fat from the surface as possible. You should have 2½ qt (2.5 l) broth. Skin the chicken pieces, then pull the meat from the bones and shred it. Add the shredded chicken to the broth.

3 Cut the tortillas in half. Cut each half crosswise into strips ¼ inch (6 mm) wide. Pour corn oil to a depth of 2 inches (5 cm) into a deep, heavy frying pan and heat over medium-high heat. Working in 2 batches, fry the strips, stirring once or twice, until crisp, about 1 minute. Using a slotted spoon, transfer to paper towels to drain. Season lightly with salt.

4 Bring the soup to a simmer. Taste and adjust the seasoning. Divide the cheese and tortilla strips evenly among warmed soup bowls. Put the avocado, green onions, cilantro, limes, and red pepper flakes in separate small bowls and place on the table. Ladle the simmering soup into the soup bowls. Diners garnish their servings as desired.

Pickled Cucumber Salad

Midwest · America

America's summer cucumber choices are growing. Thanks to local farm stands, progressive truck farmers, and a growing interest in gardening, many heirloom varieties are available. Some have strange shapes. Others come in unusual colors and sizes. Nearly all, even the customary "pickling" varieties, benefit from a brief treatment with brine.

¼ cup (2 fl oz/60 ml) safflower oil

3 tablespoons cider vinegar

1 tablespoon water

1 tablespoon sugar

½ teaspoon kosher salt or coarse sea salt

2½–3 lb (1.25–1.5 kg) cucumbers

1 teaspoon chopped fresh dill, or ½ teaspoon dried dill

1 small red onion, cut into paper-thin rings (optional)

Serves 4–6

1 In a small stainless-steel or enameled saucepan over medium-low heat, combine the safflower oil, vinegar, water, sugar, and salt. Heat just until the mixture begins to bubble. Keep warm.

2 If the skins of the cucumbers are waxed or thick, peel them. If you are not peeling the cucumbers, you can score the skins with a citrus zester, if desired. Slice the cucumbers crosswise into pieces about ½ inch (12 mm) thick. Place in a heatproof glass or ceramic bowl. Sprinkle with the dill.

3 Pour the warm dressing over the cucumbers and toss to coat for several seconds. Allow to cool, then cover and refrigerate. Chill for at least 2 hours or for up to 2 days, stirring often. The cucumbers will continue to absorb more flavor, although they will become somewhat more limp.

4 Just before serving, taste and adjust the seasoning. Line individual plates with the onion rings, if using, and top with the cucumbers and dressing.

Poblano Chile Soup

Sopa de Chile Poblano • Puebla • Mexico

The large poblano chile is extremely versatile. It can be stuffed, cut into *rajas* (strips), which are used in a variety of ways, or made into this simple yet elegant traditional soup. The peas lend a brighter green hue to the finished soup.

4 tablespoons (2 oz/60 g) unsalted butter

1 teaspoon safflower or canola oil

4 poblano chiles, roasted, peeled, seeded, and deveined (pages 222–223), then cut into long, narrow strips

1 white onion, chopped

3 cloves garlic, chopped

6 cups (48 fl oz/1.5 l) chicken stock

1 cup (5 oz/155 g) fresh or frozen English peas

Sea salt and freshly ground pepper to taste

½ cup (2½ oz/75 g) blanched almonds, finely ground

5 tablespoons (2½ fl oz/75 ml) *crema* (page 223)

Serves 4–6

1 In a large saucepan over medium heat, melt the butter with the oil. Stir in the chiles, onion, and garlic and sauté, stirring, until well softened, about 3 minutes. Add the chicken stock, peas, salt, and pepper, and simmer, uncovered, to allow the flavors to blend, about 10 minutes. Remove from the heat and let cool slightly.

2 Working in batches, pour the chile mixture into a blender, add the ground almonds, and process until smooth. Taste and adjust the seasoning. Reheat the soup if necessary.

3 Ladle into warmed bowls and garnish with the *crema*. Serve at once.

BLENDERS AND MORTARS

Every Sunday, outside the city of Oaxaca, there is a Zapotec Indian market in Tlacolula so large that it spills through most of the town. The streets are choked with men leading goats past women seated on blankets with carefully constructed pyramids of chiles in front of them, stalls of cassettes with music blaring, and tables spread with medicinal herbs. It is a chaotic wonderland that links past and present.

The clearest evidence of this are the numerous displays of blender parts, which are prominent among the locks, nails, coils of rope, and batteries being hawked. *Licuadoras*, or blenders, are now among the most important cooking utensils in the Mexican kitchen. All but the very poorest or very traditional families consider this time-saving tool essential.

The *molcajete*, the three-legged mortar of dark volcanic rock that has been used throughout the centuries for grinding, is less evident at the market. Of course, the *molcajetes* that most families already have at home seldom need to be replaced, and except for the making of guacamole and salsas and the grinding of small amounts of whole spices and seeds, the blender is now the main workhorse.

Summer Salad

Ensalada de Verano • Mexico, D.F. • Mexico

More and more of the women in Mexico City are serving salads for *comida*, with perhaps some tasty *antojitos* and a bowl of soup. Especially in the summer, tart tomatillos with tangy *chiles chipotles en adobo* make an unusual salad. It is an ideal dish to start a meal.

1 lb (500 g) tomatillos, husked, rinsed, and chopped into ½-inch (12-mm) pieces

½ white onion, finely chopped

3 tablespoons finely chopped fresh cilantro (fresh coriander)

¼ cup (2 fl oz/60 ml) olive oil

1 or 2 *chiles chipotles en adobo*, finely chopped

1 teaspoon brown sugar

Sea salt to taste

1 cup (5 oz/155 g) crumbled *queso añejo*

Tortilla chips

Serves 6

1 In a bowl, toss together the tomatillos, onion, and cilantro.

2 Pour the olive oil into a small bowl, add 1 of the chiles, the brown sugar, and the salt, and whisk vigorously until well blended. Taste and add the other chile, if desired. Remember, the dressing will not taste as potent after it is mixed with the tomatillos.

3 Spoon on enough of the dressing to coat the tomatillos thoroughly. Arrange on a platter and sprinkle with the cheese. The tortilla chips can be served alongside the salad or in a separate bowl.

Cilantro Soup

Sopa de Cilantro • Puebla • Mexico

The bright, distinctive flavor of fresh cilantro is the main component of this light, willow green soup. It is the perfect dish to serve at dinner parties.

2 cups (16 fl oz/500 ml) milk

2 bay leaves

2 tablespoons unsalted butter

1 teaspoon safflower or canola oil

⅓ white onion, coarsely chopped

3 tablespoons all-purpose (plain) flour

2 bunches fresh cilantro (fresh coriander), main stems removed

4 cups (32 fl oz/1 l) chicken stock

¼ teaspoon ground white pepper

Sea salt to taste

½ cup (4 fl oz/125 ml) *crema* (page 223)

1 cup (1 oz/30 g) tortilla strips

¼ lb (125 g) *queso fresco*, crumbled

Serves 6

1 In a saucepan, combine the milk and bay leaves and bring slowly to a gentle boil. Remove from the heat and set aside to cool slightly.

2 In a heavy frying pan over medium heat, melt the butter with the oil. Add the onion and sauté until translucent, about 3 minutes. Add the flour and cook, stirring often, for several minutes until quite thick.

3 Remove the bay leaves from the milk and discard. Gradually add the hot milk to the onion mixture, stirring constantly. Cook over medium heat, continuing to stir, until slightly thickened, about 5 minutes. Remove from the heat and let cool slightly.

4 Working in batches, pour the onion-milk mixture into a blender, add the cilantro, and process until smooth. Pour the purée into a large saucepan and place over medium heat. Gradually stir in the chicken stock, white pepper, and salt and cook, stirring occasionally, for 10 minutes. Stir in the *crema* and simmer only until heated through.

5 Ladle into warmed bowls and sprinkle with the tortilla strips and cheese. Serve at once.

Corn and Black-Eyed Pea Salad

The South • America

Native to Asia, black-eyed peas were likely introduced to the American South from Africa. The field peas were initially grown for animal feed, but in the years after the Civil War, black-eyed peas became a popular and relatively inexpensive protein source for the devastated region. Today, the beige beans, each with a distinctive black "eye," are a pantry staple, used in soups, main dishes, and salads like this starter. If fresh peas are unavailable, use 2 cups (14 oz/440 g) frozen shelled peas in this salad.

2 lb (1 kg) fresh black-eyed peas, shelled

4 cups (32 fl oz/1 l) water

Salt and freshly ground pepper to taste

6 slices bacon, coarsely chopped

1 small red onion, chopped

2 cloves garlic, chopped

Kernels from 1 ear sweet yellow or white corn

⅔ cup (5 fl oz/160 ml) cider vinegar

1 tablespoon sugar

2 plum (Roma) tomatoes

1 cucumber

2 tablespoons fresh lime juice

⅓ cup (3 fl oz/80 ml) extra-virgin olive oil

¼ cup (⅓ oz/10 g) chopped fresh cilantro (fresh coriander)

2 teaspoons ground coriander

About 4 cups (4 oz/125 g) watercress sprigs, tough stems removed (2–3 bunches)

2 green (spring) onions, including tender green tops, finely chopped

Serves 6–8

1 In a saucepan over high heat, combine the black-eyed peas, water, salt, and pepper. Bring to a boil, then reduce the heat to medium. Cover and cook until the peas are tender, 25–30 minutes. Drain and cool under running cold water. Drain again and set aside.

2 In a frying pan over medium heat, fry the bacon, stirring often, until crisp and golden brown, about 10 minutes. Using a slotted spoon, transfer the bacon to absorbent paper towels to drain.

3 Add the red onion, garlic, and corn kernels to the hot drippings in the pan and cook over medium heat until tender, about 5 minutes. Stir in the vinegar and the sugar. Continue cooking until the liquid has reduced by one-third, 3–5 minutes. Using a slotted spoon, transfer the contents of the frying pan to a large bowl.

4 Seed and coarsely chop the tomatoes. Halve the cucumber lengthwise and then peel, seed, and finely dice. Add to the black-eyed peas and season with salt and pepper. Toss to mix well. Add the lime juice and the olive oil to the pan and swirl over medium heat until heated through, about 1 minute. Stir in the cilantro and ground coriander.

5 Divide the watercress among individual plates. Divide the black-eyed pea mixture evenly among the plates. Spoon the hot dressing over the salad, again dividing evenly. Garnish with the green onions and bacon and serve at once.

SOUTHERN PORTS

The South is home to four atmospheric ports, Charleston and Savannah on the Atlantic and Mobile and New Orleans on the Gulf of Mexico. From their earliest days, these lively cities pushed the region to flourish both economically and at the table. Exotic foods and spices were often part of a ship's cargo, and once off-loaded, they were put on trains, steamboats, and horse-drawn wagons and carried to the farthest reaches of the region. Later, with the completion of the Panama Canal, foods from Asia regularly turned up on the same docks.

Sesame seeds, okra, black-eyed peas, sweet potatoes, collard greens, and rice, arriving from the west coast of Africa, influenced the distinctive Low Country cuisine of South Carolina; cinnamon sticks and curry powder from India and olive oil from the Mediterranean found their way into dishes from Louisiana to Georgia; and spices and fruits from the Caribbean expanded the southern cook's dessert pantry. Legend has it that Country Captain, a southern classic that combines chicken and vegetables in a curry sauce and said to have been a favorite of President Franklin Roosevelt's, was introduced to Charleston cooks in the early 1800s by a sea captain who had spent years in Indian ports.

Lentil Soup with Pineapple, Pears, and Plantains

Sopa de Lentejas con Piña, Peras y Plátanos · San Luis Potosí · Mexico

San Luis Potosí, a state best known for the highland gold and silver mines that made it one of seventeenth-century New Spain's richest outposts, also has a small tropical region, La Huasteca, that extends down the slopes of the eastern range of the Sierra Madre. From here, the Spaniards obtained the tropical fruits that, combined with the lentils and pears of their homeland, created this earthy, soul-satisfying soup.

1½ cups (10½ oz/330 g) lentils, preferably brown, well rinsed

8 cups (64 fl oz/2 l) water

1 white onion, stuck with 2 whole cloves

4 cloves garlic, peeled but left whole

1 bay leaf

1 tablespoon olive oil

½ lb (250 g) good-quality chorizo, crumbled

4 ancho chiles, seeded and toasted (pages 222–223)

Boiling water to cover

¾ cup (4½ oz/140 g) drained canned chopped tomatoes

½-inch (12-mm) piece true cinnamon bark, or ½ teaspoon ground cinnamon

1 black-ripe plantain, peeled and cut on the diagonal into slices ¼ inch (6 mm) thick

½ cup (2 oz/60 g) chopped white onion

¼ teaspoon dried oregano, preferably Mexican

Pinch of ground allspice

Sea salt and freshly ground pepper to taste

1 small pear, peeled, cored, and cut into ½-inch (12-mm) cubes

2 fresh pineapple slices, each ½ inch (12 mm) thick, cut into small triangles

2 limes, quartered

Serves 8 as a first course, or 6 as a main course

1 In a large pot, combine the lentils, water, clove-studded onion, garlic, and bay leaf. Bring to a boil over high heat, cover, reduce the heat to medium-low, and simmer gently until the lentils are almost tender, about 30 minutes. Meanwhile, in a frying pan over medium heat, warm the oil. Add the chorizo and brown until it gives off its fat, about 5 minutes. Using a slotted spoon, transfer the chorizo to the lentils. Drain all but 1 tablespoon of fat from the pan, reserving the excess to use later if needed.

2 In a bowl, combine the ancho chiles with boiling water to cover. Let soak until the chiles are soft, about 15 minutes. Drain and put into a blender or food processor with the tomatoes, cinnamon, and 1 cup (8 fl oz/250 ml) of the lentil cooking liquid. Blend until smooth.

3 Reheat the chorizo fat in the frying pan over medium-high heat. Add the plantain slices and fry, turning as needed, until dark brown, 6–8 minutes. Using a slotted spoon, transfer to paper towels to drain. Pour some of the reserved chorizo fat into the pan if needed, add the chopped onion, and sauté over medium heat until softened, about 2 minutes. Pour in the chile mixture and add the oregano, allspice, salt, and pepper. Fry, stirring frequently, until the sauce is thickened, about 5 minutes.

4 Stir the sauce into the lentils and continue to simmer until the lentils are tender, about 15 minutes. The timing will depend on the age and type of lentil used. When tender, stir in the plantain, pear, and pineapple and simmer until the fruit is soft, about 10 minutes longer. Add more water if necessary, although the soup should be thick. Taste and adjust the seasoning.

5 Ladle into warmed large bowls and accompany with the lime wedges. Serve at once.

SOUTHWESTERN CHILES

Found in a range of brilliant colors and in widely varying heat levels, modern chiles are descendants of an ancient vine that originally grew in the Amazon forest. Compared with subtropical Mexico, the arid and sometimes chilly American Southwest relies on only a crucial handful of chile varieties. New Mexico produces the most chiles in the region, particularly in the south, along the Rio Grande, around the village of Hatch, "Chile Capital of the World." Medium-sized or larger, medium-hot or hotter, shiny green New Mexico chile pods, six to eight inches (15–20 cm) long, are the workhorse chiles of the Southwest.

When the harvest reaches its peak in late summer, many native cooks stock their freezers for the coming year. Along the roadsides, in grocery store parking lots, and at farmers' markets, a fragrant smoke rises as cylindrical wire-mesh roasters the size of oil drums turn above propane-fired burners, charring the peels of prime chiles, which are then packed into plastic bags and frozen. Later, the tough peels easily slip off the chiles as they thaw, leaving them ready to be used whole in such dishes as *chiles rellenos*, or chopped and added to everything from green chile sauce to cheeseburgers.

The same chile varieties may also ripen to bright red. As hot as the green, red chiles possess an added and attractive sweetness. They are dried whole and strung in decorative but useful bunches, called *ristras*, or are ground to powder or flaked. Whole dried red chiles must be soaked, puréed, and sieved before using. The resulting crimson paste flavors and colors the sauces and stews that are the heart of southwestern cooking.

Other essential favorites include small, thin serranos and slightly larger and plumper jalapeños, which are mostly used raw, in sauces and salsas, or are pickled. They run from hot to very hot and are found in brilliant green mounds in markets throughout the region. Pungent chipotles from Mexico are popular newcomers to the Southwest. Actually red-ripe jalapeños that have been smoked, chipotles are most useful *en adobo*, that is, canned in a tart, brick red sauce. A few go a long way, creating a fiery flavor that is habit-forming.

Buffalo Chili

The Southwest · America

Of all the exuberantly seasoned "Tex-Mex" dishes eaten throughout Texas, none is more popular than *chile con carne*, or chile with meat.

3 lb (1.5 kg) coarsely ground (minced) buffalo or lean beef, at room temperature

1 tablespoon salt

5 slices thick-cut bacon, about ¼ lb (125 g) total weight, chopped

2 large yellow onions, chopped

8 cloves garlic, chopped

3 jalapeño chiles, chopped

⅓ cup (3 oz/90 g) mild, pure powdered red chile

2 tablespoons ground cumin

1 tablespoon dried oregano, preferably Mexican

1 tablespoon freshly ground black pepper

1 teaspoon ground coriander

½ teaspoon red pepper flakes, or to taste

5 cups (40 fl oz/1.25 l) beef stock

1 can (28 oz/875 g) whole tomatoes, finely chopped, with juice

2 tablespoons cornmeal

2 cans (15 oz/470 g each) black beans, rinsed and drained

CONDIMENTS
Sour cream

Sliced green (spring) onions, including tender green tops

Chopped tomatoes

Shredded Monterey jack cheese

Serves 8–10

1 Place the ground meat in a large frying pan over medium heat and season with the salt. Cook, breaking up any clumps of meat and stirring as needed, until it is uniformly gray, 12–15 minutes.

2 Meanwhile, in a large, nonaluminum pot over medium-low heat, fry the bacon, stirring often, until lightly browned, 8–10 minutes. Add the yellow onions, garlic, and jalapeños, cover, and cook, stirring occasionally without browning, until almost tender and golden, about 10 minutes. Add the powdered red chile, cumin, oregano, black pepper, coriander, and red pepper flakes and cook, stirring constantly, for 2 minutes to blend the flavors. Gradually stir in the stock, then add the finely chopped tomatoes and the meat, including any juices, from the frying pan. Bring to a simmer, cover partially, and cook, stirring the chili occasionally, until it has thickened and the meat is tender, about 2 hours. (At this point, the chili can be completed and served immediately, but it will improve in flavor if cooled, covered, and refrigerated overnight. Reheat the chili to simmering over low heat before proceeding.)

3 Sprinkle the cornmeal over the chili, then stir it in. Stir in the beans and heat through. Taste and adjust the seasoning.

4 Place the sour cream, green onions, chopped tomatoes, and cheese in separate small bowls and place on the table. Spoon the chili into warmed bowls. Diners garnish their servings as desired.

Potato and Meatball Soup

Sopa de Bolitas de Carne y Papas • Tlaxcala • Mexico

Hearty enough to be a meal, this simple *sopa* from Tlaxcala is thick with tasty balls of meat entwined with shreds of potato. Tlaxcala, meaning "land of corn," is situated between Mexico City and Puebla, and it has a fascinating history—without the help of the Tlaxcalans, who were the archenemies of Montezuma, the Spanish would not have defeated the Aztecs. It is also an exquisite colonial city with a very distinctive cuisine.

1 Peel the potatoes and grate them on the medium holes of a handheld grater. Wrap the potatoes in a kitchen towel and squeeze out any liquid. In a bowl, combine the potatoes and meat, tossing and blending them together with the minced onion, salt, pepper, and oregano. When well mixed, add the eggs and mix again. With your hands, roll the meat-and-potato mixture into 1-inch (2.5-cm) balls.

2 Warm a Dutch oven or other large heavy pot over medium heat and add the oil. When it is sizzling hot, working in batches, gently drop in the meatballs and fry until lightly brown on all sides, about 10 minutes. Using a slotted spoon, transfer the meatballs to a plate and set aside.

3 While the meatballs are cooking, put the tomatoes and chopped onion into a blender. Process until smooth, adding a little chicken stock, if needed, to facilitate the blending.

4 Sprinkle the flour into the hot oil remaining in the pot and stir for several minutes over medium heat. Slowly pour in the tomato-onion mixture, drop in the chile, and add the parsley. Continue to cook, stirring occasionally, until the mixture thickens and darkens in color, about 3 minutes. Add the remaining stock and the meatballs and let the soup simmer, uncovered, for 10–15 minutes. Remove the chile and discard. Taste and adjust the seasoning.

5 Ladle into warmed bowls and float the cilantro leaves on the surface. Serve at once.

4 large russet potatoes, about 2 lb (1 kg) total weight

1 lb (500 g) ground (minced) lean pork

1 white onion, 1 half minced and 1 half coarsely chopped

1 teaspoon sea salt, or to taste

1 teaspoon freshly ground pepper

½ teaspoon dried oregano, preferably Mexican

2 eggs, lightly beaten

2 tablespoons safflower or canola oil

1 lb (500 g) ripe tomatoes, chopped, or 1 can (14½ oz/455 g) chopped tomatoes, drained

4 cups (32 fl oz/1 l) chicken stock

1 tablespoon all-purpose (plain) flour

1 jalapeño chile, partially slit open

1 fresh flat-leaf (Italian) parsley sprig, chopped

¼ cup (¼ oz/7 g) fresh cilantro (fresh coriander) leaves

Serves 6

Cheese Soup with Potatoes

Caldo de Queso con Papas • Sonora • Mexico

A classic northern Mexican ranch dish, this rich but simple soup is best when made from the local Sonoran cheeses. When you crave comfort food, there is nothing more satisfying.

2 tablespoons unsalted butter or safflower oil

4 small new potatoes, peeled and cut into ¾-inch (2-cm) cubes

1 white onion, finely chopped

1 clove garlic, minced

2 large, ripe tomatoes, peeled and finely chopped

4 cups (32 fl oz/1 l) beef stock

2 Anaheim chiles, roasted, peeled, seeded, and deveined (pages 222–223), then chopped, or 2 canned mild green chiles, drained and chopped

1 cup (8 fl oz/250 ml) half-and-half (half cream) or milk, slightly warmed

Sea salt and freshly ground pepper to taste

¾ lb (375 g) white Cheddar or Monterey jack cheese, shredded

4 green (spring) onions, including tender green tops, finely diced

Serves 4–6

1 In a Dutch oven or other large, heavy pot over medium heat, melt the butter or warm the oil. Stir in the potatoes and onion and sauté until they begin to soften, 6–8 minutes. Do not allow to brown. Add the garlic and sauté for another minute or so.

2 Raise the heat to medium-high and add the tomatoes. Cook, stirring, until quite thick, about 5 minutes. Pour in the stock and chiles. Simmer, uncovered, until the potatoes are soft but not breaking apart, about 4 minutes. Reduce the heat to very low and add the half-and-half or milk, salt, and pepper. Cook until heated to serving temperature.

3 Divide the cheese evenly among warmed bowls and ladle in the soup. Garnish with the green onions and serve at once.

Spinach Salad

Ensalada de Espinaca • Jalisco • Mexico

This spinach salad is tossed with a delicous rose-colored dressing made from the dried flower calyxes of *jamaica*, or hibiscus flowers. Look for the flowers in health-food stores.

1 cup (8 fl oz/250 ml) water

½ cup (1½ oz/45 g) dried *jamaica* flowers

2 teaspoons sugar, or to taste

½ teaspoon sea salt, or to taste

½ teaspoon freshly ground pepper

¼ cup (2 fl oz/60 ml) extra-virgin olive oil

¼ cup (3 fl oz/90 ml) dark honey

1 cup (8 oz/250 g) amaranth seeds

8 slices lean bacon

4 cups (4 oz/125 g) baby spinach leaves

½ small jicama, peeled and julienned

Serves 4

1 In a saucepan over medium heat, bring the water to a boil with the *jamaica* flowers and maintain a slow boil for 3–5 minutes, stirring frequently. Pour through a medium-mesh sieve into a small bowl. You should have ¼ cup (2 fl oz/60 ml). Whisk in the sugar, salt, and pepper, then whisk in the olive oil in a slow, steady stream. If the *jamaica* liquid is allowed to sit before mixing, it will thicken, but when mixed with the oil, it will return to the correct consistency.

2 In a frying pan over medium heat, warm the honey until the edges bubble. Add the amaranth seeds and stir until they start to stick together, 40–60 seconds. Immediately pour onto a sheet of waxed paper and let cool. If they are still sticking together, rub between your palms to break them apart. Place the bacon in a cold frying pan and fry over medium-low heat until crisp, 6–8 minutes. Drain on paper towels and coarsely crumble.

3 Put the spinach in a bowl with the bacon, stir the dressing well, and add just enough to moisten the leaves. Toss the salad and adjust the seasoning. Divide among individual plates, top with the jicama strips and amaranth seeds, and serve.

THE MARKETS

The narrow, multilevel market in Pochutla may be considered rather ordinary. Located in the second-largest town in Oaxaca, only a few miles from the coast, it has a comparatively meager selection of chiles, fruits, herbs, and vegetables, but for a first-time visitor to a Mexican market, it can be the start of a wondrous adventure.

Shoppers wander by open bags of wine-colored *jamaica*, the dried hibiscus flowers that make such a refreshing drink, as well as bins of bulging tamarind pods and plastic bags of the sticky sweet-and-sour paste stacked nearby. Tiny tomatoes the size of marbles might catch the eye; they are *miltomates*, the wild tomatoes that locals use to make an especially flavorful sauce. Exotic fruits are everywhere, especially the *guanábana* (soursop), a lumpy, warty green fruit with perfumed white flesh, and the *zapote negro*, which looks almost like a nearly rotten fat avocado. Both make sweet *nieves* (sorbets), but the *zapote negro* is best mixed with lime and orange juice.

Handsome women in the crowd who have come up from the Isthmus of Tehuantepec are dressed in vividly colored velvets, satins, and lace; billowing skirts; and heavy gold jewelry. On their heads they carry rush baskets of tiny dried shrimp (prawns), slabs of dried and smoked fish, and all sorts of fresh ocean fish and other sea creatures. Across the street from the market there stands a cluster of colorful men and women, gypsies who sell bundles of dried avocado leaves for flavoring black beans, as well as a tangle of dubious jewels.

Market-goers will often stop to regain their energy at one of the several *fondas* with signs that advertise the *comida corrida*, the daily lunch special. These are the perfect places to sample dishes such as the wonderful *caldo de nopales con camarón*, a tomato-based broth swimming with tiny pink shrimp and squares of green cactus.

There is no better place than a market such as the one in Pochutla to experience firsthand the fundamental vitality of Mexico.

Clam Chowder

New England · America

Northeasterners are opinionated when it comes to chowder. Defining the "authentic" bowl inevitably leads to heated discussions about what ingredients should or should not be included. In general, potatoes, corn, celery, milk or cream, and, of course, clams, are givens. The main point of friction is the tomato. While most New Englanders boast of tomatoes as an important local crop, residents of the upper region—Maine, Vermont, New Hampshire, and Massachusetts—would never dream of putting them in their chowder kettles.

1 Discard any clams that fail to close to the touch. In a heavy soup pot over high heat, combine the clams and the water and bring to a boil. Cook, shaking the pot occasionally, until the clams just begin to open, about 3 minutes. Scoop the clams into a large bowl, discarding any that failed to open; set aside to cool. Pour the remaining liquid through a fine-mesh sieve set over a 4-cup (32–fl oz/1-l) measuring pitcher. Add fish stock or clam juice as needed to make 3 cups (24 fl oz/750 ml). Set aside.

2 Wipe out the soup pot and add the diced pancetta. Place over medium heat and sauté until crisp but not dry, about 5 minutes. Using a slotted spoon, transfer the pancetta to a small bowl and set aside. Add the butter to the pot over medium-low heat and stir until melted and bubbling. Add the leeks and celery and cook, stirring frequently, until the vegetables are tender, about 10 minutes. Add the garlic and thyme and cook until fragrant, about 1 minute. Stir in the potatoes and season with pepper. Pour in the reserved clam liquid and the cream. Bring to a boil over high heat. Reduce the heat to low and simmer gently, uncovered, until the potatoes are just tender when pierced with the tip of a knife, about 10 minutes.

3 Meanwhile, remove the cooled clams from their shells, saving the juices and discarding the shells. Roughly chop the clams and add to the soup. Pour any accumulated juices through a sieve lined with cheesecloth (muslin) and add to the soup. Stir in the reserved pancetta and the corn. Simmer gently until just heated through. Taste the soup and adjust the seasoning with salt and pepper.

4 Ladle into warmed bowls and sprinkle with the chives. Serve at once.

3½ lb (1.75 kg) hard-shelled clams such as littleneck, quahog, or mahogany, scrubbed

¾ cup (6 fl oz/180 ml) water

2 cups (16 fl oz/500 ml) fish stock or bottled clam juice, or as needed

3 oz (90 g) pancetta, sliced ¼ inch (6 mm) thick and diced

2 tablespoons unsalted butter

2 small leeks, including tender green tops, diced (about 1 cup/4 oz/125 g)

2 small celery stalks, thinly sliced

1 clove garlic, minced

1 teaspoon chopped fresh thyme

½ lb (250 g) red potatoes, unpeeled and diced

Freshly ground pepper to taste

1½ cups (12 fl oz/375 ml) heavy (double) cream

1 cup (6 oz/185 g) fresh or frozen corn kernels

Salt to taste

2 tablespoons minced fresh chives

Serves 6

Warm Goat Cheese Salad

California · America

Chez Panisse, the Berkeley, California, restaurant, popularized baked goat cheese salad, which has roots in France. Panfrying the cheese instead of baking it produces a nicely browned coating. Mesclun, a mix of delicate baby greens, makes a refreshing counterpoint.

4 tablespoons (2 fl oz/60 ml) plus 5 teaspoons extra-virgin olive oil

1 tablespoon Champagne vinegar

1 shallot, finely minced

Salt and freshly ground pepper to taste

¼ cup (1 oz/30 g) very fine dried bread crumbs

½ lb (250 g) fresh goat cheese with no rind

6 oz (185 g) mesclun

½ cup (2 oz/60 g) coarsely chopped toasted walnuts

Freshly cracked pepper to taste

Serves 4

1 In a small bowl, whisk together 3 tablespoons of the olive oil with the vinegar, shallot, salt, and pepper to make a vinaigrette. Let stand for 30 minutes.

2 Spread the bread crumbs on a plate. Using a thin-bladed knife, cut the goat cheese into 4 rounds of uniform thickness. Coat each round with 1 teaspoon olive oil. Coat the rounds on all sides with the bread crumbs, patting the crumbs into place.

3 In a large bowl, combine the mesclun and the walnuts. Add enough of the vinaigrette to coat lightly, then toss well. Adjust the seasoning and divide among individual plates.

4 Heat a nonstick frying pan over medium heat. Add the remaining 1 tablespoon plus 1 teaspoon olive oil. When the oil is hot, add the goat cheese rounds. Cook on the first side until nicely browned, 45–60 seconds. Turn and cook until the cheese is quivery to the touch, 45–60 seconds longer. Do not allow it to burn or melt. Transfer the goat cheese to the plates, placing 1 round atop each pile of greens. Sprinkle the cheese with cracked pepper and serve.

Pork and Hominy Soup

Pozole Sinaloense • Sinaloa • Mexico

Pozole refers to both the dish itself and the large corn kernels processed to make hominy. Variations of this rustic soup are found in most regions of Mexico. This red version is a family recipe from the state of Sinaloa.

1 To make the soup, rinse the pig's feet in several changes of water. Place in a large pot and add water to cover. Bring the water to a boil over high heat, reduce the heat to medium, and simmer, uncovered, for 1 hour. Remove the pig's feet and set aside to cool. Reserve the liquid in the pot. With a knife, cut the meat from the feet and add to the broth.

2 Add the soup bones, pork ribs, pork loin, garlic, and onion to the broth and simmer over medium heat. Cover, reduce the heat to medium-low, and cook until the meat is tender, about 2 hours.

3 Meanwhile, in a bowl, cover the ancho chiles with the boiling water and let soak for about 15 minutes.

4 When the meat is tender, remove it from the pot along with the onion and garlic.

5 Squeeze out the garlic from the skin and place in a blender with the onion and the chiles and 1 cup (8 fl oz/250 ml) of their soaking liquid. Blend until smooth, then pour through a medium-mesh sieve and return to the simmering broth.

6 When the meat is cool enough to handle, shred with the grain into large pieces. Discard any fat, bones, and gristle. Add the *pozole*, oregano, and salt and continue to simmer, uncovered, for about 30 minutes longer to blend the flavors. Add boiling water if necessary to keep the meats immersed. Using a large spoon, skim off the fat from the surface.

7 To serve, ladle the *pozole* into warmed bowls. Serve the cabbage, radishes, onions, avocados, and limes in small bowls on the side, to be added to taste.

SOUP

4 pig's feet, cleaned and halved

3 lb (1.5 kg) pork soup bones

1 lb (500 g) country-style pork ribs

2 lb (1 kg) boneless pork loin, cut into large chunks

1 small head garlic, outside papery skin removed, then halved crosswise

1 white onion, peeled but left whole

½ lb (250 g) ancho chiles (12–14), seeded (page 222)

About 4 cups (32 fl oz/1 l) very hot water

3 lb (1.5 kg) packaged freshly prepared *pozole*, or 4 cans (14 oz/440 g each) white hominy, rinsed and drained

1 tablespoon dried oregano, preferably Mexican

Sea salt to taste

Boiling water, if needed

CONDIMENTS

½ head lettuce or cabbage, shredded

20 small radishes, thinly sliced or diced

2 white onions, finely chopped

2 avocados, preferably Hass, pitted, peeled, and cubed

8 limes, halved

Serves 12 generously

POZOLE

Corn—heart, soul, and backbone of the Mexican culinary world—becomes something entirely new when it is transformed into *pozole*, the Mexican word for what is called hominy elsewhere. Fat, meaty kernels of corn are first treated the same as for making tortillas or tamales. But, instead of being ground into *masa*, the kernels are kept gently bubbling on the fire for hours until they are very tender.

What transforms the *pozole* into a hearty and flavorful soup, one with the same name as its principal ingredient can be learned firsthand in Uruapan, Michoacán. Simply stop at an open-air *fonda* crowded with locals to see what makes the kitchen's *pozole* so popular. On the counter are bowls of chopped white onions and red radishes, thinly sliced cabbage, and dried oregano so aromatic that it can be smelled from any spot in the kitchen. When customers are perched on a stool and served a large enamel bowl filled with the fragrant chile-red broth, thick with meat and hominy, they will realize that what makes *pozole* so special is the combination of textures and flavors created when these toppings are stirred into the soup.

Red *pozole* is just one of the several varieties of this colorful soup found throughout central Mexico. In Jalisco, it will be plain white with just pork, hominy, and savory broth. It's a dish that appears rather dull until the condiments are added: a *picante* árbol chile salsa, onions, radishes, and shredded lettuce. In Acapulco and other parts of Guerrero, Thursday is green *pozole* day, and small stands serve only this earthy version, its flavor and color enhanced by ground pumpkin seeds, an assortment of greens, jalapeño chiles, and tangy tomatillos. The locals usually top the soup with pork rinds and avocado, along with chopped onion, cabbage, and pungent dried oregano. A squirt of lime juice is the final touch.

Golden Squash Blossom Cream Soup

Crema de Flor de Calabaza • Jalisco • Mexico

One of the glorious market sights of Mexico's summer rainy season is the profusion of vibrant golden squash blossoms. The delicately flavored flowers are used in elegant crepes and in soups such as this one.

4 tablespoons (2 oz/60 g) unsalted butter

2 poblano chiles, roasted, peeled, seeded, and deveined (pages 222–223), then diced

½ cup (2½ oz/75 g) finely chopped white onion

3 tablespoons all-purpose (plain) flour

1 lb (500 g) large squash blossoms (about 15, depending on size), stems and pistils removed and blossoms coarsely chopped

4 cups (32 fl oz/1 l) milk

3 cups (24 fl oz/750 ml) chicken stock

Sea salt and white pepper to taste

Serves 6

1 In a frying pan over medium-low heat, melt the butter. Add the chiles and sauté lightly until soft, about 3 minutes. Transfer to a plate. Add the onion to the butter remaining in the pan and sauté over medium-low heat until translucent, about 5 minutes. Add the flour and cook, stirring continuously, until lightly golden, about 2 minutes.

2 Set aside a handful of the chopped squash blossoms. Gently stir the remaining blossoms into the onion mixture over low heat and let them sweat, stirring occasionally, for 5 minutes. Pour in the milk and stock and bring to a gentle simmer. Taste and season with salt and white pepper. Cover and keep at a simmer for 10 minutes to blend the flavors. Remove from the heat and let cool slightly.

3 Working in batches, pour the soup into a blender or food processor and process until smooth. Pass the puréed soup through a sieve back into the pan. Gently reheat over medium-low heat.

4 Ladle into warmed bowls, top with the sautéed chiles and reserved blossoms, and serve at once.

Cactus Salad with Chile

Ensalada de Nopalitos con Chile · Tlaxcala · Mexico

Nopales, the paddles of the opuntia cactus, are a favorite vegetable in Mexico. Tlaxcala, the smallest of Mexico's states, seems to have more ways of preparing the cactus than anywhere else in the country: in soups or stews; combined with beans, rice, eggs, or meats; and even grilled whole. It is most commonly found in colorful, crunchy salads. Canned *nopales* are widely available now, but they lack the vitality of the freshly prepared ones.

1 To prepare the *nopales*, use a sharp paring knife or vegetable peeler to scrape off the stickers and their "bumps." Cut off the base end and trim the outer edge. Cut into strips ¼ inch (6 mm) wide, then into pieces about 1 inch (2.5 cm) long.

2 Bring a large saucepan three-fourths full of water to a boil. Add the cactus strips, onion slice, garlic, tomatillo husks or baking soda, and salt. Reduce the heat to medium and cook at a slow boil until tender but still green, 5–10 minutes, depending on the age of the paddles. Drain and quickly place under running cold water to remove the slimy residue and stop the cooking. Remove the onion, the garlic, and the husks, if used, and discard. Shake the cactus strips to remove as much moisture as possible and put in a bowl while they are still warm.

3 To make the salad, add the onion rings, oregano, lime juice, and Worcestershire sauce to the bowl holding the cactus strips. Then add just enough of the olive oil to bind the ingredients. Season with salt and gently mix in the chiles. Allow the salad to stand for at least 10 minutes. (The salad can be prepared several hours in advance and refrigerated. Bring to room temperature before serving.)

4 Just before serving, add the cilantro and tomato and toss to combine. Spoon onto a serving platter or individual plates and top with the avocado slices and crumbled cheese.

NOPALES

7 fresh *nopales*, the smallest available

1 thick slice white onion

2 cloves garlic, peeled but left whole

10 tomatillo husks or 1 teaspoon baking soda (bicarbonate of soda)

1 teaspoon sea salt

SALAD

1 small white onion, sliced into very thin rings

1 teaspoon dried oregano, preferably Mexican

Juice of 1 lime, or 1 tablespoon mild vinegar, or to taste

1 teaspoon Worcestershire sauce

About ¼ cup (2 fl oz/60 ml) olive oil

Sea salt to taste

3 árbol chiles, toasted (pages 222–223) and crumbled

1 cup (1½ oz/45 g) chopped fresh cilantro (fresh coriander)

1 large, ripe tomato, or 4 plum (Roma) tomatoes, finely diced

1 avocado, preferably Hass, pitted, peeled, and sliced

1 cup (5 oz/155 g) crumbled *queso fresco*

Serves 6

CACTUS

The new growth of various species of the prickly pear cactus, or nopal (*Opuntia ficusindica*), is used as a food source throughout the world. But in Mexico it is the historic symbol of the beginning of the Aztec empire.

According to legend, one of the seven tribes of the Chichimecas, nomadic Indians from the north, was instructed by their tribal god to settle wherever an eagle with a snake trapped in its talons was seen perched on a nopal. The sighting occurred at Tenochtitlán, one of two small islands in Lake Texcoco, site of present-day Mexico City. The probable date was AD 1325, and the people who settled there became known as the Aztecs. In the two hundred intervening years before Hernán Cortés arrived, the Aztecs conquered most of what is now Mexico, and today the nopal, their symbol, is depicted on the Mexican flag.

This history, combined with the abundance of the nopal and its culinary attributes—a gentle crunchy texture and a sorrel-sour flavor—make this versatile cactus a common ingredient in Mexican cooking. A favorite way to prepare it comes from Mexico's smallest state, Tlaxcala. Outside the entrance to the Mayan ruins at Cacaxtla, local vendors partially slice the tender paddles, or *nopales*, to resemble the fingers on a hand, brush them with a little oil and lime juice, and grill them over glowing coals. When they are tender and browned, the *nopales* are chopped and wrapped together with a tasty salsa in a blue corn tortilla.

Look for the egg-shaped *tuna*, or prickly pear, the fruit of the nopal cactus. It ranges in color from white, through the spectrum of greens and reds, to the exotic magenta *tuna*, which is prized for its tropical-sweet watermelon-like flavor. One light dessert combines *tunas* with other tropical fruits such as pineapple and is macerated with juice and silver tequila. For Christmas, vendors in Oaxaca sell an *horchata*, or rice drink, that is lifted out of the ordinary by the addition of the puréed *tuna*.

Chicken and Chickpea Soup

Caldo Tlalpeño • Mexico, D.F. • Mexico

The rambunctious flavor of the smoky chipotle chile is tamed in this classic soup by the addition of earthy chickpeas and a buttery rich avocado.

6 cups (48 fl oz/1.5 l) chicken stock

1 whole chicken breast, skinned

1 fresh mint sprig

1 tablespoon safflower or canola oil

½ large white onion, chopped

1 large carrot, peeled and diced

2 cloves garlic, chopped

1 *chile chipotle en adobo*, finely chopped

1 fresh epazote sprig (optional)

½ teaspoon sea salt

½ teaspoon freshly ground pepper

1 can (15 oz/470 g) chickpeas (garbanzo beans), drained and rinsed

1 avocado, preferably Hass, pitted, peeled, and diced

1 lime, cut into 6 wedges

Serves 6

1 In a saucepan over medium heat, bring the stock, chicken, and mint to a simmer and cook, partially covered, until the chicken is opaque throughout, about 15 minutes. Using tongs, lift out the chicken and mint. Discard the mint. Let the chicken cool until it can be handled, then bone the chicken and shred the meat. Set aside. Reserve the broth.

2 In a large saucepan over medium heat, warm the oil. Add the onion and carrot and sauté until the onion is translucent, about 5 minutes. Add the garlic and sauté for 1 minute longer. Pour in the reserved broth and add the chile, epazote (if using), salt, and pepper. Bring to a simmer, cover, and cook for 20 minutes. Stir in the chickpeas and simmer, uncovered, for 10 minutes longer. Add the shredded chicken and heat through.

3 Ladle the soup into warmed bowls, top with the avocado, and pass the lime wedges at the table.

Pork Stew with Chipotle Chiles

Tinga Poblana • Puebla • Mexico

Tinga is a classic regional dish. This tasty concoction of highly seasoned pork is also shredded and used as a topping for tostadas and as a filling for tacos and *tortas*.

2 lb (1 kg) boneless pork shoulder, excess fat removed, cut into 1-inch (2.5-cm) cubes

2 white onions, 1 thinly sliced and 1 finely chopped

6 cloves garlic, 3 whole and 3 chopped

1 teaspoon sea salt, plus salt to taste

2 tablespoons safflower or canola oil

¼ lb (125 g) chorizo, crumbled

1 can (14½ oz/455 g) chopped tomatoes

1 teaspoon dried oregano, preferably Mexican

1 teaspoon dried thyme

3 bay leaves

4 *chiles chipotles en adobo*, chopped

1 teaspoon sugar (optional)

2 firm avocados, preferably Hass, pitted, peeled, and sliced

Serves 8–10, with leftovers

1 In a saucepan, combine the pork, half of the onion slices, and the whole garlic cloves. Add water to cover and the 1 teaspoon salt. Bring to a boil; skim off any foam from the surface. Simmer, uncovered, over medium-low heat until tender, about 1½ hours. Transfer the pork to a bowl.

2 In a frying pan over medium heat, warm the oil. Add the chorizo and fry, stirring often, until just cooked through, about 5 minutes. Add the chopped onion and chopped garlic and sauté for about 5 minutes. Remove any excess oil. Add the pork, tomatoes, oregano, thyme, bay leaves, and chiles. Cook, stirring occasionally, for about 15 minutes, adding up to 1 cup (8 fl oz/250 ml) of the broth to keep the mixture moist. Season with salt and a little sugar, if needed, to mellow the dish.

3 Ladle the stew into bowls and garnish with the avocado and the remaining onion slices.

Cheddar and Ale Soup

Pacific Northwest • America

This easy, flavorful recipe blends the Northwest's beer tradition with that of cheese making, which also goes back more than a hundred years. Two popular Cheddars, Tillamook from Oregon and Cougar Gold from Washington, are ideal for this rich, delicious soup. In their place, use any sharp full-flavored Cheddar. For a vegetarian version, simply replace the chicken stock with vegetable stock. Serve the soup with a crisp salad and a loaf of artisanal bread for a hearty meal. If you like, pour the same ale to drink along with the soup.

3 tablespoons unsalted butter

1 large yellow onion, diced

⅓ cup (2 oz/60 g) all-purpose (plain) flour

2 teaspoons dry mustard

3 cups (24 fl oz/750 ml) chicken stock, or as needed

1 bottle (12 fl oz/375 ml) pale ale

2½ cups (10 oz/315 g) shredded sharp Cheddar cheese

Salt and freshly ground pepper to taste

2 tablespoons chopped fresh chives

Serves 4

1 In a large saucepan over medium heat, melt the butter. Add the onion and sauté until tender and aromatic, 3–5 minutes. Sprinkle the flour and mustard over the onion and stir to coat. Continue cooking, stirring often, until the mixture is quite dry, 2–3 minutes.

2 Pour in the stock, stirring until blended. Cover and simmer until thickened, about 10 minutes. Stir in the ale and then the cheese, and cook, stirring constantly, until the cheese has melted and the soup has a silky texture, 3–5 minutes. Remove from the heat. Working in batches, purée the soup in a blender. Return to the saucepan and reheat over medium heat, adding stock if the soup is too thick. Season with salt and pepper.

3 Ladle the soup into warmed bowls, scatter the chives on top, and serve at once.

NORTHWEST BEER

Since the mid-1800s, when Oregon and Washington welcomed their first breweries, people in the Pacific Northwest have been drinking local beer. The European immigrants who came to the area arrived with brewing skills in their blood and built a thriving brewery scene. Then, in the early 1980s, a new wave of small breweries, committed to high-quality beers, emerged. These operations, which produced fewer than ten thousand barrels annually, were initially called microbreweries, but today the term "craft brewery" is more common, indicating that quality of the beer is more important than production size. Washington and Oregon together are home to some 150 breweries.

At neighborhood brewpubs throughout the region, the house brew is on tap along with beer-friendly fare in a very casual, convivial setting. Bigger breweries, where the aroma of malted barley and hops wafts through the brewing rooms, can be dazzling in their stainless-steel glory. Many breweries offer tours and tastings, allowing visitors to appreciate this age-old craft up close.

Festive Chayote Salad

Ensalada de Chayotes • Veracruz • Mexico

From outside Xalapa, the capital of Veracruz, comes this simple salad of lightly dressed chayote, which recalls the clear flavors of cucumber and zucchini. With the addition of golden corn and bright red tomatoes, it makes a perfect side dish for grilled fish.

1 Place the chayotes in a large saucepan with water to cover generously. Add the salt, bring to a boil over high heat, reduce the heat to medium, and cook until tender but still firm, about 30 minutes. A fork should pierce all the way through a chayote half. If using the ears of corn, add to the pan during the last 5 minutes of cooking. Drain the chayotes and corn. When cool enough to handle, peel the chayotes and cut into ½-inch (12-mm) dice. Cut the kernels off the corn cobs. If using frozen corn kernels, cook in a small amount of boiling water for 2 minutes, then drain well. Place the chayotes, corn, and tomatoes in a bowl and set aside.

2 Place the onion slices in a heatproof bowl and add boiling water to cover. Let soak long enough for the slices to lose some of their crispness but not become limp, 2–3 minutes. Drain the onions well, cover, and refrigerate until cold.

3 To make the dressing, in a bowl, whisk together the canola and olive oils. Whisk in the vinegar and lime juice and then add the oregano, sugar, red pepper flakes, hot-pepper sauce, salt, and black pepper. Taste and adjust the seasoning. Pour ½ cup (4 fl oz/125 ml) of the dressing over the chayotes, tomatoes, and corn and toss gently. (The mixture can be covered and refrigerated for up to 1 day before continuing.)

4 Just before serving, toss the chayote mixture lightly once again. Taste and adjust the seasoning or add more dressing. Scatter the onion rings on top and serve.

3 chayotes, halved and seeded

2 teaspoons salt

3 ears corn, husks and silk removed, or 2 cups (12 oz/375 g) frozen corn kernels

1 lb (500 g) cherry tomatoes, quartered

½ red onion, thinly sliced and separated into rings

Boiling water as needed

DRESSING

¼ cup (2 fl oz/60 ml) canola oil

¼ cup (2 fl oz/60 ml) olive oil

¼ cup (2 fl oz/60 ml) pineapple or other mild vinegar (page 227)

1 tablespoon fresh lime juice

1 teaspoon dried oregano, preferably Mexican

2 teaspoons sugar

1 teaspoon red pepper flakes

3 drops Tabasco or other hot-pepper sauce

½ teaspoon sea salt

Freshly ground black pepper to taste

Serves 6–8

Green Salad with Jicama and Mango

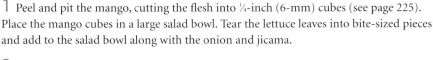

Ensalada de Lechugas con Jícama y Mango • Mexico, D.F. • Mexico

The colorful medley of ingredients in this easy-to-make salad is stunning. The mango, the spectacular color of a summer sunset, offers a sweet-tasting contrast to the crisp, ivory white jicama, the bright flecks of reddish tinted onion, and the many verdant hues of the lettuce greens and buttery Hass avocado.

1 mango

1 head red oak-leaf lettuce, leaves separated

1 head butter (Boston) lettuce, leaves separated

½ red onion, finely diced

½ jicama, cut into thin strips ¼ inch (6 mm) wide by 2 inches (5 cm) long

DRESSING

1 cup (8 fl oz/250 ml) safflower or canola oil

½ cup (4 fl oz/125 ml) olive oil

2½ tablespoons cider vinegar

1 cup (1½ oz/45 g) chopped fresh flat-leaf (Italian) parsley

½ cup (½ oz/15 g) fresh cilantro (fresh coriander) leaves, chopped

1 clove garlic, chopped

1 shallot, chopped

1½ teaspoons honey

1½ teaspoons sea salt, or to taste

¼ teaspoon freshly ground pepper

Small pinch of ground cloves

1 avocado, preferably Hass, pitted, peeled, and sliced

Serves 6

1 Peel and pit the mango, cutting the flesh into ¼-inch (6-mm) cubes (see page 225). Place the mango cubes in a large salad bowl. Tear the lettuce leaves into bite-sized pieces and add to the salad bowl along with the onion and jicama.

2 To make the dressing, in a blender, combine the oils and vinegar. Add the parsley, cilantro, garlic, shallot, honey, salt, pepper, and cloves. Blend until smooth. Pour just enough dressing over the salad to moisten it, then toss to coat evenly. Garnish with the avocado slices and serve.

Heirloom Tomato Salad with Basil Vinaigrette

Mid-Atlantic · America

The rich, loamy soil of Long Island, New York, and New Jersey supports many crops, including plenty of types of tomatoes. Some heirloom varieties are more than a century old, in distinctive and diverse sizes, shapes, colors, and flavors. Most folks are lured to these gems because of their unusual colors and shapes, but it is their flavor that sets them apart.

VINAIGRETTE

½ cup (½ oz/15 g) firmly packed fresh basil leaves

1 small clove garlic

3 tablespoons red wine vinegar

1 tablespoon Dijon mustard

⅔ cup (5 fl oz/160 ml) olive oil

Kosher salt and freshly ground pepper to taste

2 lb (1 kg) mixed heirloom tomatoes

3 large balls fresh mozzarella cheese, about 3 oz (90 g) each, drained

Kosher salt and freshly ground pepper to taste

6 fresh basil sprigs

Serves 6

1 To make the vinaigrette, in a food processor, combine the basil leaves, garlic, vinegar, and mustard. Process briefly to combine. With the machine running, gradually add the olive oil through the feed tube, processing until completely incorporated. Season with salt and pepper. Pour the vinaigrette into a small serving pitcher or bowl, cover, and refrigerate until ready to serve or for up to 2 days.

2 Cut the tomatoes and mozzarella into ¼-inch (6-mm) slices. Arrange the tomato and cheese slices on a chilled large plate or individual plates. Sprinkle with salt and pepper. Drizzle with some of the basil vinaigrette and garnish with the basil sprigs. Pass the remaining vinaigrette at the table.

HEIRLOOM TOMATOES

No one has come up with a solid definition for the heirloom vegetable. Must it have been planted first more than a century ago, or can it simply predate the arrival of hybrids on the scene? The toughest judges are the ones who insist that a true heirloom can never originate from a commercial source.

For these inflexible people, heirlooms must be planted only from seeds handed down through the generations. What everyone can agree on is that heirloom vegetables are increasingly popular. Most home gardeners and small farmers are interested in these old-timers for their flavor, but a handful of garden historians seek them out for what they can reveal about an earlier time.

Tomatoes are arguably the most common of the heirloom vegetables, but watch for the many others worth sampling, such as Early Jersey Wakefield cabbage, which sports mild, crisp leaves in the first weeks of summer, or Early Scarlet Horn carrots, tasty roots that date back to seventeenth-century gardens. Seeds for these and others can be purchased from specialty catalogs. If you lack a garden plot, look for them at roadside stands.

ASIA

*C*hinese soups are a sensation, hot or cold, winter or summer. The thick soups are chunky and full-bodied, the clear soups vibrant. No self-respecting Chinese chef would prepare a soup without using a freshly made stock, rich with the deep flavors drawn from slow, gentle simmering, with ginger for clarity, pork hocks for richness, and in some, the heady perfume of star anise and the salty-smoky savor of local ham.

In a typical Chinese menu, soup comes midway through the main meal as a palate cleanser, although it can also be served as a snack any time of the day. When a host wants to impress guests with a soup made from rare or expensive ingredients, such as shark, abalone, or snake or bamboo fungus, the soup is served first, to be appreciated without distraction. In any Chinese city or village, you will find a restaurant or street stall with a pot of soup at the ready. Soup is sucked noisily from porcelain or metal spoons. To slurp is to show due appreciation that the soup is hot and delicious—and it helps you to avoid burning your tongue.

Salads are generally a foreign concept to the Chinese, who rarely eat raw vegetables. Southeast Asian cooks, however, combine uncooked chopped or pounded vegetables (and sometimes fruits) with chopped or shredded meats, fish, or poultry; a scattering of fresh herbs; finely julienned rhizomes such as ginger; chopped peanuts; and a dressing. Sometimes noodles are tossed in as well. It arrives with all the other dishes and is eaten communally.

Shopping for these vegetable-based dishes in Asia is delightful. Throughout Southeast Asia, outdoor markets teem with people in search of provisions. Shopkeepers painstakingly arrange banana blossoms, ginger buds, clumps of leafy herbs, and bushels of exotic fruits in spiraling circles or towering pyramids. But the most intriguing marketplaces in Southeast Asia are the floating water markets in and around Bangkok. Imagine a market set up in a canal, with each stall a long wooden boat loaded down with produce, fish, shellfish, dry goods, and even a small kitchen.

In Denpasar, Bali's largest city, the market scene is nearly as exotic. Green eggplants, green and mature coconuts, lemongrass, spike-skinned fruits such as rambutan and jackfruit, snake-skinned salaks, papayas, mangoes, mangosteens, passion fruits, varieties of bananas, and grapes are piled in abundant mounds next to Western vegetables introduced by early European explorers. These imports are integral to the local cuisine, as evidenced by the popularity of *gado gado*, a salad of potatoes, cabbage, bean sprouts, beans, and cauliflower dressed with spicy peanut sauce and topped with shrimp chips.

Almost every Southeast Asian market has vendors that hawk freshly pounded salads. The scene is a swirl of activity, and the heat and humidity add to the enjoyment. Indonesian *urap*, a chilled spicy "salad" of bean sprouts, green beans, and toasted coconut, tastes best under the tropical sun.

The Burmese serve dinner with at least two salads, the ingredients for which come from a long list: mangoes and papayas, raw and cooked eggplants, cabbage, daikon, cucumbers, yard-long beans, and chickpeas, as well as chicken, shrimp, pork, fish, and pig's ears, the last mixed with sliced cucumbers and chile sauce. The Vietnamese *dia rau song* is composed of lettuce, carrots, sprouts, and cucumbers with mint, basil, and other herbs. It is often served with grilled or fried dishes.

Today, travelers dining in the restaurants of Southeast Asia will be served their soup at the beginning of a meal. But traditionally, these soups are served in a communal bowl brought to the table with the rest of the meal. In Singapore, a few open-air shops still specialize in *bak kuh teh*, or pork rib tea soup, a specialty of the Chao Zhou people. The soup is made by simmering pork spareribs in a broth with star anise, garlic, cinnamon, and green onions. The ribs are plucked out with chopsticks, dipped into a soy-chile sauce, and eaten with rice. Part of the ritual includes spooning some broth over the rice before eating it and then drinking the remaining broth.

In India, soup is part of the *chat*, or snacks, served round the clock by busy *chatwallas*. For centuries, the *chatwallas* in northern India have served bowls of soup at their stalls in place of tea. In recent years, soups have been carefully paired and served as a soup-and-savory combination. A cup of tomato or mulligatawny soup with a lentil dumpling dunked in yogurt makes a winning combination. In the south, soups are eaten from disposable *katori* (bowls) made of banana leaves, and in the north from small metal containers. Other soups, aromatic with spices and chunky with vegetables and meats, resemble stews and are centerpieces of a meal, surrounded by rice or breads, relishes and chutneys, and the cooling yogurt salads known as *raita*.

Left: A veritable rainbow of umbrellas blooms over the market stalls in Georgetown, on Penang, protecting shoppers, vendors, and goods from the searing Malaysian sun. **Above, left:** Chinese women bundle green onions for the day's customers at a vegetable market in Chengdu. **Above, right:** Individually labeled, fresh laid eggs are stacked in a basket ready for sale in a Beijing stall.

Hot-and-Sour Soup

Suan La Tang • Western • China

This fiery soup, with its ebullient flavors, is on so many Beijing restaurant menus you'd think it was invented in the capital. But Sichuan stakes its claim to the tart and peppery dish, which can be a showcase for exotic ingredients. Less esoteric family versions feature bean curd, egg shreds, chicken, and pork. This thick soup might be served as a one-dish meal or to accompany a dish of grilled pork chops or fried chicken served over rice or noodles.

¼ lb (125 g) boneless chicken breast or pork meat, very thinly sliced, then finely julienned

2 teaspoons light soy sauce

1 teaspoon ginger juice (optional; page 224)

1 cup (7 oz/220 g) cubed soft fresh bean curd (¼-inch/6-mm cubes)

5 dried black mushrooms, soaked in hot water to cover for 25 minutes

2-inch (5-cm) square dried black fungus, soaked in hot water to cover for 25 minutes

3 cups (24 fl oz/750 ml) chicken stock

¼ cup (1 oz/30 g) thinly sliced bamboo shoots

2 tablespoons black vinegar

1 tablespoon dark soy sauce

1 teaspoon peeled and finely grated fresh ginger (optional)

1 tablespoon chile oil

1 teaspoon salt

1 teaspoon freshly ground white pepper

2 tablespoons cornstarch (cornflour) dissolved in ⅓ cup (3 fl oz/80 ml) water

2 oz (60 g) squid bodies (about 2¾ oz/85 g before cleaning, page 227), very thinly sliced

1 egg, lightly beaten

2 teaspoons sesame oil (optional)

2–3 tablespoons chopped green (spring) onion tops or fresh cilantro (fresh coriander)

Serves 4–8

1 In a bowl, combine the chicken or pork, light soy sauce, and the ginger juice, if using, and mix well. Set aside for 10 minutes. In a bowl, combine the bean curd cubes with cold water to cover and set aside.

2 Drain the mushrooms and fungus, reserving 1 cup (8 fl oz/250 ml) of the soaking water. Pour the water through a fine-mesh sieve into a saucepan and set aside. Remove and discard the stems from the mushrooms and the woody parts from the fungus if necessary. Finely slice the mushroom caps and fungus and place in the saucepan holding the reserved soaking water. Add the stock, bamboo shoots, chicken or pork, vinegar, dark soy sauce, ginger (if using), chile oil, salt, and white pepper.

3 Place the pan over medium-high heat and bring just to a boil. Reduce the heat to medium and simmer for 1–2 minutes. Stir in the cornstarch mixture and continue to simmer, stirring slowly, until the soup thickens slightly, about 1½ minutes.

4 Drain the bean curd and add to the soup along with the squid. Cook gently until the bean curd is heated through, about 1 minute.

5 Pour the egg into the soup in a thin, steady stream and immediately remove the pan from the heat. Let stand for about 20 seconds to allow the egg to set in fine strands, then stir lightly.

6 Taste and adjust the seasoning with salt and white pepper. Transfer to a deep serving bowl and add the sesame oil, if using, and the green onion or cilantro. Serve at once.

Clear Soup with Chicken and Spinach

Qing Tang Ji Bocai • Southern • China

This soup exemplifies the duality of yin (light and bland) and yang (dark and flavorful). The addition of aromatic ginger imparts a fresh note of flavor.

2 or 3 whole chicken legs

½-inch (12-mm) piece fresh ginger

6 cups (48 fl oz/1.5 l) chicken stock

2 oz (60 g) chicken breast meat, thinly sliced

1 teaspoon light soy sauce

½ teaspoon rice wine

1½ oz (45 g) young, tender spinach leaves or pea shoots

1 tablespoon peeled and finely grated fresh ginger (optional)

Salt and freshly ground white pepper to taste

Serves 4–6

1 Rinse the chicken legs (drumsticks and thighs) under running cold water. In a saucepan over high heat, combine the chicken legs, ginger, and stock and bring to a boil. Reduce the heat to low and simmer gently, uncovered, skimming the surface as needed to remove any froth, until the chicken is cooked, about 35 minutes.

2 Meanwhile, in a small bowl, combine the sliced chicken breast, soy sauce, and rice wine and let marinate while the stock simmers.

3 When the stock is ready, remove the chicken legs from the pan and reserve for another use. Add the marinated chicken breast to the simmering stock and simmer briefly until cooked through. Using a slotted spoon, lift out the chicken and divide evenly among warmed individual bowls. Divide the spinach leaves or pea shoots and the ginger, if using, among the bowls.

4 Season the stock with salt and pepper, then pour through a fine-mesh sieve into the bowls, dividing it evenly. Serve at once.

Chinese New Year Salad

Yu Sang • Singapore

In China, people do not often eat raw fish or raw vegetables, but Singaporeans do. When this salad is served, it is the custom for everyone to use their chopsticks to help toss it.

¼ lb (125 g) very fresh sashimi-grade tuna, striped bass, or red snapper fillets, wrapped in plastic wrap and placed in the freezer for 1 hour

1 tablespoon fresh lemon juice

1 teaspoon Asian sesame oil

Big pinch of freshly ground white pepper

DRESSING

½ cup (5 oz/155 g) Chinese plum sauce

1 tablespoon sugar, or to taste

¼ teaspoon salt

¼ cup (2 fl oz/60 ml) hot water

2 tablespoons fresh lime juice

SALAD

1 tablespoon sesame seeds

2 cups (8 oz/250 g) finely julienned daikon, squeezed of excess water

2 cups (8 oz/250 g) finely julienned carrot

3 green (spring) onions, white part only, finely shredded into 2-inch (5-cm) lengths

6 kaffir lime leaves, spines removed and leaves shredded into hairlike threads

½ cup (½ oz/15 g) fresh cilantro (fresh coriander) leaves

4 Chinese sweet pickled shallots, thinly sliced

2 tablespoons well-drained, finely shredded pickled tea melons (2 or 3 pickled tea melons)

¼ cup (1½ oz/45 g) well-drained, finely shredded sweet pickled ginger

2 tablespoons finely slivered fresh ginger

1 tablespoon well-drained, finely shredded pickled red ginger

¼ cup (1½ oz/45 g) unsalted roasted peanuts, lightly crushed

Serves 8–10

1 Remove the partially frozen fish from the freezer and cut across the grain into paper-thin slices. Cover and refrigerate. Then, just before serving, combine the fish, lemon juice, sesame oil, and white pepper in a bowl and toss well.

2 To make the dressing, in a bowl, combine the plum sauce, sugar, salt, and hot water. Stir to dissolve the sugar, then stir in the lime juice. Set aside.

3 To assemble the salad, preheat a dry frying pan over medium heat. When the pan is hot, add the sesame seeds and stir frequently until the seeds are light golden brown and begin to pop, 2–3 minutes. Pour onto a small plate and let cool.

4 In a large bowl, toss together the daikon, carrot, green onions, lime leaves, and half of the cilantro leaves. Make a bed of the mixture on a platter. In a bowl, stir together the pickled shallots, tea melons, and the three gingers. Scatter the mixture over the daikon-carrot mixture. Mound the seasoned fish slices in the middle. Top with the peanuts and sesame seeds and then with the remaining cilantro. Pour the dressing evenly over the top.

5 Place the salad in the middle of the table. Have everyone reach in with their chopsticks to help toss the salad.

Green Papaya, Bean, and Carrot Salad

Tom Som • Laos

A green (unripe) papaya or mango is often used as a raw "vegetable" in Southeast Asian salads, as illustrated by this classic Laotian shredded salad.

¼ lb (125 g) yard-long beans or green beans, trimmed and cut into 1-inch (2.5-cm) lengths

1 small green papaya, about 1 lb (500 g), halved, seeded, and peeled

1 carrot, peeled

2 cloves garlic

3 small green serrano chiles

1 firm tomato, cut into thin wedges

2 kaffir lime leaves

2 tablespoons fresh lime juice

1 tablespoon fish sauce

1 tablespoon sugar

1 cup (1 oz/30 g) fresh cilantro (fresh coriander) leaves

½ cup (2½ oz/75 g) chopped unsalted roasted peanuts

Serves 8–10

1 Bring a saucepan three-fourths full of water to a boil. Add the beans, blanch for 1 minute, drain, and rinse under cold running water until cool. Drain again and set aside.

2 With a handheld grater or a Japanese mandoline fitted with the medium blade, shred the papaya into long, fine julienne. Repeat with the carrot.

3 In a mortar, pound together the garlic and chiles to form a coarse paste. Add the beans and bruise them slightly to break down the fiber. Transfer the mixture to a large salad bowl. In small batches, pound the papaya and carrot slivers to bruise them lightly, then add them to the beans. Finally, lightly pound the tomato wedges and add to the bean-papaya mixture.

4 Remove and discard the spines from the kaffir lime leaves, then finely shred the leaves. In a small bowl, stir together the lime juice, fish sauce, and sugar, until the sugar dissolves. Pour over the vegetables and mix thoroughly. Transfer to a serving dish, garnish with the cilantro, shredded lime leaves, and peanuts, and serve.

POUNDED SALADS

On a journey through the floating markets of Thailand, a kind of culinary music orchestrates the trip. It is the melody of vendors—stirring, pounding, cooking—preparing their edible wares for sale. Along the busy waters, the somewhat high-pitched clang of one object striking another can be heard. The source of the sound is a traditional Thai earthenware mortar, which has a deep and narrow bowl, being struck rhythmically with a hardwood pestle. The vendor's light pounding—bruising really—of shredded green papaya, dried shrimp, shallots, garlic, peanuts, fresh mint, and Thai basil tenderizes the stiff ingredients, fusing them together into a salad.

Thailand's waterborne vendors are remarkably astute cooks. They know just how hard and how long to pound, stopping precisely at the moment before a salad turns mushy.

Similar pounded salads using unripe papaya and mango are also popular in Laos, Cambodia, and Vietnam. Cambodian and Laotian cooks mix *prahok*, a creamy preserved fish paste with a flavor as pungent as overripe Brie, with the classic Southeast Asian "vinaigrette" of lime juice, fish sauce, garlic, shallots, and sugar. The Vietnamese version calls for the addition of a little *rau ram*, a pungent herb with pointed leaves and light red stems.

Spicy Chicken Soup

Soto Ayam • Indonesia

In Indonesia, a *soto* is a substantial meat-broth dish, and *soto ayam*, its most popular example, comes in nearly as many versions as there are Indonesian cooks.

SPICE PASTE

8 shallots, quartered

1-inch (2.5-cm) piece fresh ginger, peeled and quartered

5 cloves garlic, quartered

2 slices fresh galangal, peeled and chopped

2 tablespoons coriander seeds, toasted and ground (page 227)

1 tablespoon cumin seeds, toasted and ground (page 227)

1 tablespoon fennel seeds, toasted and ground (page 227)

⅓ cup (3 fl oz/80 ml) vegetable oil

2 lemongrass stalks, tender midsection only, cut into 2-inch (5-cm) lengths and smashed

1 cinnamon stick

2 cardamom pods

3 whole cloves

2 whole star anise

1 small chicken, about 2½ lb (1.25 kg), cut into serving pieces

2½ qt (2.5 l) water

2 teaspoons sugar

1 teaspoon salt, or to taste

Freshly ground white pepper to taste

3 small potatoes, quartered

2 carrots, peeled and cut into 2-inch (5-cm) lengths

ACCOMPANIMENTS

½ lb (250 g) bean sprouts

1 cup (1 oz/30 g) celery leaves

½ cup (½ oz/15 g) fresh cilantro (fresh coriander) leaves

½ cup (1½ oz/45 g) fried shallots (see sidebar, page 82)

Serves 6

1 To make the spice paste, in a blender, combine the shallots, ginger, garlic, and galangal and process to a smooth paste. If necessary, add a little water to facilitate the blending. Add the ground coriander, cumin, and fennel and blend to mix well.

2 In a large saucepan over medium-high heat, warm the oil. Add the spice paste and fry, stirring frequently, until the oil and spices are emulsified and fragrant, about 3 minutes. Add the lemongrass, cinnamon stick, cardamom pods, cloves, and star anise and stir together for 1 minute until fragrant. Add the chicken and the water and bring to a boil. Skim off any foam or other impurities from the surface. When the liquid is clear, reduce the heat to medium-low and simmer, uncovered, for 1 hour.

3 Remove the pan from the heat and, using a slotted spoon, transfer the chicken pieces to a plate. Pour the stock through a fine-mesh sieve placed over a clean saucepan. Using a large spoon, scoop off and discard any fat from the surface. Place the pan over high heat and add the sugar, salt, and white pepper. Bring to a boil, add the potatoes and carrots, reduce the heat to medium, and simmer, uncovered, until the vegetables are tender, about 15 minutes.

4 Meanwhile, hand-shred the chicken meat, discarding the skin and bones, and set the meat aside.

5 To serve, put one-sixth of the shredded chicken, bean sprouts, and celery leaves into 6 soup bowls. Ladle 1½–2 cups (12–16 fl oz/375–500 ml) of the hot stock into each bowl. Garnish with the cilantro leaves and fried shallots and serve at once.

DRIED VEGETABLES

Anyone who has visited India during the monsoon season (April to November, depending on the region) has witnessed the havoc wreaked by the torrential rains. Routine activities such as grocery shopping come to a halt as people retreat to their homes. As one waits for the deluge to end, which could be a few hours, or up to several days, dried vegetables, *sookhida*, replace their fresh counterparts on the menu.

All vegetables, even watery ones such as cucumbers, are dried.

The drying begins in March, at the end of the winter harvest season. During this period it is almost impossible to find even the smallest space around a farmhouse that is not covered with slices of drying cauliflower, eggplant, pumpkin, beet, or okra.

Dried vegetables are rehydrated by briefly soaking them in water just before use. Vegetarians have a particular fondness for *sookhida*—they have a slightly chewy texture similar to that of meat. Anyone who has breathed air still redolent with the aroma of drying cauliflower or green onions will know why many Indians helplessly crave a culinary tradition born of bad weather.

Kari Leaf–Scented Tomato Broth

Rasam • Tamil Nadu • India

Rasam, the spicy, curry-flavored lentil soup of southern India, is the classic creation from the Tamil Nadu state. Tamilians like to add a little rice to the soup, although it is delicious as is.

1 cup (7 oz/220 g) red lentils

4 cups (1½ lb/750 g) chopped tomatoes

2 teaspoons curry powder

6 cups (48 fl oz/1.5 l) water

24 fresh or 48 dried kari leaves (page 225)

1½ teaspoons salt, or to taste

2 tablespoons *usli ghee* (page 224)

1 teaspoon brown mustard seeds

1 teaspoon ground cumin

1 teaspoon minced garlic

Juice of ½ lime

Serves 6–8

1 Pick over the lentils, removing any stones or misshapen or discolored lentils. Rinse thoroughly and place in a deep pot. Add the tomatoes, curry powder, and 4 cups (32 fl oz/1 l) of the water. Bring to a boil over high heat, then reduce the heat to low and simmer, uncovered, until the lentils are soft, about 35 minutes.

2 Remove from the heat and, working in batches, purée the mixture in a food processor or blender. Return the purée to the pot and add the kari leaves, the remaining 2 cups (16 fl oz/500 ml) water, and the salt.

3 In a small frying pan over high heat, warm the *usli ghee* until very hot. Reduce the heat to medium-high, add the mustard seeds, and cover the pan. When the seeds stop making a popping noise, after about 30 seconds, uncover and add the cumin and garlic. Let the mixture sizzle for 5 seconds, then pour the entire contents of the pan over the soup. Stir to combine. Bring the soup to a boil. Stir in the lime juice and taste and adjust the seasoning. Ladle the soup into warmed bowls and serve at once.

Lentil Wafers

Pappadums • Rajasthan • India

Pappadums, or *papads*, are disks of flavored dried beans, rice, or potato that are fried or roasted before serving. A variety of flavors can be purchased at most Indian food markets.

4 store-bought *pappadums*

Peanut or corn oil for deep-frying

Serves 4

1 In a *karhai*, deep-fryer, or large frying pan, pour oil to a depth of 2 inches (5 cm) and heat to 375°F (190°C) on a deep-frying thermometer.

2 When the oil is ready, use tongs to gently slip in 1 wafer, laying it flat in the oil. The wafer will puff, buckle, and turn creamy colored. It will also expand considerably. (All this will happen in 1–3 seconds, therefore one needs to move fast.) As soon as the whole wafer is evenly cream colored, use tongs to transfer it to paper towels to drain. Fry all the wafers in the same way. Serve hot or at room temperature.

Tomato and Yogurt Salad

Takkalipayam Pachadi • Tamil Nadu • India

Pachadi is the southern Indian version of the northern Indian yogurt salad *raita*. This recipe from Tamil Nadu is made with ripe tomatoes, yogurt, and oil infused with mustard seeds. A cool and refreshing side dish, it can also be transformed into a complete meal when served with stuffed bread, a pilaf, or a grain dish.

1½ cups (12 oz/375 g) plain yogurt

½ teaspoon salt, or to taste

¾ lb (12 oz/375 g) cherry tomatoes, halved

1 tablespoon vegetable oil

½ teaspoon brown mustard seeds

½ teaspoon minced garlic

1 fresh hot green chile such as serrano, thinly sliced

8 fresh or 16 dried kari leaves (page 225)

Serves 4

1 In a bowl, combine the yogurt and salt and whisk until smooth. Add the tomatoes, mixing carefully so as not to crush them.

2 In a small frying pan over medium-high heat, warm the oil. When hot, add the mustard seeds and cover the pan. When the seeds stop sputtering, after about 30 seconds, uncover and add the garlic, chile, and kari leaves. Let the spices sizzle for 10 seconds, then pour the entire contents of the pan over the yogurt. Mix well and serve, or cover and refrigerate for up to 3 days.

Fragrant Cauliflower Stew

Gobhi Masala • Madhya Pradesh • India

Every region in India has a version of this dish. Here the cauliflower is braised in coconut sauce with onion, tomatoes, and Moghul spices. Serve the stew with rice and chutney.

1 head cauliflower, about 2 lb (1 kg)

3 tablespoons *usli ghee* (page 224) or vegetable oil

2 cassia leaves (page 222)

1 cinnamon stick

1 teaspoon cumin seeds

1 yellow onion, finely chopped

1 tablespoon peeled and grated fresh ginger

1 tablespoon ground coriander

1½ teaspoons salt

½–1 teaspoon cayenne pepper

2 tomatoes, finely chopped

1 cup (8 fl oz/250 ml) coconut milk or light (single) cream

½ cup (4 fl oz/125 ml) water

1 tablespoon tomato paste

1 boiling potato, peeled and cut into 1-inch (2.5-cm) pieces

1 teaspoon garam masala

½ cup (¾ oz/20 g) chopped fresh cilantro (fresh coriander)

Serves 6

1 Separate the cauliflower into florets and cut them into 2-inch (5-cm) pieces. Peel the stem and cut crosswise into slices ⅛ inch (3 mm) thick. Chop the tender leaves into 2-inch (5-cm) pieces. Set aside until needed.

2 In a large saucepan over medium heat, warm the *usli ghee* or oil. When hot, add the cassia leaves, cinnamon, and cumin seeds and let the spices sizzle for 30 seconds. Add the onion and cook, stirring occasionally, until light brown, about 3 minutes. Stir in the ginger, ground coriander, salt, cayenne to taste, tomatoes, ½ cup (4 fl oz/125 ml) of the coconut milk or cream, the water, and the tomato paste.

3 Add the cauliflower and potato, mix gently, and bring to a boil over high heat. Reduce the heat to low, cover, and cook until the vegetables are tender, 17–18 minutes. Uncover and add the remaining ½ cup (4 fl oz/125 ml) coconut milk or cream, the garam masala, and half of the cilantro. Mix well. Transfer to a warmed serving dish, sprinkle with the remaining cilantro, and serve at once.

Sparerib Soup

Bak Kuh Teh • Singapore

A favorite soup, *bak kuh teh* is a standard at Singaporean hawker stalls. Fried Chinese crullers, called *yu tiao*, can be purchased at Chinese markets.

1 lb (500 g) pork back rib

6 cups (48 fl oz/1.5 l) water

2 cloves garlic, crushed

3 tablespoons dark soy sauce

4 whole star anise

1 cinnamon stick

1½ teaspoons sugar

1 teaspoon *each* white peppercorns and salt

¼ cup (2 fl oz/60 ml) soy sauce

2 fresh red chiles, seeded and sliced

2 Chinese crullers, sliced on the diagonal into slices ½ inch (12 mm) thick

2 tablespoons fried shallots (see sidebar, below)

Hot steamed long-grain white rice

Serves 4

1 Chop the ribs into 1-inch (2.5-cm) lengths. In a 2-qt (2-l) clay pot or saucepan over medium-high heat, combine the ribs and water. Bring to a boil and boil gently for about 3 minutes. Skim off and discard any foam from the surface. Add the garlic, soy sauce, star anise, cinnamon stick, sugar, peppercorns, and salt. Reduce the heat to medium-low and simmer, uncovered, until the pork is tender, about 45 minutes. Using a large spoon, scoop off and discard any fat from the surface.

2 To serve, divide the soy sauce and chiles evenly among 4 dipping saucers. Place the crullers on a plate. Scald 4 soup bowls, then ladle the broth along with 4–6 pieces of pork rib into each bowl. Scatter the fried shallots evenly on top. Serve with the rice.

FRIED SHALLOTS AND GARLIC

A bowl of crispy fried shallot flakes and another of fried garlic flakes are indispensable to the Southeast Asian cook. Indonesians scatter a generous handful of them over spicy *soto ayam* (chicken soup), the Burmese strew them over coconut-milk rice, Indian cooks in Singapore add a dusting to *pilaus* (pilafs), and Thai cooks even add them to sweet dishes. They are always sprinkled on a dish at the last moment and deliver a crunch and an explosion of flavor with the first mouthful.

To make shallot or garlic flakes, slice the cloves into very thin, very uniform slices, then separate the slices. In a small frying pan, pour canola oil to a depth of about 1 inch (2.5 cm), place over medium heat, and heat to 325°F (165°C) on a deep-frying thermometer. Add the slices and fry until they turn light golden brown, about 5 minutes, reducing the heat if they color too quickly. Scoop them out with a slotted spoon, drain on a paper bag, let cool, and store in a jar in a cool cupboard.

Stuffed Crab Soup with Bamboo Shoots

Bakwan Kepiting • Malaysia

Violet Oon, a Nonya who is a popular Singaporean food writer and cooking teacher, makes a very elegant version of this classic Nonya soup. Oon stuffs the shells of small local crabs with shrimp, pork, crabmeat, and cilantro; panfries them; and then serves them in a delicately flavored broth of bamboo shoots and browned garlic bits. Inspired by Oon's dish, this recipe uses either rock crabs or blue crabs. However, if small live crabs are unavailable, you can form the filling into tiny balls and make a tasty crab-ball soup.

3 tablespoons peanut oil or corn oil, or as needed

8 large cloves garlic, finely chopped

6 live rock crabs or hard-shelled blue crabs, each about ¾ lb (375 g)

FILLING

¼ lb (125 g) shrimp (prawns), peeled, deveined, and chopped

6 oz (185 g) ground (minced) pork butt

3 tablespoons finely chopped bamboo shoots

2 tablespoons finely grated carrot

1 green (spring) onion, including 1 inch (2.5 cm) of the tender green top, minced

3 tablespoons chopped fresh cilantro (fresh coriander)

1 egg, lightly beaten

1 tablespoon cornstarch (cornflour)

1 teaspoon light soy sauce

½ teaspoon sugar

¼ teaspoon salt

1½ cups (6 oz/185 g) julienned bamboo shoots

8 cups (64 fl oz/2 l) water or light chicken stock

2 teaspoons light soy sauce, or to taste

2 teaspoons salt

1 teaspoon sugar

Big pinch of freshly ground white pepper, or to taste

Fresh cilantro (fresh coriander) leaves

Fried shallots (see sidebar, page 82)

Serves 6

1 In a small saucepan over medium heat, warm the oil. When it is hot but not smoking, add the garlic and sauté until lightly browned, about 1 minute. Pour through a fine-mesh sieve placed over a small bowl. Transfer the captured garlic to paper towels to drain. Set aside. Reserve the garlic oil.

2 Rinse the crabs with cold water. Bring a large pot three-fourths full of water to a boil. With a pair of long-handled tongs, pick up the crabs and drop them into the water. Boil for 2 minutes, then lift out and rinse under cold water to cool. Working with 1 crab at a time, remove the top shell. Scrub the outside and reserve. Clean the crab (see page 223). Pick out the meat from the body and legs and transfer to a bowl. Set the shells aside.

3 To make the filling, add the shrimp, pork, chopped bamboo shoots, carrot, green onion, chopped cilantro, egg, cornstarch, soy sauce, sugar, salt, and 2 tablespoons of the fried garlic to the crabmeat and mix well. Stuff into the cleaned shells, but do not pack too firmly. Use leftover filling to make meatballs, each ¾ inch (2 cm) in diameter, and set aside.

4 Warm a wide, heavy pot or wok over medium heat and add the reserved garlic oil. When hot, put the stuffed shells, filling side down, into the pot or wok. If they do not fit comfortably, fry in batches. When the bottoms are golden brown, after about 3 minutes, use tongs to transfer the shells to a plate.

5 Add the julienned bamboo shoots to the pot or wok and stir-fry for 1 minute. Return the stuffed shells, filling side up, to the pot or wok in a single layer and add enough water or stock to reach to the tops of the shells, but do not submerge them. (Reserve the remaining liquid to add later.) Bring to a rolling boil over high heat. Reduce the heat so the liquid boils gently and simmer for about 8 minutes. To test for doneness, press down on the filling; it should feel firm to the touch. Again using the tongs, transfer the shells to a plate and keep warm.

6 Add the remaining water or stock to the pot or wok and bring to a boil. Add the reserved meatballs and boil until they float to the surface, 3–5 minutes. Season to taste with soy sauce, salt, sugar, and white pepper.

7 To serve, put 1 stuffed crab shell, filling side up, into each individual shallow soup bowl. Ladle the hot soup, including some bamboo shoots and meatballs, into each bowl. Garnish with cilantro leaves and sprinkle with fried shallots. Serve at once.

GANESHA, THE ELEPHANT GOD

Most Indian households have a ritual altar, known as the family *pujamandapam*. The altar consists of the *kuttivalaku*, the holy lamp; family photographs; a small mat; and a statue of a pudgy figure with a human body and an elephant's head. This is Ganesha, a Hindu god. He is known to love food and sweets (it is no surprise that Ganesha is the god of food). As you might expect, he is fat, with a pot belly. In the Indian ethos, fatness is viewed as a good thing. It signifies abundance and prosperity and often represents an appetite for good living and good cooking.

Statues of Ganesha are most common in home kitchens and by the cash register in restaurants, where they are thought to bring prosperity. Although today prosperity is associated with money, in ancient times it meant more cattle, more land, and therefore more food. Food and prosperity are inextricably linked in the Indian psyche, so Ganesha is worshipped as the provider of both. Good fortune is often attributed to Ganesha's grace, and people offer him food so he will bless them and provide them with more food.

On Ganesha Chaturthi, which falls during the month of Bhadon (corresponding to August or September in the Western calendar), Ganesha is celebrated with great festivities that include the consumption of *modakum*, considered to be one of his favorite sweets. *Modakum*, also known as *modak*, literally means "dumpling," and is similar to the Chinese dim sum. The wheat or rice flour dough is shaped into 2-inch (5-cm) rounds, stuffed with a sweet coconut mixture or with spicy beans, and then steamed.

Hindu children love the tale of Ganesha, whose father, Lord Shiva, one day mistook his son for an intruder and accidentally beheaded him. Ganesha's distraught mother, Parvati, demanded that he be restored, but even the gods could not find all the pieces. After searching the universe for the head of a newborn with the intelligence of a man, Lord Vishnu returned with that of an elephant, and thus Ganesha was reborn with a new identity.

Because of his association with prosperity, Ganesha is revered by the business community. Whenever the stockmarket drops, the statue of him is turned around in every brokerage house to symbolize his unhappiness at not having taken care of his subjects.

Malabar Pumpkin Coconut Stew

Kalan · Kerala · India

A traditional dish of the Namboodaris, Malabar Brahmins of Kerala, *kalan* is a delicately seasoned vegetable stew. The seasoning mixture of chiles, turmeric, mustard seeds, fenugreek, and kari leaves transforms the yogurt-coconut sauce into a sublime dish.

1-lb (500-g) piece pumpkin or 1 small butternut squash, about 1 lb (500 g)

1 zucchini (courgette)

1 cup (4 oz/125 g) firmly packed unsweetened flaked coconut, preferably fresh

4 fresh hot green chiles such as serrano, stemmed

1 teaspoon cumin seeds

1 teaspoon salt

½ cup (4 fl oz/125 ml) water, as needed, plus 1 cup (8 fl oz/250 ml)

1½ cups (12 oz/375 g) plain yogurt, whipped with a fork until smooth

½ teaspoon ground turmeric

½ teaspoon freshly ground black pepper

3 tablespoons coconut oil or canola oil

1 teaspoon brown mustard seeds

1 dried red chile, broken in half and seeds discarded

¼ teaspoon fenugreek seeds

12 fresh or 24 dried kari leaves, finely shredded, plus fresh sprigs for garnish (optional; page 225)

Serves 6

1 If using a piece of pumpkin, peel it, scrape out the seeds, and cut it into 1-inch (2.5-cm) pieces. If using a whole squash, first cut it in half using a kitchen mallet to drive the knife through the tough skin, then proceed as before. Halve the zucchini lengthwise, then cut it into 2-inch (5-cm) pieces.

2 In a food processor or blender, combine the coconut, chiles, cumin seeds, and salt and process until smooth. If necessary, gradually add a little water, but not more than ½ cup (4 fl oz/125 ml). Transfer to a small bowl and stir in the yogurt.

3 In a saucepan over high heat, bring the 1 cup (8 fl oz/250 ml) water to a boil. Stir in the turmeric and pepper, then add the pumpkin and zucchini and mix to coat the vegetables with the turmeric water. Reduce the heat to low, cover, and simmer until the vegetables are soft, about 10 minutes. Add the coconut-yogurt mixture and mix carefully so as not to crush the vegetables. Taste and adjust the seasoning. Remove from the heat.

4 In a small frying pan over high heat, warm the oil. When hot, add the mustard seeds and cover the pan. When the seeds stop sputtering, after about 30 seconds, uncover and add the chile pieces and fenugreek. Cook, stirring, until the fenugreek turns darker brown, about 15 seconds. Remove from the heat. Stir in the kari leaves and pour the entire contents of the pan over the pumpkin. Mix well, taking care not to crush the vegetables. If desired, serve garnished with kari sprigs.

Raw Beef Salad with Lemongrass

Pleah Sach Ko • Cambodia

Raw beef salads are common in Cambodia, Laos, Thailand, and Vietnam. For some salads the beef is thinly sliced, while for others it is finely minced. It is usually mixed with crunchy raw vegetables and a garden of fresh herbs. This Cambodian dressing has a touch of *prahok*, or preserved fish paste. Although optional, it adds depth to the dressing and is a uniquely Cambodian touch. Packed in jars, *prahok* can be found in Southeast Asian markets.

1 lb (500 g) round or rump steak, wrapped in plastic wrap and placed in the freezer for 1 hour

¼ cup (2 fl oz/60 ml) fresh lime juice

2 lemongrass stalks, tender midsection only, very thinly sliced

DRESSING

2 shallots, unpeeled

2 cloves garlic, unpeeled

8 fresh cilantro (fresh coriander) sprigs

1 teaspoon galangal powder

½ cup (4 fl oz/125 ml) fresh lime juice

2–3 tablespoons fish sauce

1 tablespoon *prahok* juice (optional; page 226)

3 tablespoons sugar

¾ cup (4½ oz/140 g) unsalted roasted peanuts, coarsely chopped

2 shallots, very thinly sliced

1 small daikon or jicama, peeled and cut into very thin julienne

2 cups (4 oz/125 g) bean sprouts, brown root tips pinched off

½ red bell pepper (capsicum), cut into fine julienne

½ carrot, peeled and cut into fine julienne

½ cup (½ oz/15 g) small fresh mint leaves

½ cup (½ oz/15 g) small fresh Thai basil leaves

Serves 6

1 Remove the partially frozen beef from the freezer and cut across the grain into paper-thin slices. In a bowl, combine the beef with the lime juice and lemongrass. Set aside to marinate and "cook" for 30 minutes.

2 Meanwhile, to make the dressing, preheat a broiler (grill). Place the shallots and garlic cloves on a baking sheet and slip under the broiler 3–4 inches (7.5–10 cm) from the heat source. Broil (grill) the shallots and garlic, turning as necessary, until evenly charred on all sides, 3–5 minutes. Remove from the broiler, let cool, and remove the skins.

3 Strip the leaves from the cilantro stems and set the leaves aside to use for the garnish. In a mortar, combine the shallots, garlic cloves, cilantro stems, and galangal powder and pound together to form a paste. Transfer the pounded mixture to a bowl. Add the lime juice, fish sauce to taste, the *prahok* juice (if using), the sugar, and half of the peanuts.

4 Using your hands, squeeze the beef of excess liquid. You can reserve these juices, if desired, and stir them into the dressing. In a large bowl, toss together the beef, sliced shallots, daikon or jicama, bean sprouts, bell pepper, carrot, mint leaves, and basil leaves. Add the dressing and toss well.

5 Transfer the salad to a serving platter and garnish with the remaining peanuts and reserved cilantro leaves. Serve at once.

Chopped Winged Bean Salad

Yam Tua Poo • Thailand

All the ingredients in this salad must be chopped into small, uniform pieces, as size is important to the overall flavor and texture of the dish. The salad is traditionally made with winged beans, a popular Thai bean with four lengthwise ribs. When cut crosswise, the pieces look like they have wings, thus the name. Yard-long beans, sometimes called Chinese long beans, or regular green beans may be substituted.

1 tablespoon salt

1 boneless, skinless chicken breast, about 6 oz (185 g)

½ lb (250 g) winged beans, yard-long beans, or green beans, trimmed

¼ cup (1 oz/30 g) unsweetened grated dried coconut

1 red jalapeño chile, seeded and thinly sliced

DRESSING

⅓ cup (3 fl oz/80 ml) coconut cream (page 223)

2 teaspoons roasted chile paste (page 222)

2 tablespoons fresh lime juice

1 tablespoon fish sauce

1 tablespoon sugar

2 tablespoons fried shallots (see sidebar, page 82)

1½ tablespoons fried garlic (see sidebar, page 82)

3 tablespoons unsalted roasted peanuts, crushed

Coconut cream for garnish (optional)

Serves 4–6

1 Bring a small saucepan three-fourths full of water to a boil. Add ½ tablespoon of the salt and the chicken and bring to a second boil. Reduce the heat to medium-low, cover, and simmer the chicken until it is cooked through, about 10 minutes. Remove the chicken from the pan and discard the cooking liquid. Let cool, then cut into ¼-inch (6-mm) pieces.

2 Bring a large saucepan three-fourths full of water to a boil. If using yard-long beans, cut into 6-inch (15-cm) lengths. Add the remaining ½ tablespoon salt and the beans and boil until tender but still very crisp, about 1 minute. Lift out with a wire skimmer and rinse well under running cold water to stop the cooking. Cut the beans into ¼-inch (6-mm) pieces and set aside.

3 In a dry frying pan over medium heat, toast the coconut, stirring occasionally, until it turns a light golden brown, 1–2 minutes. Pour onto a plate and let cool. Set aside.

4 In a large bowl, combine the cooled chicken, green beans, and chile. (The salad can be made up to this point and refrigerated, covered, until ready to continue.)

5 To make the dressing, put the coconut cream into a bowl. Stir in the roasted chile paste, lime juice, fish sauce, and sugar, mixing until the sugar dissolves.

6 Add the dressing to the chicken-bean mixture and toss to mix well. Sprinkle with the toasted coconut, fried shallots, fried garlic, and peanuts. Toss once or twice to mix.

7 Turn out onto a serving platter. Garnish with coconut cream, if desired, and serve.

Fragrant Spinach Soup with Cumin-Scented Potato Croutons

Palak Shorva · Delhi · India

This soup can be made with many types of greens, including Swiss chard, purslane, and regular or red spinach. Rinse them thoroughly to remove any grit.

2 lb (1 kg) fresh spinach or other leafy greens (see note), or 2 packages (10 oz/310 g each) frozen spinach

1 boiling potato, peeled and chopped

1 yellow onion, chopped

1 large clove garlic, chopped

2 teaspoons ground coriander

5 cups (40 fl oz/1.25 l) chicken stock

¾ teaspoon freshly ground pepper

Salt to taste

POTATO CROUTONS

3 tablespoons *usli ghee* (page 224) or olive oil

1½ cups (7½ oz/235 g) finely diced potato

1½ teaspoons ground cumin

Salt to taste

Lemon wedges (optional)

Serves 6

1 Remove the stems from the spinach and discard. If you are using frozen spinach, thaw it thoroughly, then separate the leaves and remove and discard the stems. Set the spinach leaves aside.

2 In a large saucepan, combine the potato, onion, garlic, ground coriander, and stock and bring to a boil over high heat. Reduce the heat to low, cover, and simmer until the vegetables are very soft, about 30 minutes.

3 Stir in the spinach, a portion at a time, so that the leaves quickly come in contact with the hot liquid and wilt. Cook until the spinach is heated through, about 2 minutes. Remove from the heat and, working in batches, purée in a food processor or blender until smooth. Return the soup to the pan. Stir in the pepper and salt and warm the soup until piping hot. Simmer gently while you make the potato croutons.

4 To make the potato croutons, in a large frying pan over medium-high heat, warm the *usli ghee* or olive oil. Add the potatoes and sauté, tossing, until cooked through and brown, about 15 minutes. Sprinkle with the cumin and salt and continue sautéing, tossing, for 2 more minutes.

5 To serve, ladle the hot soup into warmed bowls. Top with the croutons and drizzle with the seasoned butter from the frying pan. Serve with lemon wedges, if desired.

COCONUT CREAM AND MILK

Cracking a coconut demands technique and practice. First, select a mature coconut with a brown husk. Shake it: you should hear juice sloshing inside. Soak the coconut in water for a minute, to tame the brown fibers, then locate the "three-dot-face" on one end of the nut. Using an ice pick or a slim screwdriver, puncture one or two of the dots and pour the juice trapped inside into a bowl. You can drink the juice or, like the Vietnamese and Indonesians, use it in cooking.

Spread newspapers on a solid surface, such as a kitchen floor or sidewalk, and place the coconut on them. Using the dull edge of a cleaver or a hammer, make several quick, determined whacks across the equator of the nut until it cracks. Continue to strike with the hammer, breaking it into smaller pieces. Then, with a small knife, pry the meat from the shell and peel off the thin brown skin. Cut the meat into 1-inch (2.5-cm) pieces and pulverize it, a few pieces at a time, in a food processor. One coconut will yield about 3½ cups (1 lb/500 g) pulverized coconut.

To make coconut cream, put the pulverized coconut in a bowl with 1½ cups (12 fl oz/375 ml) hot water. Let steep for 10 minutes, then pour through a fine-mesh sieve or piece of cheesecloth (muslin) over a bowl and press or squeeze the coconut to expel as much liquid as possible. Place the squeezed coconut in another bowl. This first pressing, about 1 cup (8 fl oz/250 ml), is coconut cream and is primarily used as oil for frying spice pastes. For coconut milk, the liquid used in curries and soups, add 3 cups (24 fl oz/750 ml) hot water to the same coconut, let steep for 15 minutes, and repeat the straining and squeezing. This step yields about 2½ cups (20 fl oz/625 ml) coconut milk. Repeat this step for thin coconut milk. Refrigerate the milk and cream and use within 3 days.

Many Southeast Asians are able to avoid the messiest part of this task by buying already-grated meat from market vendors, who prepare it on the spot with a machine. Once home, cooks have only to steep the coconut to make the various grades of milk and cream.

Chicken Coconut Soup

Tom Kha Gai • Thailand

This spectacular soup is one of Thailand's best-known dishes. It is easy to make and includes many of the ingredients that distinguish classic Thai cooking: lemongrass, galangal, fish sauce, kaffir lime leaves, chiles, and coconut milk. You can use boneless chicken if you prefer. Do not eat the galangal, lemongrass, and lime leaves. They deliver a bouquet of flavors but are far too tough to consume.

1 whole chicken breast, chopped into 1-inch (2.5-cm) pieces on the bone

2 cups (16 fl oz/500 ml) chicken stock

3 cups (24 fl oz/750 ml) coconut milk (page 223)

10 slices fresh galangal, or 5 slices dried galangal

4 stalks lemongrass, tender midsection only, smashed and cut into 2-inch (5-cm) lengths

6 green Thai chiles, or 8 green serrano chiles, cut in half crosswise

8 kaffir lime leaves, spines removed

½ cup (3½ oz/105 g) drained canned straw mushrooms

½ cup (2 oz/60 g) sliced bamboo shoots

3 tablespoons fish sauce

¼ cup (2 fl oz/60 ml) fresh lime juice, or to taste

¼ cup (¼ oz/7 g) fresh cilantro (fresh coriander) leaves

Serves 6

1 In a large saucepan, combine the chicken, stock, coconut milk, galangal, lemongrass, chiles, and lime leaves. Bring to a boil over high heat, then reduce the heat to maintain a gentle boil and cook, uncovered, for 20 minutes.

2 Add the mushrooms and bamboo shoots, stir well, raise the heat to high, and bring to a boil. Add the fish sauce and lime juice, then taste and adjust the seasoning. Ladle the soup into warmed bowls, garnish with the cilantro, and serve at once.

Cashew Salad

Yam Med Mamuang • Thailand

Cashews are grown in abundance in the southern Thai province of Ranong, and this cashew-rich salad is one of the country's little-known culinary gems. Look for big whole cashews and fry them slowly in oil so that they cook evenly. If you prefer, you can toast them in the oven at 325°F (165°C) for 5–8 minutes. This is a perfect snack to serve with iced limeade or cold beer.

½ cup (4 fl oz/125 ml) canola oil

½ lb (250 g) raw large whole cashews

2 shallots, thinly sliced

1 green (spring) onion, including 1 inch (2.5 cm) of the tender green top, thinly sliced

1 lemongrass stalk, tender midsection only, finely minced

1 tablespoon coarsely chopped Chinese celery leaves or regular celery leaves

1 tablespoon chopped fresh mint

1 red jalapeño chile, seeded and thinly sliced

DRESSING

2 tablespoons fresh lime juice

1½ teaspoons fish sauce

½ teaspoon sugar

¼ cup (¼ oz/7 g) fresh cilantro (fresh coriander) leaves

Serves 4–6

1 Pour the oil into a wok and place over medium heat. Slowly heat to 325°F (165°C) on a deep-frying thermometer. When the oil is hot, add the cashews and fry, stirring frequently, until light golden brown, about 5 minutes. Using a slotted spoon, transfer the nuts to a brown paper bag to drain.

2 Place the still-warm cashews in a bowl and immediately add the shallots, green onion, lemongrass, celery leaves, mint, and chile. Toss to mix well.

3 To make the dressing, in a small bowl, combine the lime juice, fish sauce, and sugar. Stir until the sugar dissolves. Pour the dressing over the salad and toss well. Turn the salad out onto a serving plate, garnish with the cilantro leaves, and serve.

Sweet Corn Soup with Chile Oil

Bhutte ka Shorva · Madhya Pradesh · India

The use of chile oil in this modern recipe shows a Chinese influence. For a vegetarian version, replace the chicken stock with vegetable stock or water.

3 cups (18 oz/560 g) fresh or thawed frozen corn kernels

1 small boiling potato, peeled and chopped

1 small yellow onion, chopped

2 slices fresh ginger

4 cups (32 fl oz/1 l) chicken stock

1¼ cups (10 fl oz/310 ml) milk

1 tablespoon cornstarch (cornflour) dissolved in 2 tablespoons milk

1¼ teaspoons salt, or to taste

2 teaspoons chile oil

1 teaspoon sesame oil

¼ cup (¾ oz/20 g) thinly sliced green (spring) onion, including tender green top

Serves 6

1 In a deep pot, combine 2 cups (12 oz/375 g) of the corn with the potato, onion, ginger, and chicken stock and bring to a boil over medium-high heat. Reduce the heat to low and cook until the potatoes are soft, about 15 minutes. Remove from the heat and remove and discard the ginger slices.

2 Working in batches, process in a food processor or blender until coarsely puréed. Return the soup to the pot and add the remaining 1 cup (6 oz/185 g) corn and the milk. Bring to a boil over medium heat, add the cornstarch mixture, and cook, stirring, until thickened, 4–5 minutes. Stir in the salt.

3 To serve, ladle the soup into warmed bowls and top each with a little of the chile and sesame oils and a sprinkle of the green onion.

DIWALI FESTIVAL

Celebrated during the month of Kartik, which corresponds to late October through early November on the Western calendar, Diwali is India's great festival of lights. Held in honor of Lakshmi, the goddess of wealth and prosperity, the holiday combines spectacular fireworks, pageants, decorative lights, feasting, drinking, merrymaking, and even some gambling. It also celebrates a significant event in Hindu folklore.

Diwali (also known as the feast of indulgence) inspires cooks to create imaginative preparations to please the palates of honored guests. Expensive food and elaborate garnishes reflect the host's hope for abundance in the coming year. Fragrant pilafs, almond-braised *badami* dishes, creamy *kormas*, *paneer* curries, and herbed *pooris* and *kulchas* are traditional holiday mainstays, as are special sweets, candies, and savories called *mithai aur namkeen*. Until a generation ago, these latter treats were made at home, but today they are commercially produced by sweet makers, or *halwai*, and attractively displayed in shops. They are beautifully gift boxed and sent to friends and family worldwide along with Diwali greetings.

The legend that accompanies Diwali is of Rama, the god who freed his beautiful wife, Sita (who was an incarnation of Lakshmi), from Ravana, the demon king. Ravana had abducted Sita and imprisoned her in Sri Lanka for fourteen years. When Rama finally brought Sita back to India, the people rejoiced at their homecoming and welcomed them by lighting small oil lamps, *diya*, to illuminate a path along which they could travel from the southern tip of the country to Ayodhya, Rama's kingdom, in the north.

Today during Diwali, houses, churches, temples, and other buildings are ablaze with both electric lights and the more traditional oil lamps in an unmistakable sign of welcome that echoes that earlier path. Fireworks ward off evil spirits so Lakshmi may enter people's homes.

In many ways this festival of light displays some of the elements of such large Western celebrations as Christmas and New Year's Eve in a single, grand event. Indians of all religions and sects join in. For the trading communities, or *marvaris*, of India, Diwali also marks the beginning of the new financial year.

Lemongrass Soup with Shrimp

Tom Yum Goong • Thailand

In Thailand, *tom yum goong* is often served in a round metal urn that rests atop a brazier. Lemongrass carries a wonderful citrusy scent that, along with the kaffir lime leaves, beautifully balances the heat of the roasted chile paste in this signature Thai preparation. Related to the equally lemony citronella, lemongrass is one of the ingredients that give Thai dishes their characteristic aromatic quality. An added benefit: Thai cooks believe lemongrass combats head colds, making this sour, sharp soup a curative as well.

1 Peel and devein the shrimp, reserving the shells. Rinse the shrimp and set aside.

2 In a large saucepan over medium-high heat, warm the oil. When the oil is hot, add the shrimp shells and fry them, stirring, until they turn bright orange, about 1 minute. Toss in the lemongrass, galangal, green chiles, chicken stock, and 4 of the lime leaves. Raise the heat to high and bring to a boil. Reduce the heat to medium and simmer, uncovered, for 15 minutes to develop the flavors. Remove from the heat and pour the stock through a sieve placed over a clean saucepan. Discard the contents of the sieve.

3 Add the chile paste, straw mushrooms, and sliced bamboo shoot to the saucepan, stir well, and bring to a boil over medium heat. When the liquid is boiling, add the shrimp and the remaining 4 lime leaves and cook until the shrimp turn bright orange-pink, 1–2 minutes. Season with the fish sauce and lime juice, then taste and adjust the seasoning.

4 Ladle the soup into warmed bowls, garnish with the red chile slices and cilantro, and serve at once.

¾ lb (375 g) large shrimp (prawns) in the shell

2 tablespoons canola oil

4 lemongrass stalks, tender midsection only, smashed and cut into 2-inch (5-cm) lengths

6 slices fresh galangal, or 3 slices dried galangal

6 green Thai chiles, or 8 green serrano chiles, cut in half crosswise

6 cups (48 fl oz/1.5 l) chicken stock

8 kaffir lime leaves, spines removed

1–2 tablespoons roasted chile paste (page 222), or to taste

1 cup (7 oz/220 g) drained canned straw mushrooms

4-inch (10-cm) piece bamboo shoot, thinly sliced

3 tablespoons fish sauce, or to taste

¼ cup (2 fl oz/60 ml) fresh lime juice, or to taste

1 fresh red chile, sliced into rounds

¼ cup (¼ oz/7 g) fresh cilantro (fresh coriander) leaves

Serves 6

Torn Chicken and Cabbage Salad

Goi Ga · Vietnam

A Vietnamese menu that does not include this chicken and cabbage salad does not exist. Best described as Vietnamese coleslaw, this healthful salad is oil-free.

DRESSING

1 red Fresno or serrano chile, seeded and minced

1 clove garlic, finely minced

1½ tablespoons sugar, or to taste

3 tablespoons fresh lime juice

2 tablespoons fish sauce

1 whole chicken breast, about ¾ lb (375 g)

4 cups (8 oz/250 g) finely shredded green cabbage

½ carrot, peeled and finely shredded

½ cup (¾ oz/20 g) finely slivered fresh mint

2 tablespoons finely slivered fresh polygonum (page 225) or fresh cilantro (fresh coriander) leaves

2 tablespoons chopped unsalted roasted peanuts

Serves 6

1 To make the dressing, in a bowl, combine the chile, garlic, sugar, lime juice, and fish sauce. Stir together until the sugar has dissolved. Set aside.

2 Place the chicken in a saucepan and add water to cover. Bring to a simmer over medium-high heat, adjust the heat to maintain a gentle simmer, and cook until opaque throughout, about 20 minutes. Transfer the chicken to a plate, let cool, then remove the skin and bones. With your fingers, tear the meat along the grain into long, thin shreds and place in a large bowl. Discard the cooking liquid or reserve for another use.

3 Add the cabbage, carrot, mint, polygonum or cilantro, and dressing and toss gently to mix well.

4 Arrange the salad on a platter. Sprinkle with the peanuts, and serve.

Green Mango and Grilled Shrimp Salad

Goi Xoai • Vietnam

To make a green mango salad, street hawkers in Vietnam use a short-bladed cleaver to cut the fruit into julienned slivers with pointed ends. These are put in a mortar and bruised with a pestle to mix with the dressing. When served a green mango salad, check for the pointed ends. If you see them, the mango was cut by hand. If not, it was done by machine.

½ lb (250 g) large shrimp (prawns), peeled and deveined

1 tablespoon canola oil

½ teaspoon coarse salt

Freshly ground pepper to taste

2 green mangoes, peeled and grated, preferably by hand

1 carrot, peeled and finely grated

1 tablespoon chopped fresh polygonum (page 225) or cilantro (coriander) leaves

1 red Fresno or serrano chile, chopped

¼ cup (2 fl oz/60 ml) *nuoc cham* dipping sauce (page 225)

2 tablespoons fried shallots (see sidebar, page 82)

Serves 4–6

1 Prepare a hot fire in a charcoal grill. In a bowl, toss the shrimp with the oil, salt, and pepper to taste.

2 Place the shrimp over the hottest part of the fire and grill, turning as needed, until they turn bright orange-pink and feel firm to the touch, about 2 minutes. Transfer to a plate and set aside to cool.

3 In a large bowl, combine the mangoes, the carrot, the chopped polygonum or cilantro, the chile, and the dipping sauce and toss well. Alternatively, lightly pound the vegetables with the salad dressing in a mortar.

4 Arrange the salad on a platter and top with the grilled shrimp. Sprinkle with the fried shallots and serve.

HERBS

Every Vietnamese meal includes a *dia rau song*, a fresh vegetable platter that accompanies one or more of the dishes being served. It carries several whole lettuce leaves; an assortment of crisp raw vegetables such as bean sprouts, carrots, and cucumbers; and an abundance of fresh herbs such as mint, fresh cilantro (fresh coriander), and basil. The diner layers the lettuce leaf with the vegetables and herbs and then tops it with a strip of grilled meat, a tiny spring roll, or other small bite. Finally, he or she rolls up the leaf into a bundle, plunges it into a dipping sauce, and then eats it.

Fresh herbs are also ubiquitous in a Nonya meal. Indeed, every Southeast Asian kitchen relies upon a gardenful of herbs, whether it be that of a Thai cook preparing *tom kha gai* (chicken coconut soup), a Burmese cook composing a curry, or an Indonesian cook assembling a *rempah*.

Curried Chicken and Vegetable Soup

Mulligatawny • Karnataka • India

Mulligatawny means "pepper-water," and this soup, from the Mangalore Christians of Karnataka, is traditionally spicy hot. Half a duck may replace the chicken; the cooking times will be the same. If desired, serve the soup over hot cooked rice.

1 Place the chicken pieces in a large, heavy pot and scatter the cilantro, cardamom, and cassia leaves on top. Add 2 cups (16 fl oz/500 ml) of the water and bring to a boil over high heat. Reduce the heat to low, cover, and cook, occasionally skimming off any foam that rises to the surface, until the chicken is opaque throughout and firm to the touch, about 30 minutes. Using tongs, transfer the chicken pieces to a plate. When cool enough to handle, pull the meat from the bones and return the bones to the pot. Shred the meat neatly, cover, and set aside.

2 Add the remaining 4 cups (32 fl oz/1 l) water to the cooking liquid and bring to a gentle boil over medium-high heat. Reduce the heat to low, cover, and boil gently for 30 minutes. Remove from the heat, strain through a fine-mesh sieve, and return the stock to the pot. Discard the contents of the sieve.

3 Add 1 cup (5 oz/155 g) of the onion along with the carrots, potatoes, and tomato and bring to a boil over high heat. Cover, reduce the heat to medium-low, and cook until the vegetables are very soft, about 25 minutes. Remove from the heat and, working in batches, purée the soup in a food processor or blender until smooth. Strain the soup, if necessary, to remove lumps, and return it to the pot. It should be the consistency of a cream soup. If it is not, stir in as much of the cornstarch solution as needed to thicken it. Warm the soup until it is piping hot. Add the coconut milk, light cream, or milk and salt. Simmer gently over very low heat while you make the garnish.

4 In a small frying pan over medium-high heat, melt the *usli ghee* or butter. Add the remaining 1 cup (5 oz/155 g) onion, the garlic, and the cumin, garam masala, or curry powder. Sauté, stirring, until the onion is nicely browned, about 5 minutes. Add the shredded chicken and salt and pepper to taste. Sauté, tossing the chicken, until lightly seared and well coated with spices, about 3 minutes.

5 To serve, ladle the hot soup into warmed bowls. Place the chicken on top and sprinkle with the lemon juice and almonds. Serve at once.

1 chicken, about 3 lb (1.5 kg), cut into 8–10 serving pieces and skinned

1 bunch fresh cilantro (fresh coriander)

2 black or 4 green cardamom pods, lightly bruised

2 cassia leaves (page 222), broken into bits

6 cups (48 fl oz/1.5 l) water

2 cups (10 oz/310 g) finely chopped yellow onion

2 carrots, peeled and chopped

2 boiling potatoes, peeled and chopped

1½ cups (9 oz/280 g) chopped tomato

2 tablespoons cornstarch (cornflour) dissolved in ¼ cup (2 fl oz/60 ml) water, if needed

1 cup (8 fl oz/250 ml) coconut milk, light (single) cream, or milk

1½ teaspoons salt, or to taste

¼ cup (2 oz/60 g) *usli ghee* (page 224) or unsalted butter

1 tablespoon minced garlic

2 teaspoons ground cumin, garam masala, or curry powder

Freshly ground pepper to taste

Juice of 1 lemon

½ cup (2 oz/60 g) sliced (flaked) almonds, toasted

Serves 8

Hot Sour Fish Soup with Pineapple

Canh Chua Ca • Vietnam

The intensely sour flavor of tamarind gives this everyday soup its distinctive character. Tamarind concentrate, which dissolves instantly in hot water, is available in Asian markets.

1 tablespoon canola oil

2 cloves garlic, minced

1 yellow onion, thinly sliced

3 lemongrass stalks, tender midsection only, smashed and cut into 2-inch (5-cm) lengths

3 slices fresh galangal, or 2 slices dried galangal

¼ lb (125 g) fresh white mushrooms, brushed clean, stems removed, and caps halved

½ cup (2 oz/60 g) thinly sliced bamboo shoots

½ cup (3 oz/90 g) cubed pineapple

6 cups (48 fl oz/1.5 l) chicken stock or fish stock

⅓ cup (3 fl oz/80 ml) tamarind water (page 227)

2–3 tablespoons fish sauce, or to taste

1½ tablespoons sugar

1 teaspoon salt

¾ lb (375 g) catfish fillets, cut into 1½-inch (4-cm) chunks

1 cup (2 oz/60 g) bean sprouts

1 green (spring) onion, including tender green top, thinly sliced

¼ cup (¼ oz/7 g) fresh mint leaves

¼ cup (¼ oz/7 g) fresh cilantro (fresh coriander) leaves

2 red Fresno or serrano chiles, sliced

Serves 6–8

1 In a large saucepan over medium-high heat, warm the oil. Add the garlic, onion, lemongrass, and galangal and sauté until the onion is soft, 2–3 minutes. Do not allow the onion to brown. Add the mushrooms, bamboo shoots, and pineapple and cook, stirring, for 1 minute.

2 Raise the heat to high, add the stock, and bring to a boil. Stir in the tamarind water, fish sauce, sugar, and salt. Stir well, taste, and adjust the seasoning. Add the fish and boil gently until opaque throughout, about 5 minutes. Add the bean sprouts, green onion, and mint and ladle into individual bowls. Garnish with the cilantro and chiles. Serve at once.

Lentil Dumplings and Yogurt Salad

Dahi Bhalla · Punjab · India

In this composed raita, fried beans puffs are combined with spiced yogurt and fresh herbs. *Dahi bhalla* is not an everyday dish, as one needs to have the ready-made bean puffs on hand. Also, raisins and yogurt are expensive items in India and are used with discretion.

Fried Bean Puffs with Ginger and Raisins (below)

3 cups (24 oz/750 g) plain yogurt

1½ teaspoons sugar

1 teaspoon cumin seeds, toasted and lightly crushed (page 227)

½ teaspoon salt

½ teaspoon freshly ground black pepper

2 teaspoons peeled and shredded fresh ginger

1 teaspoon sliced fresh hot green chiles

½ teaspoon cayenne pepper or paprika

2 tablespoons chopped fresh cilantro (fresh coriander)

Serves 8–12

1 Place the bean puffs in a large bowl, add hot water to cover, and let soak for 30 minutes. Drain them, then gently squeeze out the excess water.

2 In another large bowl, combine the yogurt, sugar, half of the cumin, the salt, and black pepper and whisk until blended. Add the bean puffs, cover, and set aside for 1 hour at room temperature so that the bean puffs absorb some of the yogurt.

3 To serve, arrange the bean puffs in a shallow dish. Pour any remaining yogurt over them. Sprinkle with the remaining cumin, the ginger, chiles, cayenne pepper or paprika, and cilantro. Serve immediately or refrigerate, covered, for up to 3 days.

Fried Bean Puffs with Ginger and Raisins

Bare · Punjab · India

1 cup (7 oz/220 g) white split gram beans

3 cups (24 fl oz/750 ml) hot water, plus ½ cup (4 fl oz/125 ml) cold water

¼ cup (1 oz/30 g) chopped walnuts

⅓ cup (2 oz/60 g) raisins

1 tablespoon peeled and finely chopped fresh ginger

2 fresh green hot chiles, thinly sliced

1 teaspoon salt, or to taste

¾ teaspoon cumin seeds

Canola oil for deep frying

Makes 16–24

1 Pick over the beans, removing any stones or misshapen or discolored beans. Rinse thoroughly and place in a bowl. Add the hot water and soak for 8 hours or overnight.

2 Drain the beans and transfer them to a food processor or blender. Process, gradually adding the cold water and stopping the machine often to scrape down the bowl, until smoothly puréed. (This will take a few minutes, as the mixture contains very little liquid.) Transfer the purée to a bowl and stir in the walnuts, raisins, ginger, chiles, salt, and cumin.

3 In a *karhai*, deep-fryer, or large frying pan, pour oil to a depth of 2 inches (5 cm) and heat to 375°F (190°C) on a deep-frying thermometer. Using a small ice-cream scoop or melon baller, scoop out balls of the batter and slip them gently into the oil, a few at a time. Do not crowd the pan. Fry, turning frequently, until nicely browned on all sides, about 3 minutes. Using a slotted spoon, transfer to paper towels to drain. Keep warm in a low oven while you cook the remaining balls. Serve hot or at room temperature.

Hand-Shredded White Chicken Salad

Siche Bai Ji Sela • Western • China

To prepare this chicken dish is to understand the underlying philosophy of Chinese cooking. This unique method of steeping chicken, developed centuries ago in the imperial kitchens, ensures supreme tenderness and accentuates the chicken's subtle flavors.

1 chicken, about 3 lb (1.5 kg)

2 green (spring) onions, including tender green tops, finely chopped

2 tablespoons peeled and grated fresh ginger

1 tablespoon rice wine

1 tablespoon light soy sauce

1 tablespoon salt

About 5 qt (5 l) water

1 tray ice cubes

1 tablespoon chicken bouillon granules (optional)

4 or 5 slices fresh ginger

1 green (spring) onion, trimmed and chopped

¼ cup (2 fl oz/60 ml) rice wine

SALAD

1 cup (3 oz/90 g) julienned cucumber

1 cup (3 oz/90 g) julienned carrot

1 teaspoon salt

1 teaspoon superfine (caster) sugar

1 tablespoon rice vinegar

DRESSING

2 tablespoons sesame paste

¼ cup (2 fl oz/60 ml) water or chicken stock, or as needed

1 tablespoon light soy sauce

1 tablespoon fresh lemon juice

2 teaspoons sesame oil

Salt and freshly ground white or Sichuan pepper

1–2 teaspoons peanut oil or sesame oil

Fresh cilantro (fresh coriander) sprigs

Serves 4–8

1 Rinse the chicken and pat dry. Place the finely chopped green onions, ginger, rice wine, soy sauce, and salt in the cavity. Cover and refrigerate the chicken for 1 hour.

2 In a large pot over high heat, bring the water to a rolling boil. Loop a piece of kitchen string around the chicken wings and tie firmly, leaving a loop at the top large enough to provide a firm grip. Holding the loop, lower the chicken into the boiling water for 1 minute, then lift out. Repeat this dipping 4 times, then set the chicken in a colander to drain briefly. Skim any froth from the surface.

3 Fill a large bowl with water and add the ice cubes. Lower the chicken into the ice water and leave for 1 minute, then remove and drain. Reheat the water in the pot over high heat and add the bouillon granules, if using, the ginger slices, the chopped green onion, and the rice wine. Bring to a boil over high heat. Again lower the chicken into the hot liquid for 1 minute, and lift out. Repeat this 4 times, then submerge the chicken in the liquid and bring to a boil. Skim any froth from the surface.

4 Remove the pot from the heat. Allow the chicken to remain in the hot liquid until the chicken feels firm, 25–30 minutes. To test for doneness, insert a thin skewer into the thickest part of a thigh; no pink juices should flow. Carefully lift out the chicken, holding a broad ladle or a wire skimmer under it for support. Drain the liquid from the cavity and place the chicken on a plate to cool. Do not attempt to shred the chicken for at least 20 minutes.

5 Meanwhile, to prepare the salad, in a bowl, combine the cucumber, carrot, salt, sugar, and vinegar. Using your fingers, knead and mash the sugar and salt into the vegetables to soften them partially, then let stand for 20 minutes. Drain just before serving.

6 To prepare the dressing, in a small bowl, whisk together the sesame paste, the ¼ cup (2 fl oz/60 ml) water or stock, soy sauce, lemon juice, and sesame oil. Season to taste with salt and pepper. Add more water or stock if needed to make a creamy dressing.

7 Remove either the whole breast or 2 whole legs (drumsticks and thighs) from the chicken. Reserve the remaining chicken for another use. Pull the chicken meat from its bones with your fingers, then tear the meat into bite-sized strips. Place the strips in a bowl, sprinkle with the peanut or sesame oil, and toss to coat evenly.

8 To serve, mound the drained vegetables in the center of a platter. Drape the shredded chicken over the vegetables in a mound. Drizzle the dressing over the chicken, scatter the cilantro over the top, and serve.

Spicy Green Beans, Bean Sprouts, and Coconut Salad

Urap · Indonesia

Urap, a salad combining crunchy textures, sizzling bites of chile, and cooling watercress, spinach, and green beans, is often served as part of an Indonesian *selamatan*, a feast held to celebrate meaningful occasions. In Malaysia and Thailand, versions of *urap* use regional vegetables and seasonings. Serve the salad cold or at room temperature.

1 Bring a large saucepan three-fourths full of salted water to a boil. Add the beans and blanch for 2 minutes, then scoop out with a wire skimmer and place under running cold water to halt the cooking. Drain well and set aside. Repeat with the bean sprouts, spinach, and watercress, blanching them one at a time: the bean sprouts for 10 seconds, the spinach for 1 minute, and the watercress for 30 seconds. Rinse each one with cold water, wrap in a kitchen towel, and squeeze out as much excess water as possible. Gather the spinach into a bunch and cut into thirds. Repeat with the watercress. Put all the vegetables into a large bowl and set aside.

2 To make the dressing, wrap the dried shrimp paste in aluminum foil and place the packet directly on a stove-top burner turned on to medium-high heat. Toast the packet, turning it once or twice, until fragrant, 1–2 minutes. Remove the packet and open it; if the shrimp paste crumbles, it is ready. Let cool.

3 In a mortar, combine the toasted shrimp paste, garlic, galangal, chile, and lime leaves. Pound until a smooth paste forms. Mix in the sugar, salt, coconut, lime juice, and oil. Add to the vegetables, mix well, cover, and refrigerate until ready to serve.

4 Just before serving, transfer the salad to a serving platter and top with the fried shallots.

⅓ lb (155 g) yard-long beans or green beans, trimmed and cut into 1-inch (2.5-cm) lengths

⅓ lb (155 g) bean sprouts

½ lb (250 g) spinach, tough stems removed

1 bunch watercress, tough stems removed

DRESSING

1 slice dried shrimp paste, ⅛ inch (3 mm) thick

2 cloves garlic, quartered

2 thin slices fresh galangal, peeled and chopped

1 large red Fresno or serrano chile, seeded and coarsely chopped

3 kaffir lime leaves, spines removed and leaves minced

1 teaspoon sugar

¼ teaspoon salt

3 tablespoons grated fresh or unsweetened dried coconut

2 tablespoons fresh lime juice

1 tablespoon canola oil

2 tablespoons fried shallots (see sidebar, page 82)

Serves 6

Eight Treasures Vegetarian Soup

Babao Sucai Tang • Southern • China

"Eight treasures" describes dishes featuring many (not always eight) special ingredients, such as winter melon. Winter melon looks just like a watermelon, but cut it open and you will find a fine-textured, pale green, mildly flavored flesh. It is especially appreciated in soups and steamed dishes, where it absorbs the flavors of other ingredients. For a banquet, eight treasures soup is sometimes served in the decoratively carved shell of a large melon.

2 cups (9 oz/280 g) cubed, peeled winter melon (½-inch/12-mm cubes; about 14 oz/440 g unpeeled)

¼ cup (1½ oz/45 g) cubed carrot (½-inch/12-mm cubes)

¼ cup (1¼ oz/40 g) cubed bamboo shoots (½-inch/12-mm cubes)

¼ cup (1½ oz/45 g) raw peanuts or ginkgo nuts

⅓ cup (2 oz/60 g) cubed zucchini (courgette) (½-inch/12-mm cubes)

⅓ cup (2½ oz/75 g) canned small straw mushrooms

4-inch (10-cm) piece dried bean curd stick, soaked in hot water to cover for 2 minutes, drained, and cut into small pieces

1 teaspoon peeled and grated fresh ginger

1 teaspoon salt, plus salt to taste

1 tablespoon light soy sauce

6 cups (48 fl oz/1.5 l) hot water or warmed chicken stock or vegetable stock

½ cup (3½ oz/105 g) cubed fresh soft bean curd (½-inch/12-mm cubes)

¼ cup (¾ oz/20 g) sliced green (spring) onion, including tender green top

1 tablespoon cornstarch (cornflour) dissolved in 1 tablespoon water

Freshly ground white pepper to taste (optional)

Serves 4–8

1 In a saucepan, combine the winter melon, carrot, bamboo shoots, peanuts or ginkgo nuts, zucchini, mushrooms, bean curd stick, ginger, the 1 teaspoon salt, and the soy sauce. Pour in the hot water or stock, place over medium-high heat, and bring slowly to a boil, stirring occasionally. Reduce the heat to medium and simmer gently, uncovered, until the vegetables are tender, about 15 minutes.

2 Add the cubed bean curd and green onion, then taste and adjust the seasoning with salt. Stir in the cornstarch mixture and boil gently, stirring slowly, until the soup thickens only very lightly, about 1½ minutes.

3 Pour into a deep serving bowl, season with white pepper, and serve at once.

Spicy Yellow Lentil Stew

Dal • Malaysia

In traditional Indian cooking, *dal* refers to any dried peas or beans and to the many dishes made from them. In Malaysia and Singapore, *dal* refers to a spicy stew made of yellow lentils (*toovar dal*) that typically accompanies Indian breads. The cooking time will vary with the age of the lentil.

1 cup (7 oz/220 g) dried yellow lentils (see note)

2 cups (16 fl oz/500 ml) water

½ teaspoon ground turmeric

1 teaspoon plus 2 tablespoons ghee (page 224) or canola oil

1 teaspoon black mustard seeds

2 dried red chiles, cut up

1 yellow onion, sliced

2 cloves garlic, minced

2 slices fresh ginger, peeled and minced

20 fresh or dried curry leaves (page 223)

1 teaspoon garam masala

2 small tomatoes, quartered lengthwise

½ teaspoon salt, or to taste

Serves 4

1 Pick over the lentils, discarding any misshapen lentils or stones. Rinse the lentils until the water runs clear, then drain.

2 In a saucepan over high heat, combine the lentils, water, turmeric, and the 1 teaspoon ghee or oil. Bring to a boil, stirring occasionally. Reduce the heat to medium, cover, and simmer until the lentils are soft and tender, about 30 minutes.

3 In a frying pan over medium-high heat, warm the remaining 2 tablespoons ghee or oil. When hot, add the mustard seeds and fry until they turn gray, spatter, and pop, about 2 minutes. Add the chiles, onion, garlic, ginger, and curry leaves and sauté until the onion is soft and golden, about 5 minutes. Stir in the garam masala and tomatoes and cook for 1 minute.

4 Pour the onion mixture into the pan of cooked lentils, add the salt, and simmer for 5 minutes to blend the flavors. Transfer to a serving dish and serve at once.

KRUPUK CRACKERS

The crisp, translucent crackers called *krupuk* are found in every Indonesian and Malaysian kitchen—and in other Southeast Asian pantries as well. Although many different varieties exist—fish (*krupuk palembang*), tapioca (*krupuk miller*), malingo nut (*emping malinjo*)—*krupuk udang*, made from shrimp, are the most common. They come in the form of brittle disks in various colors, and they puff into tasty, featherlight wafers when deep-fried.

Most are only as large as a potato chip and are used as garnishes or snacks, but others expand to the size of a dinner plate. In Kukup, a small fishing village built on stilts in Johor, Malaysia, the locals make their own dough for *krupuk*. It is a very dense mixture, which they shape into logs and then cut crosswise into thin slices. They spread the slices over a bamboo mat and leave them under the hot tropical sun until they are bone dry. Few people make their own dough nowadays. Instead, the chips are bought at the market and fried at home.

FRANCE

S easonality is the key to the soups and salads of the French table. Thus, in spring, look for asparagus, artichokes, and cherries; in summer, tomatoes, eggplants, zucchini, peppers, and melons; in fall, mushrooms, figs, and apples; in winter, leeks, pumpkins, and truffles. Sometimes, with seasonal vegetables, the best way to serve them is as simply as possible, allowing the flavor of perfect ripeness to have full impact. Cubes of sweet melon and ripe figs drizzled with basil cream, thick slices of tomato and red onion with a few drops of wine vinegar and olive oil, peppery young dandelion greens tossed with crunchy bits of bacon: all are uncomplicated preparations designed to show off the wonderfully fresh ingredients.

Composed and mixed salads are frequently assertive expressions of *cuisine du terroir*, both in traditional and in more innovative treatments. *Salade niçoise* with anchovies, tuna, tomatoes, salty olives, and beans, all perfumed with olive oil and fresh herbs, is redolent of the flavors of Mediterranean France, while a *salade de savoie* is lavished with generous chunks of Emmentaler or Beaufort cheese, along with walnuts and lardons, all tossed with a local walnut oil and a wine vinegar. Near the borders of Spain, around Perpignan and Biarritz, look for salads made with fish and seasoned with saffron and peppers, while fish salads of the northern coasts are more likely to be full of *coquillage*, local shellfish.

While salads allow a collection of perfect ingredients shine, French soups are an opportunity for transformation. Even the most rustic and humble elements can be turned into something sublime. Onions, bread, stock, and cheese are pantry staples, but let the onions melt in butter and olive oil until they are a thick mass of caramelized sweetness, then add a swig of hearty beef stock. Ladle it into individual bowls and add a slice of bread and grated Gruyère to each one. Bake until a golden crust forms and enjoy a classic French onion soup beloved by late-night revelers and hungry working folks alike. A summer vegetable soup with beans, potatoes, and pasta is transformed by the addition of *pistou*, a thick basil-garlic sauce.

Or consider *bourride*; it starts with a potful of fish heads and bones, vegetables, and wine. Then add chunks of fish from the catch and poach them in the liquid. Next beat aioli, a garlicky mayonnaise, and a few egg yolks into the broth to produce a delicate cream to be ladled over bread in soup plates. For a crowning touch, set a bowl of aioli on the table to spoon into the soup.

Foremost among the bounty of France is certainly the olive, valued for its mouth-watering, salty succulence as well as for its invaluable oil. In general, ripe olives are harvested by shaking the tree around the turn of the year. Many of those used for cooking are brined for long conservation. For a more interesting flavor, they may be drained and marinated with herbs and olive oil or combined with other flavorings to make them all the more appealing for use in salads. Oils pressed as extra virgin (those with less than 1 percent acidity), and those from the areas that have gained an *appellation d'origine contrôlée* (A.O.C.)—Nyons, in the Drôme Provençal was the first to gain the status in 1994—are the most aromatic, perfect for drizzling over ripe tomatoes with shredded basil or to add a gloss of aromatic richness to any dish.

To start a meal, simple combinations are among the most loved: a plate of grated or sliced raw vegetables (crudités) with either a vinaigrette or, more commonly, a bowl of sunny aioli. The French love their vegetables uncooked, and not just the usual carrots, cucumbers, and tomatoes. The first of the season's tiny purple artichokes are preferred raw. It is thought better to boil them in vinegared water and maintain their youth under oil, so that one might bring them out preserved for the rest of the year, rather than eat them after they form a hairy choke in the center. The case is much the same for tiny *fèvettes*, the first fava (broad) beans of spring. These are peeled, dipped in salt, and slipped into the mouth raw.

Composed salads are popular, with the colorful *salade niçoise* of romaine lettuce, thin green beans, artichokes, favas, tomatoes, and tuna probably the best known. But also popular are small mesclun salads of field greens and anything the market or the pantry can offer, from mushrooms to slivers of smoked or roasted chicken or duck, and from a scattering of mixed vegetables and hard-boiled egg to goat cheese laid over an oil-fried crouton.

Soups from France come in all forms. Puréed soups can be made from a variety of vegetables: carrots, tomatoes, leeks, red peppers, white beans, radish leaves, nettles, and even garlic. A broth might contain a garden of vegetables (*soupe au pistou* being the most renowned) or something as simple as leeks and potatoes. Rabbit soup, chicken soup, and all manner of seafood soups, including bouillabaisse, the undisputed queen of Marseilles, are all equally popular.

Left: The medieval church of Saint-André, built in the twelfth century, watches over the Provençal village of Comps-sur-Artuby in the Var. **Above, left:** The color of asparagus depends on the amount of light it receives as it grows. White spears have been completely shielded, whereas shoots exposed to sunlight are gradually tinged purple and then turn green. **Above, right:** The best French poultry is raised outdoors, and the birds are thus labeled in the marketplace as *"élevés en plein air"*.

Salad of Panfried Tomme de Savoie with Hazelnuts

Salade de Tomme de Savoie aux Noisettes · The Alps · France

Hazelnuts, which grow wild on the mountainsides in the valleys of Savoy, are gathered in fall and stored as part of the winter larder. The taste for local products remains strong in the area, especially for cheeses such as the mild, round, firm *tommes* made with cow's milk. If you can't find it, use another supple cheese.

½ cup (2½ oz/75 g) hazelnuts (filberts)

¼ cup (2 fl oz/60 ml) hazelnut oil or extra-virgin olive oil

1 teaspoon Dijon mustard

3 tablespoons red wine vinegar

¼ teaspoon salt

¼ teaspoon freshly ground pepper

6 cups (6 oz/185 g) red-leaf, green-leaf, or butter lettuce leaves, or a mixture, torn into bite-sized pieces

½ cup (2½ oz/75 g) all-purpose (plain) flour

1 tomme de Savoie, 5 oz (155 g), rind trimmed and cheese cut into 4 slices, each ¼ inch (6 mm) thick

Sunflower oil or other light vegetable oil for frying

Serves 4

1 Preheat the oven to 350°F (180°C). Spread the nuts in a pan and bake for 15 minutes. Stir and continue to bake until lightly golden throughout, about 10 minutes longer. Set aside.

2 In a large bowl, stir together the hazelnut or olive oil and the mustard until blended. Stir in the vinegar, salt, and pepper to form a vinaigrette. Set aside.

3 Put the lettuce in the bowl with the vinaigrette and toss to coat. Add half of the nuts and toss again. Divide evenly among individual plates.

4 Spread the flour on a plate and coat the cheese slices on both sides. In a frying pan over medium-high heat, pour in just enough vegetable oil to form a thin layer. When hot, add the cheese slices, spacing them 1 inch (2.5 cm) apart. Cook, turning once, until golden on both sides, 2–4 minutes total.

5 Place a piece of cheese atop each salad, sprinkle evenly with the remaining nuts, and serve at once.

Melon and Fig Salad with Basil Cream

Melon et Figues avec Crème au Basilic • Pays de la Loire • France

Very ripe, intensely sweet figs and melons, both daily summer fare in the warm regions of France, are often lightly dressed with a sauce made of cream and basil.

½ cup (4 fl oz/125 ml) heavy (double) cream

2½ tablespoons fresh lemon juice

¼ cup (⅓ oz/10 g) minced fresh basil, plus sprigs for garnish

1½ teaspoons sugar

3 cups (18 oz/560 g) cubed cantaloupe, honeydew, or other sweet melon (1-inch/2.5-cm cubes)

1–1½ lb (500–750 g) very ripe figs, each quartered lengthwise

Serves 4

1 In a bowl, stir together the cream, lemon juice, minced basil, and sugar. Cover and refrigerate for at least 1 hour or for up to 6 hours.

2 When ready to serve, divide the melon and figs among 4 individual plates. Pour a little of the cream mixture over each plate of fruit, then garnish each with a basil sprig.

Cucumber and Fennel Salad

Salade de Concombres et Fenouil • Provence • France

The textures and flavors of fennel and cucumber are combined in this light salad. The fennel can also be sliced even more finely and used raw.

2 large, round fennel bulbs

12 tablespoons (6 fl oz/180 ml) olive oil

6 cloves garlic, unpeeled

1 large English (hothouse) cucumber, peeled

1 heaping tablespoon salt-packed capers, rinsed

Juice of 1 lemon, or to taste

Salt and freshly ground coarse pepper to taste

2 tablespoons chopped fresh flat-leaf (Italian) parsley

Serves 6

1 Preheat the oven to 375°F (190°C). Lightly oil a baking sheet. Trim off the feathery tops and the stalks from each fennel bulb. Remove any bruised areas and trim the base of the core. Stand the bulb on its base and cut vertically into slices ⅛ inch (3 mm) thick. The stalks may be sliced on the diagonal and baked with the sliced bulbs, or they may be reserved for another use along with the tops.

2 Place the fennel slices in a single layer on the prepared baking sheet, then drizzle with 4 tablespoons (2 fl oz/60 ml) of the olive oil. Rub the garlic cloves with 2 tablespoons of the oil and place on top of the fennel. Bake, turning the fennel slices 2 or 3 times, until they soften slightly, about 20 minutes. Remove the garlic and set aside. Transfer the fennel to a platter and let cool.

3 Halve the cucumber lengthwise. Scoop out any seeds. Cut the flesh into small, even dice. Place in a bowl, add the capers, and spoon over the fennel.

4 Squeeze the roasted garlic cloves, forcing out the soft garlic into a bowl. Discard the skin. Mash with a fork. Add the remaining 6 tablespoons (3 fl oz/90 ml) olive oil and the lemon juice and whisk together. Season with salt and pepper and stir in the parsley. Drizzle the dressing over the cucumber and fennel. Toss in the kitchen or at the table and serve.

Oyster Soup with Three Herbs

Soupe aux Huîtres Trois Herbes • Brittany • France

Depending on which wine you choose, this simple yet astonishingly elegant soup will have a slightly different flavor. It's wonderful made with a Meursault from Burgundy.

12 oysters

2 tablespoons unsalted butter

1 shallot, minced

¾ cup (6 fl oz/180 ml) good-quality dry white wine such as Burgundy, Riesling, or Muscadet

1 teaspoon salt dissolved in ½ cup (4 fl oz/125 ml) water

¾ cup (6 oz/185 g) crème fraîche

1 teaspoon minced fresh chives

1 teaspoon minced fresh chervil

1 teaspoon minced fresh tarragon

½ teaspoon freshly ground pepper

Serves 4

1 First, shuck the oysters: Working with 1 oyster at a time and gripping it flat side up, push the tip of an oyster knife into one side of the hinge (opposite the shell's concentric ridges) and pry upward to open the shell. Run the knife blade along the upper shell to free the oyster from it, then lift off and discard the top shell. Run the knife underneath the oyster to free it from the bottom shell, then slip the oyster and its liquor into a bowl.

2 In a saucepan over medium heat, melt the butter. When it foams, add the shallot and sauté just until translucent, 1–2 minutes. Add the wine and the oysters and their liquor, then pour the salted water over them. When tiny bubbles begin to form around the edges, stir in the crème fraîche, chives, chervil, and tarragon and sprinkle with the pepper. Continue to cook just long enough to heat through, about 1 minute longer.

3 Ladle the hot soup into warmed bowls and serve at once.

Savoy Salad

Salade de Savoie • Franche-Comté and The Alps • France

Of the important *produits du terroir*, Beaufort is the pride of Savoy and one of the most distinguished cheeses in France. It is pressed from raw milk, aged for at least six months or up to two years, and has a firm, dense texture and a faintly nutty flavor.

¼ lb (125 g) lardons or thick-cut bacon (¼ inch/6 mm thick), cut 1 inch (2.5 cm) long and ¼ inch (6 mm) wide

3 tablespoons walnut oil

2 tablespoons raspberry vinegar

½ teaspoon freshly ground pepper

¼ teaspoon salt

5 cups (5 oz/155 g) escarole (Batavian endive), pale yellow inner leaves only (from about 2 heads)

¼ lb (125 g) Beaufort or Gruyère cheese, cubed

¼ cup (1 oz/30 g) coarsely chopped walnuts

Serves 4

1 In a frying pan over medium heat, fry the lardons or bacon pieces until they are golden brown and have released much of their fat, 7–8 minutes. Using a slotted spoon, transfer to a plate lined with paper towels to drain.

2 Scoop out ½ teaspoon of the fat from the pan and place in the bottom of a salad bowl. Add the walnut oil, vinegar, pepper, and salt to the salad bowl and mix well with a fork. Tear the escarole into bite-sized pieces, add it to the bowl, and toss well to coat. Add the cheese, walnuts, and lardons or bacon, reserving a little of each for garnish. Toss again.

3 Garnish the salad with the reserved cheese, walnuts, and lardons. Serve at once.

BOUILLABAISSE

The best Provençal cooks will tell you that producing a respectable bouillabaisse is a costly and time-consuming undertaking. But the dish itself has humble origins. It was the creation of Marseilles fishermen, who filled pots with diluted seawater, placed them over wood fires on the beach, and then added local herbs and the discards from their day's catch. When ready, fish and broth were ladled over slices of bread, and the fishermen ate.

Today, this simplicity has given way to a more complicated formula. Purists insist that at least eight species are necessary for the correct complexity of flavor, most importantly the *rascasse* (scorpion fish), without which, locals insist, it is not a bouillabaisse at all but merely a fish soup. Garlic-rubbed toasted or fried croutons topped with *sauce rouille* have now replaced the bread, and saffron is de rigueur. Cooks around Toulon, which hotly challenges Marseilles for the right to call the soup its own, add mussels and shellfish. Only Parisians, say the fishermen snobbishly—and for them that includes the restaurants of the expensive resorts—add crayfish and lobster. In traditional recipes, water and a little wine are the primary liquids, but classic variations sometimes substitute fish stock.

Fish Soup of Marseilles

La Bouillabaisse • Provence • France

Originated by the fishermen who sailed out of the busy port of Marseilles, bouillabaisse has become a classic of the southern French table. For the requisite complexity of flavor, choose eight or more types of fish, such as scorpion fish, monkfish, snapper, conger eel, whiting, sea robin, ocean perch, and John Dory.

ROUILLE SAUCE

3 large cloves garlic, chopped

1 red chile, seeded and chopped

Salt and freshly ground pepper to taste

3 egg yolks

1¼ cups (14 fl oz/430 ml) olive oil

Olive oil for sautéing

2 large yellow onions, sliced

2 large tomatoes, peeled, seeded, and coarsely chopped

1 leek, white part only, halved lengthwise

3 cloves garlic, chopped

½ fennel bulb, cut into 3 wedges

Zest from ½ orange, cut into wide strips

1 small lemon, cut into wedges

2½–3 qt (2.5–3 l) water or fish stock and dry white wine, in a ratio of 3 parts water or stock to 5 parts wine

2 fresh thyme sprigs

1 bay leaf

½ teaspoon saffron threads, crushed and steeped in 2 teaspoons hot water

2 teaspoons tomato paste, or to taste

Salt and freshly ground pepper to taste

6–7 lb (3–3.5 kg) whole fish (see note)

2 lb (1 kg) crayfish, cut into medallions if large, halved if small (optional)

4 small crabs, cleaned and quartered (optional)

16 mussels, scrubbed and debearded (optional)

3 tablespoons chopped fresh flat-leaf (Italian) parsley

20 croutons made from baguette slices

Serves 8–10

1 To make the rouille sauce, in a mortar, crush the garlic and the chile with a pestle, sprinkling in a pinch of salt to help the pestle grip the mixture. Add the egg yolks and whisk to combine. Add the olive oil, drop by drop, whisking constantly. When an emulsion has formed, add the oil in a slow, steady stream, whisking continuously. Season with salt and pepper. Cover and refrigerate.

2 Pour olive oil to a depth of ⅓ inch (9 mm) in a large, wide soup pot over medium heat. Add the onions and sauté for about 1 minute. Add the tomatoes, leek, garlic, fennel, orange zest, and lemon wedges. Add 3 ladlefuls of the water or stock and wine along with the thyme, bay leaf, saffron, 2 teaspoons tomato paste, salt, and pepper. Raise the heat to high, bring the soup to a rapid boil, and cook for 10 minutes.

3 Leave the fish whole except for the scorpion fish and the conger eel, which should be in chunks. Start adding the firmer-fleshed fish to the pot. Ladle in enough water or stock and wine to keep the seafood almost covered with liquid. Add the crayfish and crabs, if using. Boil rapidly for 10 minutes, then add the more delicate-fleshed fish. Reduce the heat to medium-low and simmer for 10 minutes, adding the mussels, if using, during the last 4–5 minutes of cooking (discard any mussels that fail to close to the touch). Taste and adjust the seasoning with tomato paste, salt, and pepper.

4 Using a large spatula, carefully transfer the seafood to a warmed serving platter, arranging the pieces attractively and discarding any mussels that failed to open. Sprinkle the fish with the parsley. Pass the soup through a fine-meshed sieve into a large tureen. Put a dollop of the sauce on each of 8–10 croutons and float the croutons on the soup. Place the remaining sauce in a bowl and the remaining croutons on a plate.

5 Bring the tureen, the platter of seafood, and the sauce and croutons to the table and serve at once in shallow bowls.

Vegetable Broth with Pesto

Soupe au Pistou • Provence • France

It is the last-minute addition of the wonderfully pungent basil paste known as *pistou* that both gives this dish its name and moves an otherwise simple vegetable soup into the realm of the sublime. Named for the pestle with which it is traditionally ground into a paste, *pistou* is a specialty of Nice, with obvious links to the Italian pesto that originated in nearby Genoa. The closer one is to the Italian frontier, notably in the area of Nice, the more the local *pistou* resembles its Italian counterpart.

1 Pick over the dried beans, discarding any grit or misshapen beans. Rinse well, place in a large bowl, and add water to cover generously. Let the beans stand overnight.

2 Drain the beans and place in a large soup pot. Add the 4 qt (4 l) water and bring to a boil over high heat. Reduce the heat to low and cook, uncovered, for 30 minutes. Add the onion, celery, green beans, zucchini, and tomatoes and season lightly with salt and pepper. Continue to cook, uncovered, until the beans are nearly tender, about 30 minutes longer.

3 Meanwhile, to make the *pistou*, combine the garlic and basil in a mortar and grind with a pestle until a paste begins to form. Add the tomato, if using, and fully incorporate into the mixture. Add the oil, a little at a time, working it into the basil mixture until a smooth paste forms. Mix in the Parmesan and season with salt and pepper. Alternatively, combine the garlic and basil in a food processor and process until finely chopped. Add the tomato, if using, and process until fully incorporated. With the motor running, slowly add the oil, processing until a smooth mixture forms. Add the Parmesan and process to mix, then season with salt and pepper. Set aside.

4 Add the pasta to the soup pot and cook until the pasta and the beans are tender, 12–15 minutes longer. Taste and adjust the seasoning with salt and pepper, then stir in the tomato paste.

5 Stir 2 tablespoons of the *pistou* into the soup until well blended. Ladle the soup into warmed wide soup bowls or into a tureen. Swirl 1 heaping tablespoon of the *pistou* into the soup in each bowl, or swirl 3 or 4 heaping tablespoons into the tureen. Pass the remaining *pistou* at the table.

1 cup (7 oz/220 g) dried beans, preferably half cannellini and half red kidney beans or black-eyed peas

4 qt (4 l) water

1 large yellow onion, chopped

2 celery stalks, sliced

½ lb (250 g) green beans, trimmed, left whole if thin or cut into 1-inch (2.5-cm) lengths if large

2 large zucchini (courgettes), trimmed, halved lengthwise, and then sliced crosswise

3 large, very red tomatoes, peeled, seeded, and coarsely chopped

Salt and freshly ground pepper to taste

PISTOU

3 cloves garlic, sliced

40 fresh basil leaves

1 small tomato, peeled, seeded, and chopped (optional)

3 tablespoons extra-virgin olive oil

½ cup (2 oz/60 g) grated Parmesan cheese

Salt and freshly ground pepper to taste

3½ oz (105 g) vermicelli, broken into 3-inch (7.5-cm) lengths, or small macaroni

2 tablespoons tomato paste, or to taste

Serves 10

Ratatouille

Ratatouille • Provence • France

Perfumed with the region's olive oil, wild thyme, and garlic, ratatouille is the summer vegetable stew of Provence, cooked up when *potagers* and market gardens are full of tomatoes, peppers, eggplants, and zucchini. The proportions of each might vary, but the dish is always well spiced with herbs. Ratatouille, though always a popular first course, is sometimes served as a side dish, a main course, or as a topping for egg dishes.

2 generous tablespoons extra-virgin olive oil

2 small yellow or white onions, chopped

2 eggplants (aubergines), cut into 1-inch (2.5-cm) cubes

4 cloves garlic, minced

2 zucchini (courgettes), cut into 1-inch (2.5-cm) cubes

2 large green, red, or yellow bell peppers (capsicums), seeded and cut into 1-inch (2.5-cm) pieces

8–10 ripe tomatoes, peeled, seeded, and coarsely chopped

3 fresh thyme sprigs

1 fresh rosemary sprig

1 bay leaf

½ teaspoon salt

½ teaspoon freshly ground pepper

¼ cup (⅓ oz/10 g) minced fresh basil

Serves 10

1 In a large, heavy saucepan or soup pot over medium heat, warm the olive oil. When it is hot, reduce the heat to medium-low, add the onions, and sauté until translucent, about 2 minutes. Add the eggplants and garlic and sauté, stirring often, until the eggplant cubes are slightly softened, 3–4 minutes.

2 Add the zucchini and bell peppers and continue to sauté, stirring and turning, until softened, another 4–5 minutes. Add the tomatoes, thyme, rosemary, bay leaf, salt, and pepper and stir and turn for another 2–3 minutes.

3 Cover, reduce the heat to low, and cook, stirring occasionally, until the vegetables are soft and have somewhat blended together, about 40 minutes.

4 Stir in the basil and remove from the heat. Transfer to a serving bowl and serve hot, at room temperature, or cold.

Mushroom, Celery, and Goat Cheese Salad

Salade de Champignons, Celeris et Fromage • Champagne • France

A refreshing, easy-to-prepare salad frequently made in French households combines thinly sliced mushrooms with celery, more common in the north, or with fennel, the custom in the south. The important thing is that the mushroom caps must still be tightly closed.

¼ cup (2 fl oz/60 ml) extra-virgin olive oil

3 tablespoons fresh lemon juice

Scant ½ teaspoon salt

Scant ½ teaspoon freshly ground pepper

4 tablespoons (⅓ oz/10 g) chopped fresh flat-leaf (Italian) parsley

¾ lb (375 g) firm fresh white button mushrooms, brushed clean

4 celery stalks, trimmed

1 2-oz (60-g) piece hard, aged goat cheese

Serves 4

1 In a large bowl, stir together the olive oil, lemon juice, salt, pepper, and 2 tablespoons of the parsley to form a vinaigrette. Set aside.

2 Using a mandoline or a very sharp knife, slice the mushrooms paper-thin. Repeat with the celery. Using a vegetable peeler, shave the cheese into paper-thin slices or curls.

3 Add the mushrooms, celery, and half of the cheese to the bowl holding the vinaigrette and toss well to coat the vegetables.

4 Divide the salad evenly among individual plates. Garnish with the remaining cheese and parsley. Serve at once.

Cream of Winter Squash Soup

Crème de Potiron au Cerfeuil • Central • France

Chervil, one of the classic herbs of French cooking, adds a delicate and slightly surprising licorice flavor to this smooth, light soup. Traditionally a cooking pumpkin would be used, but dense, meaty butternut and acorn squashes are now popular as well.

1 butternut squash, about 2 lb (1 kg)

1 teaspoon plus 1 tablespoon unsalted butter

1 yellow or white onion, chopped

1 cup (8 fl oz/250 ml) chicken stock

⅔ cup (5 fl oz/160 ml) water

3 tablespoons minced fresh chervil

½ teaspoon salt

½ teaspoon freshly ground pepper

1⅓ cups (11 fl oz/340 ml) milk

Serves 4

1 Preheat the oven to 350°F (180°C). Cut the squash in half lengthwise. Scoop out and discard the seeds and fibers. Using the 1 teaspoon butter, rub the cavities and cut edges of the squash. Place the squash halves cut sides down on a baking sheet.

2 Bake until the flesh is very soft when pierced with a fork, 45–50 minutes. Remove from the oven and, when cool enough to handle, scrape the pulp into a bowl; discard the skin. In a saucepan over medium heat, melt the 1 tablespoon butter. When it foams, add the onion and sauté until soft, 4–5 minutes. Add the stock, water, 2 tablespoons of the chervil, and ¼ teaspoon each of the salt and pepper. Simmer, uncovered, for 15 minutes to blend the flavors. Add the squash, stir well, and simmer for another 5 minutes to heat through.

3 Remove from the heat and let cool slightly. Working in batches, transfer the squash mixture to a blender or food processor. With the machine running, add the milk in a steady stream and process until smooth. Return the purée to the saucepan over medium heat and add the remaining ¼ teaspoon each salt and pepper. Cook, stirring continuously, until hot but not boiling.

4 To serve, ladle the soup into warmed bowls. Garnish each bowl with an equal amount of the remaining chervil.

Springtime Lamb Stew

Navarin d'Agneau • Provence • France

A *navarin* is a lamb dish that celebrates the spring harvest. It brings together young, tender lamb and the first of the new season's baby vegetables. The sauce is lighter and less complex than those in the more robust winter casseroles. This brothlike sauce is well suited to the subtle flavors of the baby carrots, baby turnips, peas, and asparagus tips. Fava (broad) beans or haricots verts are optional additions. The most typical accompaniment is boiled new potatoes tossed in butter and parsley.

1 In a Dutch oven over medium heat, melt the butter. Working in batches, add the meat and brown well on all sides, about 15 minutes for each batch. Return all of the browned meat to the pan, add the onion, and sauté until translucent, about 1 minute. Scatter the flour over all and cook, stirring, until some of the flour browns, about 30 seconds.

2 Add the wine, the stock or water, and the bouquet garni and bring to a boil. Reduce the heat to low and simmer, uncovered, for 15 minutes. Stir the meat, add the garlic and sugar, and season lightly with salt and pepper. Cover and continue to simmer over low heat for about 30 minutes.

3 Add the carrots, turnips, radishes, and shallots, cover, and cook at a gentle simmer until the meat is tender, about 40 minutes. Add the asparagus and peas 6–8 minutes before the end of the cooking time.

4 Using a slotted spoon, transfer the meat and vegetables to a warmed serving dish and keep warm. Raise the heat to high, bring the liquid in the pot to a boil, and boil rapidly, stirring, until reduced to a light sauce consistency. Taste and adjust the seasoning with salt and pepper.

5 Spoon the sauce over the meat and vegetables. Garnish with the parsley and serve.

¼ cup (2 oz/60 g) unsalted butter

1 boneless leg of lamb, cut into 2-inch (5-cm) cubes

1 large yellow onion, chopped

2 tablespoons all-purpose (plain) flour

2 cups (16 fl oz/500 ml) dry white wine

2½ cups (20 fl oz/625 ml) light chicken stock or water

Bouquet garni (page 222)

4 cloves garlic, finely chopped

2 teaspoons sugar

Salt and freshly ground pepper to taste

1 lb (500 g) baby carrots, peeled

16 baby turnips, peeled

1 bunch small radishes, trimmed

½ lb (250 g) shallots

24 asparagus tips, each 3 inches (7.5 cm) long

1 lb (500 g) English peas, shelled

2 tablespoons chopped fresh flat-leaf (Italian) parsley

Serves 6

LAMB

Almost everywhere in Provence where flat land gives way to undulating hillsides and mountain foothills is the domain of the lamb. The craggy scrubland and meager grasses in the region are compensated by fragrant herbal bushes that give the lamb a distinctive taste, which translates into a premium price at the market second only to that of the lamb of the salt marshes of Normandy.

Historically, the merino of the Bouches-du-Rhône was proudly raised for wool around Arles and across the open spaces of the Crau Plains. But wool prices have declined, and now almost all sheep in Provence are raised for meat. The capital of the lamb-producing regions is Sisteron, an imposing town on the Durance River. Its perched eleventh-century citadel overlooks the gaping, vertically incised gorges that make one side of the river inaccessible, while the town nestles on the other. Formerly a distribution center for both wool and meat, Sisteron now boasts the second largest abattoir in Europe in the nearby Jabron Valley, making it a large center for the export of Provençal lamb to the European market.

In the past, sheep from as far away as Arles and the Crau Plains were herded from their sun-dried pastures into the Durance Valley and the lower Alps to partake of the rich highland herbal pasture for the summer months. At that time, around June 15, shepherds would begin to herd over half a million sheep from the plains, leading them across villages, down roadways, along the river's banks, and up into the higher pastures. Lack of shepherds has transformed this once-romantic procession known as the transhumance to one of trucks and trains.

Lamb has always been the luxury meat of France and sells well throughout the country as well as locally. But meat is a smaller part of the diet in France than many outsiders realize. Leg of lamb and large joints are traditionally reserved for wedding banquets and special occasions. The smaller, less expensive cuts are cooked in classic dishes like *navarin* along with an assortment of vegetables or are simmered in daubes. Prime cuts, although more affordable now, are still eaten in small quantities as part of a larger meal.

Mussel Soup

Soupe aux Moules • Provence • France

Every region of France with a coastline also has a mussel soup. Most are simple broths that aim to catch the juice as the mussels open; transform its flavor with a little garlic, onion, or parsley; and soften the salty sea brine with a little white wine, beer, or cream. This version of mussel soup is a little more complicated than many, with rich results.

1 In a large saucepan over low heat, melt 3 tablespoons of the butter. Add three-fourths each of the carrots, leeks, and celery and sauté until shiny and well coated with butter, about 2 minutes. Add the potatoes, tomatoes, bouquet garni, and 3 cups (24 fl oz/750 ml) of the water. Raise the heat to high and bring to a boil. Reduce the heat to low, cover, and simmer slowly until the vegetables are tender, about 30 minutes.

2 Meanwhile, in a large soup pot over high heat, bring the wine to a boil. Add the mussels, discarding any that fail to close to the touch, cover, and cook over high heat, stirring once, until the mussels open, 2–3 minutes. Remove from the heat and discard any mussels that failed to open.

3 Set aside 24 mussels in their shells for garnish. Pluck the remainder from their shells and set the meats on a plate. Strain the mussel liquor through a fine-mesh sieve lined with cheesecloth (muslin) set over a bowl. Set aside.

4 Rinse the soup pot, add the remaining 1 tablespoon butter, and place over medium heat. Add the bacon and sauté until the fat is rendered and the bacon begins to crisp, about 1 minute. Add the remaining carrots, leeks, and celery and stir over medium heat until shiny and half-cooked, about 2 minutes.

5 Remove the bouquet garni from the saucepan and discard. Add about ¼ cup (2 oz/60 g) of the shelled mussels and half of the mussel liquor and mix well. Purée with a handheld blender in the pan, or transfer to a blender or food processor and purée. Slowly add the remaining mussel liquor, tasting as you do. Stop adding it if the soup becomes too salty. You will need 3–4 cups (24–32 fl oz/750 ml–1 l) liquid in all. If the liquor is too salty, use some of the remaining 2 cups (16 fl oz/500 ml) water instead. Pour the puréed soup through a medium-mesh sieve onto the vegetables and bacon. Taste and season with salt, if needed, and pepper.

6 Add the remaining mussels, both shelled and unshelled, to the soup and reheat gently to serving temperature. Ladle into wide soup bowls, placing 3 mussels in their shells in the center of each bowl. Serve at once.

4 tablespoons (2 oz/60 g) unsalted butter

2 carrots, peeled and finely diced

2 leeks, white part only, finely diced

2 celery stalks, finely diced

2 potatoes, peeled and diced

2 tomatoes, peeled, seeded, and diced

Bouquet garni (page 222)

3–5 cups (24–40 fl oz/
750 ml–1.25 l) water

1 cup (8 fl oz/250 ml) dry white wine

4 lb (2 kg) mussels, scrubbed
and debearded

¼ lb (125 g) slab bacon, cut crosswise
into pieces ½ inch (12 mm) wide

Salt and freshly ground pepper to taste

Serves 8

Salad of Baby Spinach

Salade d'Épinards • Provence • France

When tender, young spinach is available, the Provençaux like to eat the leaves raw, as in this well-crafted salad. Since Provence produces few cow's milk cheeses, Parmesan cheese from Italy is the likely choice for this dish. Cantal from the Auvergne and Beaufort, a slightly softer, Emmentaler-style cheese from the Savoy, are also excellent.

2 tablespoons pine nuts

5 tablespoons (2½ fl oz/75 ml) extra-virgin olive oil

2 tablespoons sherry vinegar or red wine vinegar

Salt and freshly ground coarse pepper to taste

½ lb (250 g) young, tender spinach leaves, stems removed

Small wedge of Parmesan cheese

2 tablespoons chopped fresh chervil

Serves 6

1 Preheat the oven to 325°F (165°C). Spread the pine nuts in a small pan and toast in the oven, shaking the pan occasionally, until crisp and golden, about 10 minutes. Alternatively, toast the pine nuts in a small frying pan over medium-low heat, stirring constantly, until crisp and golden, about 2 minutes. Pour onto a plate to cool.

2 In a small bowl, whisk together the oil and vinegar. Season with salt and pepper.

3 Place the spinach in a salad bowl or spread in a large, two-handled porcelain dish. Scatter with the pine nuts and drizzle with the dressing.

4 Using a small, sharp knife or a vegetable peeler, shave pieces of the cheese over the top. Sprinkle with the chervil and serve at once without tossing.

Tomato Soup with Fines Herbes

Soupe à la Tomate aux Fines Herbes • Provence • France

Tomato soup is only as good as the tomatoes that are used to make it, so it is no wonder that this soup is synonymous with the summer months, when the reddest, juiciest, most flavorful specimens are in the market. Also best in this season are the pungent, leafy green herbs that the French call *fines herbes*: parsley, chervil, chives, basil, and tarragon.

3 tablespoons olive oil

1 large yellow onion, finely chopped

2 lb (1 kg) ripe tomatoes, peeled, seeded, and coarsely chopped

1 tablespoon sugar

½ celery stalk, finely chopped

6 cups (48 fl oz/1.5 l) water

1 tablespoon tomato paste, or to taste

Salt and freshly ground pepper to taste

5 green (spring) onions, including tender green tops, thinly sliced

⅓ cup (½ oz/15 g) chopped fresh flat-leaf (Italian) parsley

⅓ cup (½ oz/15 g) chopped fresh chervil

12 fresh basil leaves, chopped

Serves 6

1 In a large soup pot over medium heat, warm the oil. Add the onion and sauté until softened, about 1 minute. Add the tomatoes and stir until they release their liquid, about 2 minutes. Add the sugar and continue stirring until all the liquid evaporates and the tomatoes begin to stick—or even caramelize—a little on the bottom of the pot, 2–3 minutes. Add half of the celery, the water, and the tomato paste and mix well. Season lightly with salt and pepper, then bring to a boil, reduce the heat to low, and simmer, uncovered, for about 30 minutes.

2 Using a handheld blender or a potato masher, partially purée the soup, leaving the tomatoes fairly chunky. Add the remaining celery and simmer for 5 minutes longer to blend the flavors.

3 Just before serving, add the green onions, parsley, chervil, and basil and stir to blend. Taste and adjust the seasoning. Ladle into warmed bowls and serve.

OLIVES

With its gnarled, twisted trunk and its narrow silver leaves blowing in the wind, the olive tree is a prevailing image of the Provençal landscape. It lives in backyards, in the wild, in hillside pastures, and in commercial groves, particularly in the Var, the Vaucluse, and the Bouches-du-Rhône.

Its fruit, bitter at birth, yields first the green olive, then the black. The unripe green olives, harvested around November, must be taken from the tree, then bathed in lye and cured in salt to render them palatable. Ripe, black olives eventually fall from the tree, but in December and January, farmers can be seen manning small tractors fitted with large rubber "arms" that grasp and shake the trunks, releasing the fruits onto large cloths spread beneath the branches. Black olives need no alkaline treatment. They can be simply sun-dried or salt-cured for the table.

In the Marché de Fourvilles in Cannes, the olive merchant's wares number no fewer than thirty-six different offerings. Green, pointed *lugnes* sit next to green, fleshy *picholines*. There are black Kalamatas, large *violettes* from Tunisia, green Sévillanes, and the aptly named huge *mamouths*. Some olives, like the *tanche*, are best known by their place of origin (Nyons), as are the Niçoise, their tiny shape and succulent flesh perfect for topping salads.

On display are pitted, smashed, bruised, and cracked olives suitable for eating and for cooking in classic daubes and ragouts. Then come those with flavorings, strictly destined for the aperitif or buffet table. These are marinated in oil; peppered or mixed with chopped chile or minced herbs; tossed with garlic and capers, garlic and orange peel, or thyme, red peppers (capsicums), onion, and capers; or even "smeared with anchovy." Also offered to tempt the palate are bowls of much-loved local specialties: *à la façon grecque* (braised with stock and lemon juice), *à la camarguaise* (with *crème d'anchois* and garlic), and *à la sicilienne* (mixed with lemon).

Niçoise Salad

Salade Niçoise · Provence · France

Arguably one of the best-known salads in the world, the *salade niçoise* appears in a host of variations. It can certainly be eaten without tuna, but the fish is a typical addition. There are those who swear that the salad should never see a potato or any cooked vegetable, and many cooks from Nice insist that it's not worth making the salad at all if the market has no fava beans or artichokes small enough to be eaten raw. The staples of the *salade niçoise*, however, are lettuce, tomatoes, green beans, eggs, anchovies, and Niçoise olives.

6 small, waxy potatoes, unpeeled (optional)

20–24 baby green beans, trimmed

½ lb (250 g) fresh tuna, or 1 can (7 oz/220 g) tuna packed in olive oil

3 tablespoons olive oil, if using fresh tuna

1 head butter (Boston) or romaine (cos) lettuce, leaves separated

9 small firm tomatoes, cut into wedges

5 small white onions, each 2 inches (5 cm) in diameter, sliced

1 green bell pepper (capsicum), seeded and cut lengthwise into narrow strips

1 celery stalk, sliced

1 small, slender English (hothouse) cucumber, peeled or unpeeled, sliced

12 olive oil–packed anchovy fillets, halved lengthwise

6 baby artichokes, trimmed (page 221) and halved lengthwise (optional)

15–18 young, tender fava (broad) beans, peeled (optional; page 223)

⅔ cup (3 oz/90 g) Niçoise olives

12 fresh basil leaves, torn into pieces

VINAIGRETTE

¾ cup (6 fl oz/180 ml) extra-virgin olive oil

3–4 tablespoons fresh lemon juice or red wine vinegar

2 cloves garlic, crushed

Salt and freshly ground pepper to taste

6 hard-boiled eggs, peeled and quartered lengthwise

Serves 6

1 If using potatoes, bring a saucepan three-fourths full of salted water to a boil. Add the potatoes and cook until tender, about 10 minutes. Drain, place under running cold water until cool, and drain again. Cut into slices ¼ inch (6 mm) thick. Set aside.

2 Refill the saucepan three-fourths full of salted water and bring to a boil. Add the green beans to the pan and blanch until tender, 2–3 minutes. Drain, place under running cold water until cool, and drain again. Set aside.

3 If using fresh tuna, cut into slices 1 inch (2.5 cm) wide. In a large frying pan over high heat, warm the olive oil. Add the tuna slices and sear lightly on both sides, about 2 minutes total. Remove from the heat, let cool, and cut into pieces 2 inches (5 cm) long. If using canned tuna, drain and separate into large flakes.

4 Line a large, wide salad bowl with the lettuce leaves. Add the green beans, tomatoes, onions, bell pepper, celery, cucumber, anchovies, and tuna. Add the potatoes, artichokes, and fava beans, if using. Scatter the olives and the basil over the top.

5 To make the vinaigrette, in a bowl, whisk together the extra-virgin olive oil, lemon juice or vinegar to taste, garlic, salt, and pepper. Pour over the salad and toss. Top the salad with the eggs and serve.

Gratinéed Onion Soup

Soupe à l'Oignon Gratinée • Ile-de-France • France

One of the renowned dishes of Paris is onion soup covered with slices of bread, topped with cheese and butter, then browned to form a crust, and served with extra slices of the garlicky toasted bread. The only trick to making this soup is to slice the onions very, very thinly. Thick slices or chopped bits simply don't create the same effect.

1 In a heavy saucepan over medium heat, melt the butter with the olive oil. When the butter foams, add the onions and stir and cook until translucent, 4–5 minutes. Reduce the heat to low, cover, and cook, stirring occasionally, until the onions turn lightly golden, about 15 minutes. Uncover, sprinkle with the sugar and salt, and raise the heat to medium. Cook uncovered, stirring often, until the onions are golden brown, 30–40 minutes.

2 Sprinkle the flour over the onions and continue to stir until the flour is browned, 2–3 minutes. Pour in the stock and the water, a little at a time, while continuing to stir. Raise the heat to high and bring to a boil. Add the wine and stir in the pepper. Reduce the heat to low, cover, and cook until the onions begin to dissolve, about 45 minutes.

3 While the soup is cooking, make the topping. Preheat the broiler (grill). Place the bread on a baking sheet and slip under the broiler 4–5 inches (10–13 cm) from the heat source. Broil (grill), turning once, just long enough to dry out, but not brown, 3–4 minutes on each side. Remove from the broiler and rub both sides with the garlic cloves. Then brush both sides with the olive oil. Return to the broiler and toast, turning once, until lightly golden, 2–3 minutes on each side. Set aside.

4 Preheat the oven to 450°F (230°C).

5 Place 6–8 individual ovenproof bowls on a baking sheet. Ladle the hot soup into them. Top each with 2 pieces of the toast, then sprinkle the cheese evenly over the tops. Dot evenly with the butter. Place in the oven and cook until a golden crust forms on the top and the soup bubbles around the edges, about 15 minutes. Serve at once.

6 tablespoons (3 oz/90 g) unsalted butter

1 tablespoon extra-virgin olive oil

2 lb (1 kg) yellow onions, very thinly sliced

½ teaspoon sugar

½ teaspoon salt

1½ tablespoons all-purpose (plain) flour

8 cups (64 fl oz/2 l) beef stock

2 cups (16 fl oz/500 ml) water

1 cup (8 fl oz/250 ml) dry white wine

1 teaspoon freshly ground pepper

TOPPING

12–16 slices coarse country bread, each ½ inch (12 mm) thick

2 cloves garlic, halved

3 tablespoons extra-virgin olive oil

2 cups (8 oz/250 g) shredded Gruyère or Emmentaler cheese

2 tablespoons unsalted butter, cut into small bits

Serves 6–8

Dandelion Salad with Poached Eggs

Salade de Pissenlit aux Oeufs Pochès • Languedoc • France

Throughout France, from the Alps to the Pyrenees, from Normandy to Alsace, the wild greens that have traditionally been part of the regional rural cuisine are the harbingers of spring. Dandelion is among the most pervasive of them and is used in both soups and salads. To be at their most tender and flavorful, the leaves must be picked before the flower shoots have formed, when the plant is still only a rosette. Dandelion leaves are sometimes mixed with other greens such as endive, as in this salad.

¼ cup (2 fl oz/60 ml) extra-virgin olive oil

3 tablespoons Banyuls or other red wine vinegar

½ shallot, minced

Scant ½ teaspoon salt

Scant ½ teaspoon freshly ground pepper

2 cups (2 oz/60 g) young, tender dandelion leaves, each 3–4 inches (7.5–10 cm) long, larger ones torn in half

3 cups (3 oz/90 g) curly endive (chicory), pale inner leaves only, torn into bite-sized pieces

4 eggs (see page 223)

Serves 4

1 In a large bowl, stir together the olive oil, vinegar, shallot, salt, and pepper to form a vinaigrette. Add the dandelion and curly endive and toss to coat. Divide evenly among individual salad bowls.

2 Pour water to a depth of 1 inch (2.5 cm) in a frying pan and bring to a gentle simmer over medium heat. One at a time, carefully break the eggs into the frying pan and poach them, spooning some of the hot water over them as they cook, until the whites are set and the yolks are glazed, 2–3 minutes. Using a slotted spoon, remove each egg, letting it drain a moment and blotting briefly on a kitchen towel. Place an egg on top of each salad and serve at once.

Fish Stew

Pot-au-Feu de Poisson • Provence • France

Each area of France has its own *pot-au-feu*. The Provençal version of this "pot on the fire" contains fish from the Mediterranean, tomatoes, leeks, fennel, garlic, and a pinch of saffron.

4 lb (2 kg) mixed white-fleshed whole fish such as red snapper, porgy, orange roughy, lingcod, sea perch, and Atlantic salmon, cleaned

2 small fennel bulbs, trimmed and cut lengthwise into quarters

1 leek, white part only, cut into 4-inch (10-cm) lengths

4 celery stalks, cut into 4-inch (10-cm) lengths

5 tomatoes, peeled, seeded, and quartered

¼ cup (2 fl oz/60 ml) olive oil

2 yellow onions, minced

3 cloves garlic, minced

3 tablespoons minced fresh flat-leaf (Italian) parsley

Salt and freshly ground black pepper to taste

¼ teaspoon saffron threads, crushed and steeped in 2 teaspoons hot water

Pinch of cayenne pepper

1¼ cups (10 fl oz/310 ml) dry white wine

24 small mussels, scrubbed and debearded

16 sea scallops

12 large shrimp (prawns), peeled and deveined

ROMESCO SAUCE

Fresh white bread crumbs, from 2 thick slices day-old sourdough bread

3 large red bell peppers (capsicums), roasted (page 221)

Salt and freshly ground black pepper

Tiny pinch of cayenne pepper

3 tablespoons chopped fresh flat-leaf (Italian) parsley

24 croutons made from baguette slices

Serves 8

1 Fillet most of the fish into chunky pieces about 5 by 3 inches (13 by 7.5 cm). Reserve 1 lb (500 g) of the heads and larger bones or tails for the stock. Cut larger, thicker fish across the bone into steaks.

2 Cut the fennel, leek, celery, and tomatoes as indicated, saving enough trimmings to yield about 1 cup (5 oz/155 g) finely chopped mixed vegetables. In a saucepan over medium heat, warm the olive oil. Add the onions, garlic, and parsley and sauté until fragrant. Add the finely chopped mixed vegetables and the fish heads and bones or tails. Season with salt and black pepper and add the saffron and cayenne. Pour in the white wine and 4 cups (32 fl oz/1 l) water, bring to a boil, and cook rapidly, uncovered, for about 30 minutes. Remove from the heat and strain through a sieve lined with cheesecloth (muslin) placed over a clean saucepan.

3 Place the mussels in a saucepan, discarding any that fail to close to the touch. Cover, place over high heat, and cook, shaking the pan from time to time, until the mussels open, 3–5 minutes. Transfer the mussels to a plate, discarding any that failed to open. Pass the juices through a fine-mesh sieve lined with cheesecloth placed over a bowl. Set aside. Remove 8 of the mussels from their shells.

4 Bring the strained stock to a boil over high heat. Add the fennel, leek, and celery, and cook until just tender, about 4 minutes. Add the tomatoes when the other vegetables are cooked. Reduce the heat to medium-low, lower the fish pieces into the stock, and simmer until opaque throughout, 6–8 minutes. Halfway through the cooking time, add the scallops and shrimp. Remove from the heat and add all the mussels. Season with black pepper and a little of the reserved mussel juice.

5 Meanwhile, to make the sauce, in a bowl, combine the bread crumbs with about ½ cup (4 fl oz/125 ml) water. Let stand until the water is absorbed. Squeeze out the excess water, then place the moistened crumbs in a blender or food processor. Add the bell peppers and process until puréed. Season with salt, black pepper, and cayenne. Add a small ladleful of the stock from the stew and process again. Transfer to a small saucepan and place over medium heat, stirring until heated through.

6 Transfer the fish, shellfish, and vegetables to a platter. Ladle in the stock. Drizzle with some of the sauce and sprinkle with the parsley. Serve the remaining sauce in a bowl alongside the croutons.

Roast Garlic Chicken and Walnut Salad

Salade de Poulet Rôti aux Noix • Franche-Comté • France

One of the main walnut-producing areas of France is near Grenoble, in the Dauphiné. Consequently, walnuts and walnut oil are elements in many of the regional dishes, from first courses to desserts, and they often appear in combination, as they do here, which produces a complexity of flavors. Garlic slipped beneath the skin of the chicken delicately scents the meat. Together, the walnuts and garlic form a flavorful companionship, as this dish shows. Serve as a substantial, warm main-dish salad for lunch or dinner.

1 Preheat the oven to 350°F (180°C).

2 Rinse the chicken and pat dry. Rub the chicken inside and out with the salt and pepper. Using your fingers and starting at the cavity, gently separate the skin from the breast meat, reaching as far back toward the neck and as close to the thighs as possible to create a pocket. Be careful not to tear the skin. Slip the garlic slices between the skin and the meat, spreading them evenly over the breast. Place the chicken, breast up, on a rack in a roasting pan. Add the chicken stock to the pan.

3 Roast, basting occasionally, until the juices run clear when a sharp knife is inserted into a thigh joint, about 1¼ hours. Alternatively, insert an instant-read thermometer into the thickest part of a thigh away from the bone; it should register 180°F (82°C). Transfer to a cutting board and let rest for 10 minutes before carving.

4 While the chicken is resting, begin to make the salad. In a small frying pan over low heat, toast the walnuts, shaking the pan often, until a nut piece is golden brown when cut in half, about 10 minutes. Transfer to a plate and set aside.

5 In a large bowl, stir together the walnut oil, vinegar, shallot, salt, and pepper. Tear the lettuce leaves into bite-sized pieces, add them to the bowl, and toss well to coat with the dressing.

6 Arrange the salad on a platter and sprinkle with half of the toasted walnuts.

7 Carve the chicken, slicing the breast meat and separating the thighs from the legs. Arrange the thighs, legs, wings, and the sliced breast meat on top of the salad, including any bits of garlic that slipped from beneath the skin while carving. Sprinkle with the remaining walnuts and serve warm.

1 chicken, about 3 lb (1.5 kg)

1½ teaspoons salt

1½ teaspoons freshly ground pepper

4 cloves garlic, thinly sliced lengthwise

½ cup (4 fl oz/125 ml) chicken stock

WALNUT SALAD
¾ cup (3 oz/90 g) coarsely chopped walnuts

3 tablespoons walnut oil

1½ teaspoons Champagne vinegar or white wine vinegar

1 shallot, minced

¼ teaspoon salt

¼ teaspoon freshly ground pepper

5 cups (5 oz/155 g) green-leaf, red-leaf, or other leaf lettuce, or a mixture

Serves 4

Summer Salad of Red Onions and Tomatoes

Salade de Tomates • Provence • France

It isn't a true summer in Provence unless there is some sort of tomato salad served at least once a day, if not twice. Sometimes the tomatoes will be sliced, other times they are quartered. The salad might also include anchovies, green peppers, fresh or aged goat cheese, red onions, cucumbers, or olives. It is an ideal accompaniment to a dish that includes grilled fish or chops, but it makes a fine first course on its own.

6 ripe tomatoes, thinly sliced

2 tablespoons minced red onion

½ teaspoon salt

½ teaspoon freshly ground pepper

¼ cup (⅓ oz/10 g) minced fresh basil

3 tablespoons extra-virgin olive oil

1 tablespoon red wine vinegar

Serves 4–6

1 Arrange the tomato slices on a platter. Sprinkle with the red onion, salt, and pepper and scatter the basil over the top.

2 Drizzle the tomatoes, onion, and basil with the olive oil and the vinegar. Serve at once.

Creamy Fish Soup

La Bourride • Provence • France

In southeastern Provençal ports, fishing villages, and coastal resort towns—from Saint-Raphaël to Saint-Tropez to Nice—this fish soup is served in many restaurants and, for grand occasions, at home. *Bourride* is made unique by the addition of aioli, which is whisked into the soup in large quantity to give it an essentially creamy yellow look that is very different from the region's other great fish soup, bouillabaisse. In Provence, monkfish is the most common addition, but sea bass is also often used, as are whiting and John Dory.

STOCK

2 tablespoons olive oil

1 yellow onion, sliced

4 carrots, peeled and sliced

2 leeks, white part only, sliced

2 Swiss chard leaves, stalks removed and leaves coarsely sliced (optional)

1 fresh thyme sprig

2 orange zest strips, 2½ inches (6 cm) long and ½ inch (12 mm) wide

1¾ cups (14 fl oz/430 ml) dry white wine

6–8 cups (48–64 fl oz/1.5–2 l) water or light fish stock

AIOLI

6 cloves garlic

3 egg yolks (see page 223)

2 teaspoons Dijon mustard

1–1¾ cups (8–14 fl oz/250–430 ml) olive oil

Salt and freshly ground white pepper to taste

White wine vinegar or fresh lemon juice to taste

3 lb (1.5 kg) white-fleshed fish, in fillets or thick-cut medallions

Salt and freshly ground pepper to taste

12 slices day-old baguette or dense sourdough bread

3 egg yolks (see page 223)

Serves 6

1 To make the stock, in a large saucepan over medium heat, warm the olive oil. Add the onion, carrots, and leeks and sauté until softened and shiny with oil, about 1 minute. Add the Swiss chard (if using), thyme, and orange zest, stir briefly, and then pour in the wine and the water or stock. Raise the heat to high and bring to a boil. Reduce the heat to low and simmer slowly, uncovered, for 20 minutes to infuse the liquid with flavor.

2 While the stock is simmering, make the aioli. To make the aioli, in a small bowl with a handheld electric mixer or a wire whisk, mash the garlic. Add the 3 egg yolks and mustard and beat for a few moments until blended. Begin adding the oil, drop by drop, beating constantly. When an emulsion has formed, add the oil in a very fine, steady stream, continuing to beat until the aioli has thickened to the desired consistency. The more oil used, the thicker the result. Season to taste with salt, white pepper, and vinegar or lemon juice, then cover and refrigerate. (To make the aioli in a food processor, coarsely chop the garlic, place it in the food processor, and pulse to chop as finely as possible. Add the egg yolks and mustard and pulse again briefly. With the motor running, add the oil in a very fine stream, then proceed as directed for mixer method above.)

3 Strain the stock through a fine-mesh sieve then return it to the pan. Bring to a boil and boil, uncovered, until reduced by one-third. Remove from the heat and let cool slightly, about 15 minutes, before continuing.

4 If using fillets, cut them into large chunks about 4 inches (10 cm) long. Place the fish in the cooled stock. Season lightly with salt and pepper and bring to just under a boil. Reduce the heat to low and simmer, uncovered, until the fish is opaque throughout, 8–10 minutes.

5 While the fish is cooking, arrange the bread slices in the bottom of individual soup plates, placing 2 slices in each plate. When the fish is cooked, using a slotted spoon or wide metal spatula, carefully transfer the fish to a serving platter and keep warm.

6 If the soup tastes too bland, boil it down to concentrate the flavor. Adjust the seasoning with salt and pepper. Moisten the bread with a little of the soup. Reserve about half the aioli to serve separately in a bowl. Whisk the 3 egg yolks into the remaining aioli. Ladle about ¾ cup (6 fl oz/180 ml) of the hot soup into this mixture, whisk to blend well, and then return to the soup, again whisking well. Whisking continuously, reheat the soup until the egg yolks bind and thicken the soup, being very careful not to allow the soup to boil, to avoid curdling the egg yolks. If properly done, the soup will lightly coat the back of a spoon in the manner of a custard.

7 Ladle the soup over the bread in the soup plates. Serve the fish and the reserved aioli separately. Diners alternately spoon fish and aioli into their bowls.

Dandelion Salad

Salade de Pissenlits • Provence • France

The Provençaux forage for dandelions in the wild, looking for the youngest greens, since the leaves can be bitter and tough. Perhaps that explains why this salad is always served with a hot dressing, which softens the leaves and tempers their flavor. In the dressing, bacon contrasts with the sharp acidity of the vinegar, both of which enhance the peppery dandelion leaves. If dandelions are unavailable, use other strong-textured leaves such as spinach, so the greens do not wilt when the hot dressing is poured over the salad.

6 oz (185 g) young dandelion leaves, tough stems and base ends removed

2 tablespoons blanched hazelnuts (filberts), coarsely chopped (optional)

3 oz (90 g) thick-cut sliced slab bacon, cut crosswise into pieces ½ inch (12 mm) wide

1½ tablespoons sherry vinegar or red wine vinegar

2–3 tablespoons extra-virgin olive oil

Salt and freshly ground coarse pepper to taste

Serves 6

1 Pick over the dandelion leaves, tearing the larger ones in half. Place in a wooden salad bowl. Add the hazelnuts, if using.

2 In a small frying pan over high heat, fry the bacon until crisp and its fat has been rendered, about 1 minute. Using a slotted spoon, transfer the bacon to the bowl holding the dandelions, leaving the fat in the pan.

3 Return the pan to high heat, add the vinegar, and swirl the pan or stir with a wooden spoon to remove the browned bits on the bottom.

4 Pour in as much additional oil as will be necessary to dress the salad, swirl once to heat a little, and then pour the contents of the pan over the salad. Season with salt and pepper, toss, and serve at once.

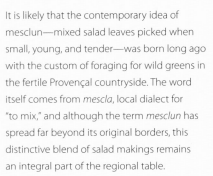

MESCLUN

It is likely that the contemporary idea of mesclun—mixed salad leaves picked when small, young, and tender—was born long ago with the custom of foraging for wild greens in the fertile Provençal countryside. The word itself comes from *mescla*, local dialect for "to mix," and although the term *mesclun* has spread far beyond its original borders, this distinctive blend of salad makings remains an integral part of the regional table.

The greens vary with the season, but mesclun generally includes frisée, arugula, red and green oak leaf lettuce, mâche (also known as lamb's lettuce), radicchio, *trévisse* (a small oval leaf similar to arugula), and herbs like chervil, cress, and purslane. In the spring, when vegetable gardens are at their most bountiful, mesclun may contain ten or more varieties of greens.

Mesclun typically appears in salads dressed with a good olive oil and a fine wine vinegar and nothing more. But mesclun has assumed another important role, and often the delicate leaves serve as the base for such familiar first courses as smoked or air-dried meats or broiled goat cheese.

ITALY

*I*n Italy, the word insalata *doesn't necessarily refer to lettuce. Glistening platters of lightly dressed, lettuce-free "salads" of fresh vegetables, grains, and cheese are the highlight of many a trattoria's antipasti table—that mouth-watering display of appetite-whetting starters cunningly laid out at the front of most Italian eateries, its appearance so alluring that it seems to pull hungry customers right into the restaurant.*

Like much of Italian cooking, the character of *insalate* changes as you travel from one region to another and pass from one season to the next. Delicate fava beans tossed with pungent arugula capture the capricious promises of springtime, while ripe tomatoes lavish their summery juices over torn crusty bread to make the popular salad known as *panzanella*. In autumn, roasted peppers touched with anchovies fill the mouth with smoky sweetness. Crunchy slices of celery tossed with new-crop green olives add a welcome freshness to the meat and bean dishes of winter. For the everyday table, there is a salad of sheer wisps of raw fennel, tangy oranges, and pecorino cheese, or a bitter-sharp combination of slivered radicchio and arugula dressed simply with olive oil and balsamic vinegar. This last combination of greens is so common on

Italian tables that it is sold, already cleaned, in clear plastic boxes in the produce section of many Italian supermarkets. Green salads are typically dressed tableside, first with a generous pour of green or golden olive oil, then with a sprinkle of sea salt and a grinding of fresh black pepper, and finally with a splash of wine vinegar. The whole process is effected with such offhand ease that it is easy to overlook the practical reasoning behind each step. The olive oil goes on first, because the leaves must be dry for the olive oil to cling to them. Once coated, the leaves can grab the salt and pepper. A sprinkle of vinegar adds just enough sharpness.

In the scenic waterside restaurants of both the Adriatic and Mediterranean coasts, summertime tourists of all nationalities sip glasses of lightly chilled *vino bianco* and enjoy forkfuls of *insalata di frutti di mare*,

Preceding pages: In Florence, the Arno passes under the Ponte Vecchio, first constructed by the early Romans and rebuilt many times since.
Top: *Radicchio di Treviso*, a bitter, red chicory, is grown in the Veneto and often served in salads.
Above: Basil is added to many Italian dishes, especially those with tomatoes and seafood.
Right: The ubiquitous motor scooter simplifies negotiation of Italy's narrow, ancient streets.

a marriage of shrimp, mussels, clams, and squid dressed with lemon and olive oil, or *carpaccio di polpo*, thinly sliced octopus scattered with slivers of celery and *cipolla di Tropea* (a sweet onion grown in the south of Italy). Following this *pranzo* (lunch) is a siesta under the welcoming shade of a wide canvas umbrella. At home, keeping a few cans of meaty Italian tuna (packed in olive oil) and imported cannellini beans on hand ensures that a quick but delicious salad, perfect for a midday lunch, can be whipped up in just a few minutes.

Soup, in Italy, has often been a stalwart answer to scarcity, a way of filling bellies when a plate of pasta or rice was beyond the family's means. In Tuscany, such necessity was raised to a fine art. Even now, if you walk into a Tuscan house and follow the enticing perfume that beckons you into the kitchen, chances are you will find a pot of gently simmering soup. Most Tuscan soups originated as peasants' dishes and embody that elemental and enviable aspect of Tuscan cooking: the ability to make something both nourishing and delicious from whatever is available, whether a handful of herbs and vegetables, a loaf of day-old bread, or a few ladlefuls of beans.

Beans and bread are at the heart of many Tuscan soups, part of the area's thrifty legacy of letting nothing go to waste. Other scraps have their place, too: a rind of Parmesan cheese, a flavorful bone scraped clean of proscuitto, handfuls of wild thyme or rosemary gleaned from the roadside: all could go into the pot to add seasoning and richness to the broth. Traditionally, *minestre* or *zuppe* appeared on Tuscan tables at least once a day, usually served as a filling first course. The former generally refers to broth-based soups but is also a generic term for first courses as a whole. The latter is used for thick soups made or served with bread, like Florence's famous *pappa al pomodoro*, a thick mash of fresh tomatoes, basil, and day-old saltless bread, and *ribollita*, a thick soup made with carrots, winter greens, white beans, and country bread that is still served in the famous central market in Florence.

Not all Italian soups were born of hard times, of course. Along the coasts of the Adriatic and the Mediterranean, each port town has its own version of fishermen's soup, from the *ciuppin* of Liguria (a dish brought by Genovese immigrants to San Francisco, where it became the city's beloved cioppino) to Livorno's famed *cacciucco* and Lazio's lusty *zuppe di pesce alla Romana*, full of clams, squid, and firm-fleshed white fish, all spiked with hot chiles and plenty of garlic. Rich game stews, or *stufato*, are part of the delights of the autumn table in the Alpine regions of Trentino and Alto Adige. Hunting was a pastime much beloved by Tuscany's noble inhabitants as well as by its peasants, and peppery meat stews are still a legacy of Tuscan gastronomy.

Left: Braids of onion brighten a pale Italian wall. **Above, left:** A sculpture of Girolamo Savonarola who was the fanatical monk that ordered the Bonfire of the Vanities in Florence's Piazza della Signoria and was himself burned at the stake in 1497 by his own disillusioned followers. **Above, right:** *Pomodori secchi sott'olio*, sun-dried tomatoes in olive oil, are a popular ingredient throughout Southern Italy.

Spring Vegetable Soup

Garmugia • Tuscany • Italy

Few recipes celebrate early spring's bounty as deliciously as Lucca's traditional *garmugia*, a beautiful soup that easily makes a complete meal on its own.

3 tablespoons extra-virgin olive oil

1 fresh Italian sausage, casing removed and meat crumbled

3 small white onions, thinly sliced

3 oz (90 g) ground (minced) lean veal or beef

2 baby artichokes, trimmed and sliced (page 221)

½ cup (2½ oz/75 g) shelled fava (broad) beans, peeled (page 223)

½ cup (2½ oz/75 g) shelled English peas

½ cup (2 oz/60 g) asparagus tips

6 cups (48 fl oz/1.5 l) chicken stock

Salt and freshly ground pepper to taste

CROUTONS

¼ cup (2 fl oz/60 ml) extra-virgin olive oil

2 cloves garlic, crushed

4 slices coarse country bread, each ½ inch (12 mm) thick, cut into ½-inch (12-mm) cubes

1 tablespoon chopped fresh flat-leaf (Italian) parsley

Serves 6

1 In a large saucepan over medium heat, warm the olive oil. Add the sausage meat and sauté until it begins to release its juices, about 3 minutes. Add the onions and the ground meat and sauté for 4 minutes. Add the artichokes, fava beans, peas, and asparagus and stir well. Pour in the stock, cover, and bring to a boil. Reduce the heat to low and cook until the flavors are blended, about 30 minutes, skimming off any froth from the surface. Halfway through the cooking time, season with salt and pepper.

2 To prepare the croutons, in a frying pan over medium heat, warm the olive oil. Add the garlic and sauté until it begins to turn golden, about 2 minutes. Discard the garlic. Add the bread cubes and stir until golden brown on all sides, about 4 minutes. Using a slotted spoon, transfer the croutons to paper towels to drain. Sprinkle with the parsley.

3 Ladle the soup into warmed bowls, garnish with the croutons, and serve at once.

Fava Bean, Arugula, and Pecorino Salad

Insalata di Fave, Rucola e Pecorino • Lazio • Italy

In Italy, this salad is made with a more flavorful pointed-leaved cousin of the arugula commonly found elsewhere. Fresh fava beans are at their best in the spring, when the pods are small and the beans are tender. Romans like to eat them right out of the pods, accompanied with wedges of sharp pecorino romano cheese and Frascati wine. If the beans are small, peeling them may not be necessary. Pecorino romano, one of the best known of Italy's many sheep's milk cheeses, is prized for its sharp taste and dense texture.

1 lb (500 g) fava (broad) beans, shelled

3 tablespoons extra-virgin olive oil

2 tablespoons fresh lemon juice

Salt and freshly ground pepper to taste

4 cups (4 oz/125 g) arugula (rocket) leaves

Wedge of pecorino romano cheese

Serves 4

1 Bring a small saucepan three-fourths full of water to a boil. Add the fava beans, blanch for 1 minute, and drain. Cool under running cold water. Using your fingertips or a small knife, slit the fava bean skins and then gently pinch them to free the beans.

2 In a large bowl, whisk together the olive oil, lemon juice, salt, and pepper. Add the arugula and fava beans and toss to coat evenly. Taste and adjust the seasoning.

3 Divide the salad among 4 individual plates. Using a vegetable peeler, shave thin curls of the cheese over the salads. Serve at once.

Bread and Tomato Soup

Pappa al Pomodoro · Tuscany · Italy

Pappa is a dish so strictly associated with easy-to-digest, healthful baby food that the word is an indispensable entry in the lexicon of Italian baby talk. *Pappa al pomodoro* is also a favorite with adults, as it combines four of the ingredients that Florentines love most: tomatoes, bread, basil, and fruity olive oil. Each bowl is usually drizzled with more oil.

¼ cup (2 fl oz/60 ml) extra-virgin olive oil

4 cloves garlic, minced

2 lb (1 kg) tomatoes, peeled, seeded, and chopped

8 fresh basil leaves

4 cups (32 fl oz/1 l) light vegetable stock or salted water

Salt to taste

½ lb (250 g) day-old, unsalted coarse country bread, cut into 1-inch (2.5-cm) slices and torn into medium-sized pieces

Freshly ground pepper to taste

Serves 4

1 In a large saucepan over medium heat, warm the olive oil. Add the garlic and sauté, stirring frequently, until the garlic begins to color, about 1 minute. Stir in the tomatoes and bring to a gentle boil. Tear 5 of the basil leaves into pieces and stir into the tomatoes. Pour in the stock or salted water, raise the heat to medium-high, and bring to a boil. Season the soup with salt, reduce the heat to low, and stir in the bread. Simmer uncovered, stirring often, until the bread softens, about 5 minutes.

2 Remove the soup from the heat, cover, and let stand for 1 hour.

3 Before serving the soup, adjust the seasoning with salt and pepper, stir well, and add the remaining 3 basil leaves. Reheat, if desired, or serve warm or at room temperature.

LA VUCCIRIA

The Vucciria, which means "voices" in the Sicilian dialect, is Palermo's oldest outdoor market. Stretched out along a warren of narrow streets, its countless stalls offer a jumble of foods and other goods, tempting the stroller at every turn. A good olive vendor sells every imaginable type—dried, brined, salted, packed in oil—as well as *sott'aceti*, pickled vegetables, and *estratto* (*'strattu* in Sicilian dialect), a brick red paste of sun-dried tomatoes that local cooks sometimes use in place of fresh tomatoes in soups or sauces. The *estratto* is molded into huge pine cone, and in one smooth, deft movement, the vendor scoops off a portion, wraps it in waxed paper, and hands it over.

An older gentleman volunteers his recipe for a quick tomato sauce using the intensely flavored extract. He explains how he sautés onions and garlic in olive oil, throws in a pinch of hot pepper flakes, and stirs in a dollop of *estratto*, a splash of white wine, and some water. He then simmers it briefly before tossing it with pasta. *Squisito!*

Strolling salesmen hawk snacks of cooked tripe, potato croquettes, and *arancine* (stuffed rice balls), while tired shoppers line up to purchase *vastedde* (also known as *guasteddu*), soft bread rolls filled with spleen and caciocavallo cheese. For a bird's-eye view of the constant swirl of activity, take a seat on the balcony of the venerable—and utterly basic—Trattoria Shanghai, overlooking the Vicolo dei Mezzani, at the heart of the market. Despite the exotic name, the kitchen serves local plates—simple pastas, seafood platters, classic cutlets, *contorni* of greens. At dusk, you can watch as the tangle of bare bulbs below comes on to light the way for shoppers making a few last-minute purchases for the evening table.

Celery and Olive Salad

Insalata di Sedano e Olive • Sicily • Italy

All olives start out green and turn black as they ripen. Green olives are picked early in the season, around September or October, then cured in brine to preserve them and remove any bitterness. Sometimes this brine, called *salamoia*, is flavored with garlic, bay leaves, or fennel stalks. The olives are ready to eat after three to four months. Serve this crunchy, colorful salad with salami or a sharp cheese such as provolone or caciocavallo.

1 small red onion, thinly sliced

½ lb (250 g) Sicilian green olives, pitted if desired

4 tender celery stalks, sliced

2 carrots, peeled and thinly sliced

2 tablespoons chopped fresh flat-leaf (Italian) parsley

½ teaspoon dried oregano

1 small dried red chile, crushed, or pinch of red pepper flakes

¼ cup (2 fl oz/60 ml) extra-virgin olive oil

2 tablespoons white wine vinegar

Serves 6

1 In a bowl, combine the onion slices with cold water to cover. Let stand for 10 minutes, then drain. If the onions still smell strong, soak them again, then drain and pat dry. Place in a bowl.

2 On a cutting board, using the flat side of a heavy knife blade, lightly crush the olives. Add to the bowl of onions along with the celery, carrots, parsley, oregano, chile, olive oil, and vinegar. Toss well, cover, and refrigerate to chill for a few hours or as long as overnight.

3 Let stand at room temperature for 30 minutes before serving.

Warm Bean Salad with Tuna and Radicchio

Insalata di Fagioli con Tonno e Radicchio • Tuscany • Italy

Radicchio is arguably the most prestigious member of the chicory family, a large group of leafy greens that grow wild throughout Italy. Here, smooth, creamy traditionally Tuscan beans are a perfect complement to the slightly bitter flavor of grilled radicchio. If you don't have the time to cook the beans, 3 cups (18 oz/560 g) canned beans may be substituted. Rinse the beans and warm them gently over medium-low heat before using.

BEANS

1 rounded cup (8 oz/250 g) dried cannellini or borlotti beans

2 tablespoons extra-virgin olive oil

1 or 2 cloves garlic

1 fresh sage sprig

Salt to taste

2 small heads radicchio

Extra-virgin olive oil for brushing, plus 2 tablespoons

Salt and freshly ground pepper to taste

1 cup (5 oz/155 g) chopped celery, including some of the leaves

½ small red onion, chopped

Pinch of dried oregano

1–2 tablespoons fresh lemon juice

1 can (7 oz/220 g) tuna in olive oil, drained and separated into chunks

Serves 4–6

1 To prepare the beans, pick over them and discard any stones or misshapen beans. Rinse the beans under running cold water and drain. Place in a large bowl with cold water to cover and let soak for at least 4 hours at room temperature or for as long as overnight in the refrigerator.

2 Drain the beans and place them in a large saucepan with fresh water to cover by about 1 inch (2.5 cm). Bring to a simmer over high heat. Add the olive oil, garlic, and sage sprig. Cover, reduce the heat to low, and simmer until the beans are tender but not falling apart, about 1 hour. Once cooked, season the beans with salt. Remove from the heat and let stand for 10 minutes.

3 Preheat the broiler (grill), or prepare a fire in a charcoal grill.

4 Cut each radicchio into 4–6 wedges through the core, so that the wedges will keep their shape. Brush with olive oil and sprinkle with salt and pepper. Broil or grill the radicchio, turning once, until wilted and lightly browned, about 5 minutes total.

5 Meanwhile, drain off the excess liquid from the beans. Add the celery, onion, oregano, the 2 tablespoons olive oil, 1 tablespoon of the lemon juice, salt, and pepper. Toss well. Taste and adjust the seasoning with more lemon juice, salt, and pepper.

6 Arrange the radicchio wedges on a platter. Pile the warm beans in the center and top with the tuna. Serve at once.

Farro Salad

Insalata di Farro · Tuscany · Italy

An ancient grain in the same family as wheat, *farro*, which long ago fell out of use in the Italian kitchen, has become popular again. Its appeal comes not only from its nutty flavor, but also because it is healthful and easy to digest, even by many people who are allergic to wheat. Residents of the Garfagnana area of eastern Tuscany where *farro* is grown claim that the grain is also an effective aphrodisiac well into old age.

1 cup (5 oz/155 g) *farro* (spelt)

4 cups (32 fl oz/1 l) water

1 teaspoon salt, plus salt to taste

4–6 radishes, trimmed and thinly sliced

2 tomatoes, chopped

1 small cucumber, chopped

⅓ cup (2 oz/60 g) chopped pitted Gaeta or other Mediterranean-style black olives

¼ cup (¼ oz/7 g) fresh basil leaves, cut into narrow strips

3 tablespoons extra-virgin olive oil

Freshly ground pepper to taste

Lettuce leaves

4 hard-boiled eggs, peeled and quartered

Serves 4

1 In a bowl, combine the *farro* with water to cover. Let soak for 2 hours. Drain, place in a large pot, and add the water. Bring to a boil over high heat and add the 1 teaspoon salt. Reduce the heat to low and cook, uncovered, until very soft, about 40 minutes. (Cooking time may vary as much as 10–20 minutes.)

2 Drain the *farro* and pour into a large bowl. Add the radishes, tomatoes, cucumber, olives, basil, olive oil, salt, and pepper and toss well. Line a platter with lettuce leaves and spoon or pour the *farro* mixture into the center. Arrange the egg quarters around the edge of the platter and serve.

Puréed White Bean Soup

Passato di Fagioli • Tuscany • Italy

The *passaverdure*, or food mill, is a common tool in the Tuscan kitchen. Passing the beans through this simple kitchen helper removes their skins and makes a smooth, velvety soup.

1 cup (7 oz/220 g) dried cannellini beans

5 cups (40 fl oz/1.25 l) water

1 fresh sage sprig

2 fresh rosemary sprigs

3 cloves garlic, 2 whole and 1 minced

2 tablespoons extra-virgin olive oil

1 yellow onion, chopped

4 fresh sage leaves, chopped

2-oz (60-g) piece pancetta

2 large tomatoes, peeled, seeded, and chopped

5 cups (40 fl oz/1.25 l) chicken stock or water

Salt and freshly ground pepper to taste

1½ teaspoons chopped fresh flat-leaf (Italian) parsley

Serves 4–6

1 Pick over the beans, discarding any stones or misshapen beans. Rinse well, place in a bowl, and add water to cover generously. Let soak overnight in the refrigerator. The next day, drain the beans, place in a large saucepan, and add the water. Bring to a boil over high heat and add the sage sprig, 1 of the rosemary sprigs, and the 2 whole garlic cloves. Reduce the heat to low, cover partially, and simmer very gently until the beans are very soft, 1½–2 hours.

2 In a frying pan over medium heat, warm the olive oil. Add the onion and sauté until fragrant, about 3 minutes. Add the sage leaves and pancetta and sauté until the pancetta is golden, about 7 minutes. Add the minced garlic and sauté until it begins to color, about 2 minutes. Remove the pancetta and discard. Reduce the heat to low, stir in the tomatoes, and simmer gently, stirring occasionally, until the tomatoes are soft, about 10 minutes.

3 Remove the herb sprigs and garlic from the beans and discard. Using a slotted spoon, transfer the beans, in batches, to a food mill fitted with the medium disk held over a soup pot and purée directly into the pot, adding cooking liquid as needed to facilitate the puréeing. Add 2 cups (16 fl oz/500 ml) of the cooking liquid to the stock and set aside. Using the food mill, purée the tomato mixture, letting it pass directly into the soup pot. Stir in the stock and place the pot over medium-low heat. Add the remaining rosemary sprig, season with salt and pepper, and cook uncovered, stirring occasionally, until the soup has thickened and the flavors are blended, about 20 minutes. Discard the rosemary.

Peppery Beef Stew

Peposo · Tuscany · Italy

This stew is remarkably effortless to make. The dish takes its name from the peppercorns, or *granello di pepe*, used to spice it. The stew comes from the hill town of Impruneta, just nine miles (15 km) from Florence and renowned for the quality of its *cotto*, or terra-cotta. Traditionally, the stew was baked in the same ovens in which the terra-cotta vases and tiles were fired. Serve it with bread so guests can mop up the juices.

1 ½ lb (750 g) beef or pork stew meat, cut into large cubes

1 pork shank, about 2 lb (1 kg)

1 ⅓ cups (8 oz/250 g) chopped and drained canned plum (Roma) tomatoes

1 yellow onion, finely chopped

1 carrot, peeled and finely chopped

1 celery stalk, finely chopped

4 cloves garlic, crushed

1 bay leaf

2 cups (16 fl oz/500 ml) dry red wine

1 tablespoon peppercorns, lightly crushed

Serves 4

1 Preheat the oven to 350°F (180°C).

2 In a baking dish, combine the stew meat, pork shank, tomatoes, onion, carrot, celery, garlic, bay leaf, wine, and peppercorns. Mix well and add enough water just to cover the meat.

3 Place in the oven and cook, stirring from time to time and adding a little hot water if the dish becomes dry, for 3 hours. At the end of the cooking time, the sauce should be dense and creamy and the meat very tender.

4 Divide the stew among warmed shallow bowls and serve at once.

TRIPE VENDORS

In the heart of Florence is the city's Mercato del Porcellino, and its stalls are filled with ceramics, embroidered linens, writing paper, and leather goods. In a corner of the market, the *trippaio*—the "tripe man"—operates from a mobile cart that is inevitably surrounded by a small crowd of people eating sandwiches—tripe sandwiches.

Tripe is the lining from one of the four chambers of a ruminant's stomach, usually a young ox. Florentines love the stuff. Although all tripe is edible, the most tender and subtly flavored type is the honeycomb tripe from the second chamber. The mobile tripe vendors cut the tripe into short strips and boil it in large vats of seasoned water. It is eaten plain on the spot, stuffed into hard-crusted rolls, or brought home to be simmered with tomatoes and other vegetables, stock, and wine or to be combined with onions, sweet peppers, and olives and then tossed with olive oil and lemon juice.

The name of the market, Porcellino, refers to the large bronze statue of a wild boar that stands to one side of the lively commercial space. Legend has it that anyone who rubs the boar's snout will be assured of returning to Florence. His snout shines smooth and golden from the touch of countless tourists who have made their wishes.

Octopus Salad

Insalata di Polpo · Tuscany · Italy

The texture of octopus is wonderfully meaty, and when it is chilled and thinly sliced, as in this delicious salad, it almost takes on the flavor of lobster.

2 lb (1 kg) octopus

2 tablespoons coarse salt, plus salt to taste

1 clove garlic, crushed

½ cup (4 fl oz/125 ml) extra-virgin olive oil

Juice of 1 lemon

2 green (spring) onions, including tender green tops, sliced crosswise

1 red bell pepper (capsicum), seeded and cut into small dice

2 inner celery stalks, thinly sliced

Freshly ground pepper to taste

Serves 4

1 A day in advance, clean each octopus. Invert the head sac and trim away the beaks visible in the mouth region, discarding these along with the eyes and all viscera. Remove and discard the ink sac. Rinse the octopus well under running cold water. Place in a large lock-top freezer bag and freeze overnight to tenderize the flesh. Thaw before continuing.

2 In a saucepan over high heat, combine the octopus with water to cover and bring to a boil. Add the 2 tablespoons salt and the garlic, cover, reduce the heat to low, and simmer, without lifting the lid, for about 45 minutes. The octopus should turn white.

3 Drain the octopus and set aside until cool enough to handle. Cut the cooked octopus into bite-sized pieces and place in a serving bowl. Add the olive oil and lemon juice, stir to coat the octopus, cover, and let marinate for at least 1 hour at room temperature or for up to 4 hours in the refrigerator.

4 Just before serving, add the green onions, bell pepper, and celery and toss well. Season with salt and pepper and toss again, then serve slightly chilled.

Roman-Style Fish Soup

Zuppa di Pesce alla Romana · Lazio · Italy

Every coastal region of Italy has its own recipe for fish soup. This Roman version is spicy with garlic and hot chile. It contains a minimum of liquid, so it is more like a stew than a soup. Use whatever fish varieties are available with the exception of strong-flavored oily fish, which would overwhelm the delicate shellfish.

2 cloves garlic, chopped

Pinch of red pepper flakes

⅓ cup (3 fl oz/80 ml) olive oil

2 lb (1 kg) squid, cleaned and cut into ½-inch (12-mm) rings (see page 227; about 1 lb/500 g cleaned)

1 cup (8 fl oz/250 ml) dry white wine

2 tomatoes, peeled, seeded, and chopped

2 tablespoons chopped fresh flat-leaf (Italian) parsley

Pinch of salt

2 cups (16 fl oz/500 ml) water

1 lb (500 g) small hard-shelled clams or cockles, soaked in cool water for 30 minutes and well scrubbed

1½ lb (750 g) assorted firm-fleshed fish fillets such as whiting, monkfish, turbot, porgy, bream, red snapper, and sea bass, cut into chunks

4 slices coarse country bread, toasted and rubbed on one side with a garlic clove

Serves 4

1 In a large saucepan over medium heat, warm the olive oil. Add the the garlic and red pepper flakes and sauté until the garlic is golden, about 2 minutes. Using a slotted spoon, remove and discard the garlic. Add the squid and cook and stir until opaque, 1–2 minutes. Add the wine and simmer for 1 minute longer. Add the tomatoes, parsley, and salt and cook until the juices evaporate, about 10 minutes longer.

2 Add the water and bring to a simmer. Add the clams (discard any that do not close to the touch) and fish, cover, and cook until the clams open and the fish is opaque, about 5 minutes. Discard any clams that failed to open. Taste and adjust the seasoning.

3 Place a bread slice in soup plates. Ladle the soup over the bread and serve at once.

Sage-Scented Olive Press Soup

Zuppa Frantoiana · Tuscany · Italy

This soup gets its name from the word *frantoio*, or "olive press." Most oils would make the soup unpleasantly heavy, but the biting flavor of just-pressed olive oil makes it exquisite.

1½ oz (45 g) dried porcino mushrooms, soaked in warm water to cover for 30 minutes

8 tablespoons (4 fl oz/125 ml) just-pressed extra-virgin olive oil

1 clove garlic, minced

Small handful of fresh sage leaves, finely chopped, plus whole leaves for garnish

1 large tomato, peeled, seeded, and chopped

8 cups (64 fl oz/2 l) light chicken stock

1 cup (3 oz/90 g) broken pappardelle or tagliatelle noodles (in large bits)

2 cups (14 oz/440 g) drained, cooked dried borlotti or cranberry beans (page 221), plus cooking liquid as needed

Salt and freshly ground pepper to taste

Serves 8

1 Drain the mushrooms. Rinse under cold water if they are gritty. Squeeze out the excess moisture. In a soup pot over medium heat, warm 3 tablespoons of the olive oil. Add the garlic, chopped sage, and mushrooms and sauté, stirring frequently, for 3 minutes. Add the tomato and cook, stirring occasionally, until the flavors are blended, about 5 minutes.

2 Pour in the stock and bring to a boil. Add the pasta and boil, uncovered, for 5 minutes. Reduce the heat to medium and pass half of the beans through a food mill fitted with the medium disk directly into the soup, adding some cooking liquid if needed to facilitate the puréeing. Stir in the remaining beans. Simmer for 5 minutes. Season with salt and pepper. Ladle the soup into warmed individual bowls, garnish with the whole sage leaves, and drizzle with the remaining 5 tablespoons (2½ fl oz/75 ml) olive oil.

OLIVE OIL

There is no ingredient more essential to Tuscan cuisine than olive oil—Tuscan olive oil. Of all the elements that make up the glorious Tuscan landscape—neatly tended rows of grapevines, timeworn stone houses atop sloping hills, roads lined with cypress trees—it is the gnarled bark and silvery green leaves of the olive tree that speak most beautifully of this place. Locals say there is something about the soil, the slope of the land, and the interplay of sun and wind and rain that conspire to produce an olive oil so unlike—so superior to—all others.

Tuscan olive oil is characterized by its ripe fruitiness and low acidity. The olives are harvested and pressed in the fall, usually sometime in November. Picking the olives is tedious and exacting work. Large tarps are spread beneath the trees, handmade ladders are propped precariously against the battered trunks, and the olives are shaken from the branches or raked off using special combs.

The *olio nuovo*—new, just-pressed oil—is jewel green and richly fruity, with a "bite" that mellows after about a month. A favorite way to enjoy new oil is by rubbing toasted bread with garlic, dipping it in the water in which cannellini beans have been cooked, and smothering it with beans and oil. Another is to rub the toasted bread with garlic and drizzle it with oil.

The finest-quality *olio d'oliva* is labeled "extra virgin," which means that the olives were crushed in stone mortars or under granite millstones (which extract the oil without heat, so as not to compromise its flavor), and the oil has an acidity level of less than 1 percent. It is the only oil ever used in Tuscany, for cooking, for drizzling over soups, for dressing salads and dipping vegetables, and for any of the other delicious uses. There is no greater contribution to the culinary well-being of any household than to keep it abundantly supplied with an olive oil so fine that it elevates the flavors of everything it touches.

Bread and Summer Vegetable Salad

Panzanella · Tuscany · Italy

Much of the success of this recipe, which some cooks identify as a soup rather than a salad, depends on the bread—it should be chewy and quite firm. The Tuscans, of course, use their beloved unsalted bread, known as *pane sciocco*, meaning "insipid". The salad can be made several hours ahead of time, but it is at its best when no more than a couple of hours old. Vary the flavors by adding arugula or capers.

2 tomatoes, cut into bite-sized pieces

1 small cucumber, peeled and sliced

1 small red onion, thinly sliced

1 cup (1 oz/30 g) fresh basil leaves, torn into small pieces, plus whole leaves for garnish

½ cup (4 fl oz/125 ml) extra-virgin olive oil, or as needed

3 tablespoons red wine vinegar, or to taste

Salt and freshly ground pepper to taste

6–8 slices coarse country bread

Serves 6

1 In a large bowl, combine the tomatoes, cucumber, onion, and torn basil. Drizzle with the ½ cup (4 fl oz/125 ml) olive oil and the 3 tablespoons vinegar and season with salt and pepper. Toss well to coat evenly.

2 Cut or tear the bread into bite-sized pieces. Place half the bread in a wide, shallow bowl. Spoon on half of the vegetables. Layer the remaining bread on top and then the remaining vegetables. Cover and refrigerate for 1 hour.

3 Toss the salad, then taste and adjust the seasoning. If the bread is dry, add a little more oil or vinegar. Garnish with a few basil leaves. Serve at once.

Venison Stew with Tomatoes and Capers

Stufato di Cervo • Trentino–Alto Adige • Italy

After World War II, the two regions of Trentino and the Alto Adige in the north of Italy were linked politically, although they have little but their location in common. Alto Adige shares its northern border with Austria, so this mountainous region has many Austro-Hungarian influences. The food also has an alpine inflection. Goulash and stews are flavored with sweet spices like cinnamon or cloves. This stew combines game accented with cloves and two typically southern Italian ingredients, capers and tomatoes.

1 Pat the meat dry a few pieces at a time. Spread the flour on a plate and lightly dust the pieces, shaking off the excess. Season with salt and pepper.

2 In a large, heavy pot over medium heat, melt the butter with the oil. Add the meat in batches and cook, turning as needed, until well browned on all sides, about 15 minutes. As the meat is ready, transfer it to a plate.

3 Add the pancetta, carrots, celery, onion, garlic, the 2 tablespoons parsley, sage, and rosemary to the pot and cook over medium heat, stirring occasionally, until the vegetables have softened, about 5 minutes. Add the wine, bring to a simmer, and deglaze the pot, stirring and scraping with a wooden spoon to remove the browned bits on the bottom. Cook for 1 minute longer.

4 Return the venison to the pot. Add the stock, tomatoes, capers, and cloves and bring to a simmer. Reduce the heat to low, cover, and cook, turning the meat occasionally, until the venison is tender, about 2 hours. Add a little water if the liquid reduces too much.

5 Using a slotted spoon, transfer the meat to a plate. Pass the contents of the pot through a food mill or a sieve placed over a bowl. Return the sauce to the pot and bring back to a simmer. If the sauce seems too thin, raise the heat and boil until reduced. Return the meat to the pot and reheat gently.

6 Transfer the stew to a warmed deep platter or serving bowl, sprinkle with parsley, and serve at once.

3 lb (1.5 kg) boneless venison stew meat, cut into 2-inch (5-cm) pieces

½ cup (2½ oz/75 g) all-purpose (plain) flour

Salt and freshly ground pepper to taste

2 tablespoons unsalted butter

1 tablespoon olive oil

2 oz (60 g) pancetta, chopped

2 carrots, peeled and chopped

1 celery stalk, chopped

1 yellow onion, chopped

1 clove garlic, chopped

2 tablespoons chopped fresh flat-leaf (Italian) parsley, plus extra for garnish

4 fresh sage leaves, chopped

1 teaspoon chopped fresh rosemary

1 cup (8 fl oz/250 ml) dry white wine

2 cups (16 fl oz/500 ml) meat stock

1 cup (6 oz/185 g) peeled, seeded, and chopped tomatoes (fresh or canned)

1 tablespoon capers, chopped

2 whole cloves

Serves 4

Roasted Pepper Salad

Insalata di Peperoni · Campania · Italy

Campania's plains and hillsides are regarded as some of the country's best areas for growing fruits and vegetables. Much of the soil is volcanic, courtesy of the region's still-active Mount Vesuvius, and even the ancient Romans envied the bountiful crops of their neighbors to the south, where the *contadini* enjoyed a year-round growing season. Here, Campania's sweet peppers balance the saltiness of anchovies. Serve the salad with bread for soaking up the delicious juices.

6 large red, yellow, or green bell peppers (capsicums), or a mixture

¼ cup (2 fl oz/60 ml) extra-virgin olive oil

6 large fresh basil leaves, torn into small pieces

2 cloves garlic, halved

2 tablespoons capers

Salt and freshly ground pepper to taste

12 anchovy fillets

Serves 6

1 Preheat the broiler (grill). Place the bell peppers on a broiler pan and slip under the heat. Broil (grill), turning as needed, until the skins are evenly blistered and lightly charred; do not allow the flesh to burn. Transfer to a bowl, cover with plastic wrap or aluminum foil, and let cool.

2 Working with 1 pepper at a time and holding it over a sieve placed over a bowl to catch the juices, remove the stem, seeds, and ribs, then peel away the charred skin. Cut or tear the peppers into long strips ½ inch (12 mm) wide.

3 Add the cut peppers to the bowl of captured juices along with the olive oil, basil, garlic, capers, salt, and pepper. Cover and refrigerate for at least 1 hour or up to overnight. (If left to chill overnight, the oil and juices will solidify. Let stand at room temperature for about 30 minutes to liquefy slightly before continuing.)

4 Place half of the peppers into a serving dish. Layer the anchovy fillets on top. Arrange the remaining peppers over the anchovies. Serve at once.

CAVOLO NERO

Literally translated, *cavolo nero* means "black cabbage," and although this handsome brassica is not black, it is as deep a green as any vegetable you'll ever see. It is an essential ingredient in the classic Tuscan soup, *ribollita*, and in the days following the olive harvest, it is boiled and heaped on toasted country bread rubbed with garlic and slathered with newly pressed oil. Some cooks chop the cooked cabbage finely, mix it with a bit of fresh ricotta cheese, and use it as pasta sauce.

Although botanically a cabbage, *cavolo nero* has a pleasant bitterness not usually associated with cabbage. The plume-shaped crinkled leaves are harvested and eaten after the first frost, which considerably softens their rather heavy texture.

Unfortunately, *cavolo nero* is nearly impossible to find outside of Italy. The good news is that it can be grown from seed in nearly any backyard garden. There's no reason not to pick up a few packets on your next trip to Tuscany. Sow the seeds during the summer and enjoy *cavolo nero* all winter long.

Twice-Boiled Soup with Black Cabbage and White Beans

Ribollita · Tuscany · Italy

Ribollita is considered a soup, but it is much thicker and denser than a soup, so much so that it is sometimes served with a fork. The dish begins as a typical Tuscan bread and vegetable soup, and it can be eaten on the first day as such. It becomes *ribollita* on the second day, when, as its name implies, it is reboiled.

BEANS

1 cup (7 oz/220 g) dried cannellini beans

5 cups (40 fl oz/1.25 l) water

1 clove garlic

1 fresh sage sprig

SOUP

8 tablespoons (4 fl oz/125 ml) extra-virgin olive oil

1 large yellow onion, chopped

1 clove garlic, finely chopped

2 leeks, white part and 1 inch (2.5 cm) of the green, chopped

2 carrots, peeled and thickly sliced

2 zucchini (courgettes), trimmed and thickly sliced

2 tomatoes, peeled, seeded, and chopped

1 celery stalk, thickly sliced

1 potato, peeled and cut into chunks

Salt to taste

4 cups (32 fl oz/1 l) hot water

½ head savoy cabbage, core removed and leaves coarsely sliced

1 bunch Swiss chard, ribs removed and leaves coarsely chopped

1 bunch black cabbage or kale, ribs removed and leaves coarsely chopped

1 fresh rosemary sprig

1 fresh thyme sprig

6 slices day-old coarse country bread, toasted

Freshly ground pepper to taste

Serves 6–8

1 Pick over the cannellini beans, discarding any stones or misshapen beans. Rinse well, place in a bowl, and add water to cover generously. Let soak overnight in the refrigerator.

2 The next day, drain the beans and place in a large saucepan along with the water, garlic, and sage sprig. Bring to a boil over high heat, reduce the heat to low, cover partially, and simmer gently until tender, 1½–2 hours, depending on the age of the beans.

3 Meanwhile, begin making the soup. In a soup pot over medium heat, warm 3 tablespoons of the olive oil. Add the onion and sauté until fragrant, about 3 minutes. Add the garlic and sauté until it begins to color, about 2 minutes. Add the leeks, carrots, zucchini, tomatoes, celery, and potato, season with salt, and sauté, stirring frequently, until the vegetables are soft, about 10 minutes.

4 Pour in the hot water and add the savoy cabbage, Swiss chard, black cabbage or kale, rosemary, and thyme. Cover and simmer over medium heat, stirring occasionally, until the soup is thick, about 1 hour.

5 Using a slotted spoon, transfer half of the beans to a food mill fitted with the medium disk held over the soup pot, and purée directly into the soup. Scoop out the remaining beans with the slotted spoon and add to the pot along with 2 cups (16 fl oz/500 ml) of the cooking liquid and the toasted bread. Season with salt and pepper, and gently stir the contents of the pot.

6 Place over medium heat, cover, and simmer for 10 minutes to blend the flavors. Remove from the heat, uncover, and let cool, then re-cover and refrigerate overnight.

7 The following day, preheat the oven to 375°F (190°C). Transfer the soup to an earthenware or other ovenproof baking dish.

8 Bake the soup, stirring occasionally for the first 20 minutes only to allow a thin crust to form, until heated through, about 30 minutes. Remove from the oven.

9 Bring the soup to the table, drizzle with the remaining 5 tablespoons (2½ fl oz/75 ml) olive oil. Season abundantly with pepper and serve.

Seafood Salad

Insalata di Frutti di Mare • Campania • Italy

The long, beautiful coastline of Campania ensures that seafood is at the heart of the local diet. *Fritto di pesce*, *zuppa di cozze*, and *polpi alla luciana* are classics of the region, with the latter, octopus in a sauce of olive oil, parsley, garlic, tomatoes, and red chiles, a favorite of the Neapolitan table. This seafood salad, with its marriage of shellfish and fennel, is part of that seaside tradition. It can also be served as a main course for a light summer meal. Vary the seafood according to what is available, such as lobster, octopus, scallops, or clams.

DRESSING

¼ cup (2 fl oz/60 ml) extra-virgin olive oil, or more to taste

2 tablespoons fresh lemon juice, or more to taste

½ teaspoon grated lemon zest

1 clove garlic, minced

Salt to taste

1 small dried red chile, crushed, or pinch of red pepper flakes

2 lb (1 kg) squid

1 lb (500 g) shrimp (prawns), peeled and deveined

24 mussels, scrubbed and debearded

½ cup (4 fl oz/125 ml) water

1 small fennel bulb, trimmed and thinly sliced crosswise

1 cup (5 oz/155 g) Gaeta or other Mediterranean-style black olives, pitted and sliced

3 tablespoons chopped fresh flat-leaf (Italian) parsley

Salt and freshly ground pepper to taste

Radicchio and lettuce leaves

Lemon wedges

Serves 8

1 To make the dressing, in a large bowl, whisk together the ¼ cup (2 fl oz/60 ml) olive oil, the 2 tablespoons lemon juice, lemon zest, garlic, salt, and chile. Set aside.

2 Clean the squid as directed on page 227. You should have about 1 lb (500 g) once they are cleaned. Leave the tentacles whole, but cut the bodies crosswise into rings ½ inch (12 mm) wide. Set aside.

3 Bring a saucepan three-fourths full of salted water to a boil. Add the shrimp and cook just until they turn bright pink and are cooked through, about 2 minutes.

4 Using a slotted spoon, transfer the shrimp to a colander to drain. Add to the dressing and toss to coat evenly.

5 Add the squid to the boiling water and cook until opaque, about 1 minute. Drain well, add to the dressing, and toss to coat evenly.

6 Discard any mussels that do not close to the touch. In the same saucepan over medium heat, combine the mussels and the ½ cup (4 fl oz/125 ml) water. Cover and cook until the mussels begin to open, about 5 minutes. Remove from the heat and discard any mussels that failed to open. Remove the mussels from their shells and discard the shells.

7 Add the mussels to the dressing along with the fennel, olives, and parsley. Taste and adjust the seasoning as needed with more olive oil, lemon juice, salt, and pepper.

8 Make a bed of the radicchio and lettuce leaves on a platter. Spoon the seafood mixture into the center. Garnish with lemon wedges and serve at once.

Onion Soup

Carabaccia • Tuscany • Italy

Carabaccia (also known as *cipollata* and *zuppa di cipolle*) is a mysterious name of disputed origin for what is essentially a humble—and extraordinarily tasty—onion soup. The dish has evolved over the centuries. During the Renaissance, when the recipes of the court were highly spiced and elaborate, *carabaccia* included ground almonds, vinegar, sugar, and cinnamon. The modern version is much simplified and arguably as good as any *soupe à l'oignon* you'll eat at a bistro in Paris.

6 tablespoons (3 fl oz/90 ml) extra-virgin olive oil

2 lb (1 kg) yellow onions, quartered, then sliced

2 celery stalks, minced

2 carrots, peeled and minced

6 cups (48 fl oz/1.5 l) chicken stock

Salt and freshly ground pepper to taste

6 slices day-old coarse country bread, toasted

1 clove garlic, halved lengthwise

½ cup (2 oz/60 g) grated Parmesan cheese

Serves 6

1 In a soup pot over medium heat, warm the olive oil. Stir in the onions, celery, and carrots and sauté, stirring often, until the onions break apart easily with a wooden spoon, about 30 minutes.

2 Pour in the stock, season with salt and pepper, and simmer for 30 minutes.

3 Rub the toast with the cut sides of the garlic clove and distribute among warmed individual soup bowls.

4 Taste the soup and adjust the seasoning with salt and pepper. Ladle the hot soup over the toast and sprinkle with the Parmesan, dividing it evenly. Serve at once.

Orange and Fennel Salad

Insalata di Arance e Finocchio • Sicily • Italy

Oranges are plentiful in Sicily, where they are often used in salads during the winter months when good tomatoes, lettuces, and other typical salad vegetables are not as abundant.

2 navel oranges

1 fennel bulb

1 red onion, thinly sliced

Salt and freshly ground pepper to taste

½ cup (2 oz/60 g) sliced radishes

½ cup (2½ oz/75 g) oil-cured Mediterranean-style black olives, pitted if desired

¼ cup (2 fl oz/60 ml) extra-virgin olive oil

Serves 4

1 Working with 1 orange at a time, cut a thin slice off the top and bottom to expose the fruit. Place the orange upright on a cutting board and thickly slice off the peel in strips, cutting around the contour of the orange to expose the fruit. Repeat with the second orange. Cut the oranges crosswise into slices ¼ inch (6 mm) thick.

2 Cut off the stems and feathery tops and any bruised outer stalks from the fennel bulb. Halve the bulb lengthwise, then thinly slice each half crosswise.

3 Arrange the oranges, fennel, and onion on a platter. Sprinkle with salt and pepper. Scatter the radishes and olives over all. Drizzle the olive oil over the top and serve at once.

Farro Soup

Minestra di Farro • Tuscany • Italy

In the charming town of Lucca, *trattorie* such as the bustling Da Giulio serve traditional Tuscan home cooking, including steaming bowlfuls of *minestra di farro*.

FARRO

2 cups (10 oz/315 g) *farro*, soaked in water to cover for 20 minutes and drained

6 cups (48 fl oz/1.5 l) water

SOUP

¼ cup (2 fl oz/60 ml) extra-virgin olive oil, plus more for serving

1 small yellow onion, finely chopped

2 cloves garlic, minced

1 leek, white part and 1 inch (2.5 cm) of the green, thinly sliced

1 celery stalk, finely chopped

1 carrot, peeled and diced

2 tomatoes, peeled, seeded, and chopped

8 cups (64 fl oz/2 l) water

1 fresh rosemary sprig

Salt to taste

2 cups (14 oz/440 g) drained, cooked dried borlotti or cranberry beans (page 221), plus cooking liquid as needed

Freshly ground pepper to taste

Serves 6

1 To cook the *farro*, in a large saucepan, combine the *farro* and water and bring to a boil over high heat. Reduce the heat to medium-low, cover, and simmer the *farro* until the grains swell and are lighter in color, about 35 minutes.

2 Meanwhile, begin making the soup. In a soup pot over medium heat, warm the ¼ cup (2 fl oz/60 ml) olive oil. Add the onion, garlic, leek, celery, and carrot and sauté until the vegetables are soft, about 8 minutes.

3 Stir the tomatoes into the vegetables, cook for 1 minute, and then add the water and rosemary sprig and season with salt. Cover partially and simmer gently until the flavors are blended, about 30 minutes.

4 Drain the *farro* and add it to the soup pot. Re-cover partially and simmer, stirring often, until the *farro* absorbs the flavors, about 20 minutes.

5 Uncover the pot and, using a food mill fitted with the medium disk, pass half of the beans through the mill directly into the soup, adding some cooking liquid if needed to facilitate the puréeing. Stir in the remaining whole beans.

6 Re-cover partially and simmer until the *farro* is tender but not mushy, about 20 minutes longer. Remove and discard the rosemary sprig. Adjust the seasoning with salt and pepper.

7 Transfer the soup to a warmed tureen, or ladle it into warmed individual bowls. Top each serving with a swirl of olive oil.

FARRO

You wouldn't know it from all the fanfare it has been receiving the past few years, but *farro* has been around a very long time. One of the oldest grains in the world, it was known in ancient Palestine and Egypt, and it was the first grain to be introduced to Italy. When wheat began to be widely grown in the country around the first century BC, *farro* was almost abandoned, except in those places where it grew best, such as the low mountains of the Garfagnana, an area in which it has been cultivated for millennia.

Until fairly recently, it was quite unusual to find *farro* on a menu far from the Garfagnana or nearby Lucchesia, and even then the grain was used primarily in soups and porridges.

All that has now changed. The delights and usefulness of *farro* has been rediscovered not only throughout Tuscany, but in places outside Italy as well. The oval grain adds a faintly sweet and nutty flavor to dishes and maintains a firm texture when it is cooked. You will find it in Florence replacing the bread in *panzanella*, and in the Maremma it is often cooked like risotto and served with fresh fish. The grain can also be ground into flour, which is used in Italian desserts.

Cornmeal, Cabbage, and Herb Soup

Infarinata · Tuscany · Italy

Variations of this cornmeal and cabbage soup, each with its own colorful name and culinary twists, are common throughout the Garfagnana, Versilia, Lunigiana, and Livorno.

½ cup (4 fl oz/125 ml) extra-virgin olive oil

1 yellow onion, finely chopped

2 carrots, peeled and finely chopped

1 celery stalk, finely chopped

Leaves from 1 fresh sage sprig, chopped

2 cups (12 oz/375 g) crushed canned plum (Roma) tomatoes with juice

Salt and freshly ground pepper to taste

8 cups (64 fl oz/2 l) hot water

2 potatoes, peeled and cut into large cubes

1 lb (500 g) savoy cabbage, cored, halved, and sliced

1 cup (5 oz/155 g) polenta

2 cups (14 oz/440 g) drained, cooked dried cannellini beans (page 221)

Serves 6

1 In a large saucepan over medium heat, warm the oil. Add the onion, carrots, celery, and sage and sauté, stirring frequently, until the vegetables begin to soften, about 8 minutes. Stir in the tomatoes and their juice, season lightly with salt, and simmer until thick, about 15 minutes.

2 Pour in the hot water, raise the heat to medium-high, bring the mixture to a boil, and add the potatoes and cabbage. Reduce the heat to medium-low, cover, and simmer until the potatoes are tender, about 20 minutes. Uncover and pour in the polenta in a thin, steady stream, stirring with a wooden spoon. Stir continuously for 40 minutes while the polenta bubbles and thickens.

3 Stir in the beans and adjust the seasoning with salt and pepper. The *infarinata* should be fluid and soft. Add a bit of hot water if it appears too dense. Ladle into warmed individual bowls and serve at once.

Italian Chesnut Soup

Minestra di Castagne • Siena • Italy

Wherever there are mountains in Tuscany, there are usually large chestnut woods. Mount Amiata, southern Tuscany's highest mountain, is covered with chestnut trees, as are the mountains near Pistoia and Arezzo and in the Mugello. Historically, dried chestnuts, which have the virtue of an extraordinarily long shelf life, were an important winter staple.

2 tablespoons extra-virgin olive oil

2 oz (60 g) pancetta, cubed

½ red onion, chopped

3 cloves garlic, minced

1 celery stalk, chopped

1 cup (4 oz/125 g) dried chestnuts, soaked overnight in lightly salted water and drained

¼ teaspoon fennel seeds, lightly crushed

Leaves from 1 fresh rosemary sprig

8 cups (64 fl oz/2 l) light chicken stock or water

Salt and freshly ground pepper to taste

1 cup (7 oz/220 g) short-grain white rice

2 oz (60 g) aged pecorino cheese, grated

Serves 6–8

1 In a large saucepan over medium heat, warm the olive oil. Add the pancetta cubes and sauté until they begin to soften, about 5 minutes. Add the onion, garlic, and celery and sauté, stirring frequently, until the vegetables begin to soften. Sprinkle in the chestnuts, fennel seeds, and rosemary and stir well for a couple of minutes to combine.

2 Pour in the stock or water and bring to a boil. Reduce the heat to low, cover, and simmer until the chestnuts almost begin to fall apart, 1½–2 hours, seasoning with salt and pepper after the first hour.

3 Stir in the rice and continue to simmer until the rice is cooked, about 20 minutes. Taste and adjust the seasoning. Ladle into warmed individual bowls and serve at once. Pass the pecorino cheese at the table.

SPAIN AND PORTUGAL

While it may seem odd to open a chapter of soup and salad recipes with a discussion about bread, it is actually quite appropriate, for bread forms the basis of many Iberian soups. Bread has traditionally been a common means for extending meager rations, so it is not surprising that frugal cooks in Spain and Portugal, like their thrifty counterparts in Tuscany, have created a sizable repertoire of bread-thickened soups.

The Portuguese *açorda*, a dish little known outside Iberia, is a "dry" soup made by thickening broth with bread and enriching it with egg. *Açorda de mariscos* (shellfish and bread soup), from Estremadura, and *açorda à alentejana* (bread soup with cilantro, garlic, and egg), a specialty of the south, are the two most popular examples.

The earliest Spanish gazpacho called for bread as well. Bread, oil, vinegar, and garlic were pounded together, thinned with water, and seasoned. Today, gazpacho is at home in the Levante, La Mancha, and Catalonia, but Andalusia is the true capital of this summer soup, offering more than thirty distinctive versions, including the medieval *ajo blanco*, usually made with garlic, bread, almonds, and fresh grapes. New World exploration expanded the Iberian pantry, and tomatoes and peppers (capsicums) soon became a part of the basic mixture of bread and garlic, creating the memorable cold soup that most of us now associate with the name. On a hot summer evening, seated in a tile-lined Andalusian courtyard under a full August moon, few travelers can resist a cooling bowl of this Spanish classic.

Bread also plays an important role in the rustic *sopa de ajo* (garlic soup). A mixture of bread, garlic, olive oil, and water, it is not far removed from the original gazpacho and *açorda*, and, as with all traditional dishes, its style varies with the region. Most Spaniards agree, however, that the best versions are served in the south and southeast, where garlic is cultivated extensively, and intricately woven strings of the pungent bulbs hang in every farmhouse and restaurant kitchen.

When cold winds begin to blow, Iberian cooks know it's time for a long-simmered

stew of meats or seafood and vegetables. Called *cocido* in Spain and *cozido* in Portugal, these hearty one-pot meals are welcome sights on a wintry evening. They recall the *pot-au-feu* of France, the *bollito misto* of Italy, and the *adafina* of Morocco, with the last their likely origin.

The Jewish *adafina*, a slow-cooked dish of vegetables, beef or chicken, and eggs, was born out of two traditions: kosher law that proscribes cooking on the Sabbath and the Moorish preference for stewing. In Spain, this dish evolved into a Christian one with the advent of the Inquisition. Jews who did not flee the Iberian Peninsula were forced to renounce Judaism and became Catholics. An important test of loyalty to the new faith was the consumption of pork or foods cooked with lard. To avoid being branded infidels, converts added pork to *adafinas*, often replacing the eggs and sometimes the other meats. With that culinary innovation, the *cocido* and *cozido* were established.

The simplest peasant versions of *cocido* are eaten from a single bowl. In more elaborate presentations, the broth is strained and served with rice or noodles as a first course. Then the other ingredients are served, sometimes in two courses. In some regions, a *cocido* takes on the name of the pot in which it is served, such as the *puchero* in La Mancha or the *olla* in Catalonia.

The Portuguese *cozido*, a close cousin to Spanish *cocido*, is primarily a dish of the north, where brutal winters demand a hearty table. *Cozido à portuguesa* is thick with meat, poultry, sausages, root vegetables, and cabbage but no beans. The broth can be ladled up as a first course, and the meats and vegetables sit atop a bed of rice.

Because Iberia is surrounded on three sides by water, a large repertoire of fish and shellfish soups and stews grace coastal tables. In Spain, *zarzuela de mariscos* is an all-shellfish specialty of Catalonia. Catalonia's prized *romesco* sauce of peppers, nuts, and olive oil is thinned with broth and loaded with local, seasonal fish and shellfish to produce Tarragona's celebrated *romesco de peix*. A classic of the Algarve, *amêijoas na cataplana* combines clams and sausage with chiles in a dish named for the saucer-shaped pan in which it is cooked. The Catalonian *suquet de peix* and the northern Portuguese *caldeirada* are seafood soups hearty enough to be declared stews. Most diners use a piece of thick-crusted rustic bread to mop up the broth at the bottom of the bowl.

Salads, usually simple, are meant to pique the appetite at the beginning of a meal. The Romans introduced salads to the peninsula, but it was the Arabs who began serving them at the start of the repast. While you will find simple green salads, they are often embellished with sliced oranges, cooked eggs, strips of ham, canned tuna, olives, or pimientos. They are served on platters in the center of the table and eaten communally.

Left: Evidence of Spain's Catholic heritage is visible in its simple sidewalk shrines, tranquil cloisters, and richly ornamented altars. **Above, left:** Many of Madrid's tapas bars are decorated with murals rendered in painted tiles. Here, a colorful portrayal of bulls rises above rows of regional wines. **Above, right:** Brilliant and fragrant yellow sunflower fields blanket vast stretches of Catalonia and Old Castile.

Cold Tomato Soup

Gazpacho Andaluz · Andalusia · Spain

After the Spaniards returned from the New World with tomatoes and peppers, the original bread, oil, and water gazpacho evolved into this refreshing summer soup. Myriad variations exist on this specialty of Andalusia. Some have bread incorporated into the mix; others use bread as a garnish of garlic croutons. In some, all the vegetables are puréed; in others, only half are puréed, and finely chopped vegetables are served as a garnish. But all gazpachos have one common element: ripe and flavorful tomatoes.

2 slices day-old coarse country bread, crusts removed, soaked in water just to cover, and squeezed dry

2 small cucumbers, peeled, seeded, and coarsely chopped

1 small yellow or red onion, chopped

2 cloves garlic, minced

2½ lb (1.25 kg) ripe tomatoes, peeled, seeded, and coarsely chopped

2 small green bell peppers (capsicums), seeded and coarsely chopped

6 tablespoons (3 fl oz/90 ml) extra-virgin olive oil

3 tablespoons red wine vinegar, or to taste

Salt and freshly ground pepper to taste

Ice water or tomato juice (optional)

GARNISHES

4–6 tablespoons (2–3 fl oz/60–90 ml) extra-virgin olive oil

2 tablespoons minced garlic

2 slices coarse country bread, cut into ½-inch (12-mm) cubes

2 cups (12 oz/375 g) diced, peeled ripe tomatoes

½ cup (2½ oz/75 g) diced, peeled, and seeded cucumber

½ cup (2½ oz/75 g) minced green bell pepper (capsicum)

¼ cup (1½ oz/45 g) finely minced red onion

Serves 6–8

1 Put the soaked bread, cucumbers, onion, garlic, most of the chopped tomatoes, and 1 of the bell peppers in a food processor or blender. Purée until smooth and pour into a bowl.

2 Finely chop the rest of the chopped tomatoes and the remaining bell pepper and add to the soup. Stir in the olive oil and vinegar and season with salt and pepper. If the soup is too thick, add a little ice water, or, if the tomatoes are not perfect, add a little tomato juice. Cover and refrigerate until well chilled, for up to a day before serving.

3 To prepare the garnishes, in a frying pan over medium heat, warm the olive oil. Add the garlic and sauté briefly until fragrant. Add the bread cubes and fry, turning as needed, until golden brown on all sides, 4–5 minutes. Transfer the croutons to paper towels to drain.

4 Put the croutons, tomatoes, cucumber, bell pepper, and onion in separate bowls and set on the table. Ladle the gazpacho into chilled bowls and let diners add garnishes as desired.

"Green" Soup

Caldo Verde · Minho · Portugal

A specialty of Minho, *caldo verde* is served all over Portugal. It calls for *couve*, a dark green cabbage rarely found beyond the Iberian Peninsula, so you will need to substitute kale or collard greens. If you choose to purchase a dry sausage, you may skip the first step.

½ lb (250 g) *linguiça* or *chouriço*

¼ cup (2 fl oz/60 ml) olive oil, plus 4 teaspoons

1 large yellow onion, chopped

3 potatoes, about 1 lb (500 g) total weight, peeled and cut into slices ¼ inch (6 mm) thick

2 cloves garlic, finely minced

6 cups (48 fl oz/1.5 l) water

2 teaspoons salt, plus salt to taste

¾ lb (375 g) kale or collard greens, stems removed and leaves finely shredded

Freshly ground pepper to taste

Serves 4

1 If using fresh sausages (see note), preheat the oven to 375°F (190°C). Prick the sausages with a fork and place on a baking sheet. Bake until firm, about 25 minutes. Remove from the oven, let cool slightly, then slice ¼ inch (6 mm) thick; set aside.

2 In a large saucepan over medium heat, warm the ¼ cup (2 fl oz/60 ml) olive oil. Add the onion and sauté until tender, about 8 minutes. Add the potatoes and garlic and sauté for a few minutes, stirring often. Add the water and the 2 teaspoons salt, cover, reduce the heat to low, and simmer until the potatoes are very soft, about 20 minutes.

3 Mash the potatoes to a purée with a wooden spoon or potato masher. Add the sausage and cook over low heat for 5 minutes longer to warm through. Add the greens, stir well, and simmer, uncovered, for 3–5 minutes. Do not overcook. The greens should stay bright green and slightly crunchy. Season with salt and pepper.

4 Ladle the soup into bowls, drizzle each serving with 1 teaspoon of the remaining olive oil, and serve at once.

Green Salad with Serrano Ham and Tomato Vinaigrette

Ensalada Andaluza · Andalusia · Spain

As early as 500 AD, lettuces, asparagus, leeks, garlic, and wild herbs and greens were used in salads around the Mediterranean. Vinegars were made from grapes, figs, or peaches and salt. During the years when the Moors planted the first market gardens and orchards in Spain, spring onions and citrus juices were added to the mix. With the discovery of the New World, tomatoes and peppers became salad standbys.

VINAIGRETTE

1 lb (500 g) ripe tomatoes, peeled, seeded, and coarsely chopped

3 cloves garlic, minced

1 tablespoon sweet paprika

1½ teaspoons ground cumin

1 teaspoon salt

½ cup (4 fl oz/125 ml) extra-virgin olive oil

6–8 tablespoons (3–4 fl oz/90–125 ml) red wine vinegar

2 heads romaine (cos) or butter (Boston) lettuce, leaves separated and torn into bite-sized pieces

2 hard-boiled eggs, peeled and sliced

2 or 3 green (spring) onions, thinly sliced

¼ lb (125 g) serrano ham, thinly sliced and cut into narrow strips

⅓ cup (2 oz/60 g) mixed black and green olives

Serves 4

1 To make the vinaigrette, in a food processor or blender, combine the tomatoes, garlic, paprika, cumin, and salt and pulse to purée. With the motor running, slowly add the olive oil and vinegar, processing until fully incorporated.

2 Place the lettuce in a bowl. Drizzle on just enough of the vinaigrette to coat, toss well, and transfer to a platter. Top with the eggs, green onions, ham, and olives. Spoon the rest of the vinaigrette on top.

Galician Chestnut Soup

Sopa de Castañas • Galicia • Spain

Until the eighteenth century, chestnuts played a significant role in the Galician diet. But then disease wiped out the region's vast stands of chestnut trees, and potatoes quickly replaced the once-abundant nuts in everyday cooking.

1 lb (500 g) fresh chestnuts, or about 10 oz (315 g) canned or vacuum-packed chestnuts, without sugar

7 cups (56 fl oz/1.75 l) water

1 yellow onion, chopped, plus 3 tablespoons chopped

1 clove garlic, chopped

¼ lb (125 g) serrano ham, chopped

3 oz (90 g) salt pork, chopped

1 teaspoon salt, plus salt to taste

3 tablespoons olive oil

Freshly ground pepper to taste

3 tablespoons fresh lemon juice

3 thin slices coarse country bread, cut in half and toasted

Serves 6

1 If using fresh chestnuts, cut a deep X in the flat side of each nut. Bring a saucepan three-fourths full of water to a boil, add the chestnuts, and boil for 15 minutes. Drain and, while the nuts are still warm, remove the thin shell and the furry inner lining. Cut the nuts in half and return them to the saucepan. If using canned chestnuts, drain them; if using vacuum-packed chestnuts, unwrap. Halve the nuts and place in a saucepan.

2 Add about 6 cups (48 fl oz/1.5 l) of the water, the 1 chopped onion, garlic, ham, salt pork, and the 1 teaspoon salt to the chestnuts and bring to a boil over high heat. Cover partially, reduce the heat to low, and simmer until the nuts are very soft, about 1½ hours.

3 In a small frying pan over medium heat, warm the oil. Add the 3 tablespoons chopped onion and sauté until tender, about 8 minutes. Stir the onion into the soup. Season with salt and pepper, then stir in the lemon juice. To serve, divide the toasted bread among individual soup bowls and ladle the hot soup over the bread.

LODGING IN SPAIN AND PORTUGAL

Most travelers insist they experience a country's authentic regional dishes. The Spanish system of *paradores*, government-operated hotels, ensures that visitors can do just that. These hostelries are primarily housed in landmark buildings such as convents, monasteries, manor houses, palaces, and, in the case of the lovely Parador El Molino Viejo, the ruins of an Asturian cider mill. Guests are invariably treated to an exquisite table of local dishes, whether it be the roast suckling pig at the fifteenth-century Parador de Avila or the *caldereta extremeña* (goat stew) at the richly landscaped Parador de Trujillo.

The Portuguese, seeing the value of the *parador* system, borrowed the concept and established their own accommodations called *pousadas*. Like their Spanish counterparts, these operations tend to be housed in historic structures, such as the Pousada do Castelo in Obidos, once a medieval castle, or the Pousada de Santa Marinha in Guimarães, where today sixteenth-century monks' cells shelter a steady stream of guests.

Salt Cod and Potato Salad with Olives and Peppers

Rin Ran · Andalusia · Spain

This hearty salad originates in Jaén, a provincial capital surrounded by vast olive groves. Another musical name for the dish is *poti-poti*, or "a jumble."

½ lb (250 g) boneless salt cod, soaked (page 227)

1 lb (500 g) small new potatoes

2 red bell peppers (capsicums), seeded and diced

½ cup (2½ oz/75 g) green olives, pitted

DRESSING

6 tablespoons (3 fl oz/90 ml) extra-virgin olive oil

2 tablespoons red wine vinegar

1 teaspoon ground cumin

1 teaspoon sweet paprika

Salt and freshly ground pepper to taste

¼ cup (⅓ oz/10 g) fresh flat-leaf (Italian) parsley

Serves 4

1 Drain the cod and place in a saucepan with water to cover. Bring to a gentle simmer over medium heat and cook until tender, 10–15 minutes. Drain and, when cool enough to handle, shred, removing any bits of skin and small bones. Place in a large bowl.

2 Meanwhile, combine the potatoes with water to cover, bring to a boil, and boil until tender but still firm enough to hold their shape when diced, about 20 minutes. Drain and, when cool enough to handle, peel and cut into ½-inch (12-mm) dice. Add the potatoes, bell peppers, and olives to the salt cod.

3 To make the dressing, in a small bowl, whisk together the olive oil, vinegar, cumin, and paprika. Season with salt and pepper. Pour the dressing over the salt cod mixture and toss well. Garnish with the parsley and serve.

Gypsy Stew

Olla Gitana · Andalusia · Spain

This rich stew, a favorite of the Gypsy table, is made in an earthenware or iron pot called an *olla*. The almond *picada* belies a Moorish influence, while the pear is a Gypsy touch.

1 cup (7 oz/220 g) dried chickpeas (garbanzo beans)

1½ lb (750 g) meaty pork spareribs

½ lb (250 g) green beans, trimmed and cut into 2-inch (5-cm) lengths

1½ cups (7½ oz/235 g) diced or coarsely chopped peeled pumpkin

2 or 3 pears, peeled, halved, cored, and cut into chunks

1 bunch Swiss chard, coarsely chopped

½ cup (4 fl oz/125 ml) olive oil

10 almonds, toasted

1 slice coarse country bread, crusts removed

1 clove garlic

2 tablespoons red or white wine vinegar

1 yellow onion, diced

1 tablespoon sweet paprika

2 tomatoes, peeled, seeded, and diced

Pinch of saffron threads steeped in ¼ cup (2 fl oz/60 ml) hot chicken stock

Serves 6–8

1 Pick over the chickpeas, discarding any stones or misshapen beans. Rinse well and place in a bowl with water to cover generously. Let soak overnight in the refrigerator.

2 The next day, drain the chickpeas and place in a deep saucepan. Add the pork ribs and cold water to cover. Bring to a boil over high heat, reduce the heat to low, and skim off any foam. Simmer until the chickpeas are almost tender, about 1 hour. Add the green beans, pumpkin, pears, and Swiss chard and simmer for 10 minutes.

3 Meanwhile, in a sauté pan over medium heat, warm the olive oil. Add the almonds, bread, and garlic and cook, stirring the almonds and garlic and turning the bread as needed, until golden, about 5 minutes. Using a slotted spoon, transfer the almonds, bread, and garlic to a mortar and grind with a pestle. Set the pan of oil aside. Add the vinegar to the mortar and mix well. This is the *picada*.

4 Add the onion to the oil remaining in the pan and sauté over medium heat until pale gold, 10–12 minutes. Stir in the paprika and then the tomatoes. Cook for 10 minutes to soften the tomatoes, then add the saffron and stock and mix well.

5 Add the *picada* and the tomato mixture to the soup and simmer over low heat for about 10 minutes to blend the flavors. Taste and adjust the seasoning.

6 Ladle into warmed bowls and serve at once.

Green Bean Soup

Sopa de Feijão Verde à moda da Beira • Beira Alta • Portugal

This peasant soup, from the mountainous Beira Alta, is traditionally made with water. However, using vegetable stock allows the flavors of the vegetables to be more distinct.

5 tablespoons (2½ fl oz/75 ml) extra-virgin olive oil

2 yellow onions, chopped

1 lb (500 g) tomatoes, peeled, seeded, and chopped

1 lb (500 g) boiling potatoes, peeled and diced

4 cups (32 fl oz/1 l) vegetable or chicken stock

1 lb (500 g) green beans, trimmed and cut on the diagonal into 1-inch (2.5-cm) pieces

Salt and freshly ground pepper to taste

3 tablespoons chopped fresh mint (optional)

Serves 4–6

1 In a large saucepan over medium heat, warm the olive oil. Add the onions and sauté until tender, 8–10 minutes. Add the tomatoes and potatoes and sauté, stirring, until well combined, 3–5 minutes. Add the stock, raise the heat to high, and bring to a boil. Reduce the heat to low and simmer, uncovered, until the potatoes are tender, about 20 minutes. Remove from the heat and let cool slightly. Working in batches, ladle the soup into a food processor or blender and purée until smooth. Return the purée to the saucepan.

2 Bring a saucepan three-fourths full of salted water to a boil. Add the green beans and cook until tender-crisp, about 5 minutes. Drain, reserving a bit of the cooking water to add to the purée if it is too thick.

3 Reheat the purée and season with salt and pepper. Add the green beans and simmer over medium heat until heated through, about 5 minutes. Thin with the reserved cooking water if needed. Ladle into warmed soup bowls and garnish with the chopped mint, if desired. Serve at once.

Bread Soup with Cilantro, Garlic, and Egg

Açorda à Alentejana • Alentejo • Portugal

Each serving of this well-known southern Portuguese bread soup is crowned with a poached egg that the diner swirls into the hot soup before enjoying the first spoonful.

3 tablespoons finely minced garlic, plus 1 whole clove garlic

1 teaspoon kosher or sea salt

1 cup (1½ oz/45 g) chopped fresh cilantro (fresh coriander)

¾ cup (6 fl oz/180 ml) extra-virgin olive oil

6 thick slices coarse country bread, each about 1 inch (2.5 cm) thick, crusts removed

6 eggs

5–6 cups (40–48 fl oz/1.25–1.5 l) chicken stock or water

Serves 6

1 In a mortar, combine the minced garlic, salt, and half of the cilantro and mash to a coarse paste. Add ¼ cup (2 fl oz/60 ml) of the olive oil, 1 tablespoon at a time, mixing until well blended. Spoon into 6 warmed ovenproof soup bowls and keep warm.

2 In a large frying pan over medium heat, warm about ¼ cup (2 fl oz/60 ml) of the remaining oil. Add half of the bread slices without crowding and sauté, turning, until golden, 5–6 minutes. Transfer to paper towels to drain. Repeat with the remaining bread and oil. While the bread is still hot, rub both sides with the whole garlic clove, then cut into cubes. Distribute the cubes evenly among the bowls and toss with the garlic mixture.

3 In a large sauté pan, pour water to a depth of 1½ inches (4 cm). Bring the liquid to just under a boil. One at a time, break the eggs and carefully slip into the water. Cook until the whites are barely firm and the yolks are just glazed, 3–5 minutes. Using a slotted spoon, transfer them to a bowl of cold water. In a saucepan, bring the stock or water to a boil and then ladle most of it over the bread mixture in the bowls. Using the slotted spoon, place 1 egg on top of the bread mixture in each bowl. Gently ladle on the remaining hot stock or water. Sprinkle with the remaining cilantro and serve at once.

SOFRITO, REFOGADO, AND PICADA

A trinity of mixtures, the *sofrito*, the *refogado*, and the *picada*, contributes its distinctive character to countless Portuguese and Spanish dishes.

Spanish cooks use the *sofrito*, a kind of base sauce, to give body and richness to soups, stews, braises, and fricassees. At its most basic, a *sofrito* is made of onions and garlic cooked slowly in olive oil until soft and golden. Tomatoes are usually added, and sometimes chiles, peppers (capsicums), and herbs broaden the flavors.

The Portuguese *refogado*, also known as a *cebolada*, is a close cousin to the *sofrito*. Cooks from Oporto to Faro begin a myriad of dishes with a splash of olive oil and a shower of onions. The onions are cooked until they form a thick, sweet golden purée, then garlic and tomatoes may be added.

Finally, the *picada* is a traditional Catalan preparation. Made from nuts, fried bread, garlic, and freshly ground spices, crushed together to a paste, the fragrant mixture is added during the final stages of cooking to thicken a sauce and heighten its bouquet.

Chickpea and Spinach Soup

Potaje de Garbanzos y Espinacas • New Castile • Spain

This is a Lenten dish, served on Good Friday and other fast days in Madrid, where chickpeas are a popular addition to soups and *cocidos*. Salt cod is typically added to round out the flavors. The calendar of the Catholic Church traditionally includes many such holy days on which believers are required to abstain from eating meat—indeed, nearly one-third of the days of the year—thus, meatless soups are not unusual in the Spanish kitchen. A *picada* of fried bread and garlic is added to enrich the soup, producing a fairly thick result.

2 cups (14 oz/440 g) dried chickpeas (garbanzos)

7 cloves garlic

2 yellow onions

1 bay leaf

2 teaspoons salt, plus salt to taste

½ lb (250 g) boneless salt cod, soaked (optional; page 227)

1½ lb (750 g) spinach, stems removed

3 tablespoons olive oil

2 slices coarse country bread, crusts removed

Pinch of saffron threads

Water or vegetable stock, if needed

Freshly ground pepper to taste

½–1 cup (3–6 oz/90–185 g) diced cooked ham (optional)

2 hard-boiled eggs, peeled and chopped

Serves 6–8

1 Pick over the chickpeas and discard any stones or misshapen beans. Rinse well and place in a bowl with water to cover generously. Let soak overnight in the refrigerator.

2 The next day, drain the chickpeas and place them in a saucepan with water to cover. Add 4 garlic cloves, the onions, and the bay leaf and bring the mixture to a boil over high heat. Reduce the heat to low, cover, and simmer, adding the 2 teaspoons salt after the first 15 minutes of cooking, until the chickpeas are tender, about 1 hour.

3 Meanwhile, if using the cod, drain it and place in a saucepan with water to cover. Bring to a gentle simmer over medium heat and cook until tender, 10–15 minutes. Drain well and, when cool enough to handle, using your fingers, break the cod into bite-sized pieces, removing and discarding any bits of skin and any small bones. Set the pieces of cod aside.

4 When the chickpeas are done, using a slotted spoon, remove the onions and garlic cloves and set aside. Remove and discard the bay leaf. Leave the chickpeas in their liquid off the heat.

5 Place the spinach in a sauté pan with just the rinsing water clinging to the leaves. Place over medium heat and cook, turning occasionally, until wilted, 3–4 minutes. Remove the pan from the heat, drain the spinach well, pressing out excess moisture, and drain and chop the spinach coarsely. Set aside.

6 In a small sauté pan over medium heat, warm the olive oil. Add the bread and the remaining 3 garlic cloves and sauté until the bread and garlic are golden, 5–6 minutes. Transfer to a food processor or blender and add the saffron, the reserved cooked onions and garlic, and 1 cup (8 fl oz/250 ml) of the chickpea liquid. Process until the mixture is a smooth purée. This is the *picada*.

7 Pour the *picada* into the chickpeas and add the spinach. Stir well and bring to a simmer over medium heat. If the mixture is too thick, thin with water or vegetable stock. Season to taste with salt and lots of pepper. Add the salt cod or ham, if using, and heat through.

8 To serve, ladle the soup into warmed bowls. Garnish each serving with the chopped eggs, and serve at once.

Beef Stew with Vegetables and Spices

Estofado de Buey a la Catalana • Catalonia • Spain

While beef is not widely served in Spain and Portugal, this hearty stew is a superb member of the relatively small repertoire of beef recipes. The use of unsweetened chocolate might seem a bit unusual, but the Spaniards quickly took to this food from the New World. Some Catalan *picadas* include a dose of bitter chocolate called *xocolata a la pedra*, "chocolate on the stone," which contains cinnamon. Although not traditional, marinating the meat overnight in spices and wine results in maximum flavor and tenderness.

4 cups (32 fl oz/1 l) dry red wine

2 teaspoons freshly ground pepper, plus pepper to taste

1 teaspoon ground cinnamon

½ teaspoon ground cloves

3 lb (1.5 kg) beef chuck or other stewing beef, cut into 2-inch (5-cm) cubes

½ cup (4 fl oz/125 ml) olive oil or ½ cup (4 oz/125 g) lard

¼ lb (125 g) bacon, cut into ¼-inch (6-mm) dice

4 large yellow onions, chopped

Salt to taste

2 tablespoons finely minced garlic

3 bay leaves, crumbled

1 large tomato, peeled and diced (optional)

1 cup (8 fl oz/250 ml) veal or beef stock

24 baby carrots or carrot chunks, peeled (optional)

24 small new potatoes, peeled

½ cup (4 fl oz/125 ml) dry sherry

1 oz (30 g) unsweetened chocolate, grated

6 tablespoons (½ oz/15 g) chopped fresh flat-leaf (Italian) parsley

Serves 6–8

1 In a nonreactive pan, combine 2 cups (16 fl oz/ 500 ml) of the wine, 1 teaspoon of the pepper, ½ teaspoon of the cinnamon, and the cloves. Add the beef cubes, mix well, cover, and refrigerate overnight.

2 The next day, bring the meat to room temperature. Using a slotted spoon, lift the meat from the marinade and discard the marinade. In a large frying pan over high heat, warm half of the olive oil or melt half of the lard. Working in batches, brown the meat on all sides, 8–10 minutes. Using the slotted spoon, transfer the meat to a plate.

3 When all the meat is browned, add the remaining olive oil or lard to the pan over medium heat. Add the bacon and cook, stirring, until lightly browned, about 5 minutes. Add the onions and a bit of salt and sauté until tender, about 10 minutes. Add the garlic, the remaining 1 teaspoon pepper and ½ teaspoon cinnamon, the bay leaves, the tomato (if using), the remaining 2 cups (16 fl oz/500 ml) wine, and the stock. Return the meat to the pan, raise the heat to high, and bring to a boil. Reduce the heat to low, cover, and cook until the meat is tender but not falling apart, about 2 hours.

4 Meanwhile, if using the carrots, bring a large saucepan two-thirds full of salted water to a boil. Add the carrots and parboil for about 10 minutes, then drain and set aside. Place the potatoes in the same saucepan with salted water to cover generously, bring to a boil, and boil until nearly tender, about 15 minutes. Drain and set aside.

5 When the beef is ready, using a slotted spoon, transfer it to a large *cazuela* or heavy pot. Using a large spoon, skim the fat off the top of the stewing liquids and discard. Pass the contents of the frying pan through a food mill or sieve placed over a bowl. Add the sherry and the chocolate and mix well. Pour this sauce over the beef and add the potatoes and the carrots, if using. Place over medium heat and bring to a simmer. Adjust the heat to maintain a gentle simmer and cook, uncovered, for about 15 minutes to blend the flavors.

6 Taste and adjust the seasoning. Sprinkle with the parsley and serve at once.

Garlic Soup

Sopa de Ajo • New Castile • Spain

Sopa de ajo was probably the inspiration for the original gazpacho. Traditionally, it was a mixture of chopped garlic, crumbled stale bread, olive oil, and water, the pantry staples of the poor, but it has evolved to have many regional variations. In Málaga, cooks might use fish stock, and in Galicia, rye bread is used. The addition of paprika earmarks this recipe as the Madrid version. Sometimes the eggs are beaten and then whisked into the soup. In every case, however, the garlicky creation is believed to be a surefire cure for hangovers.

6 tablespoons (3 fl oz/90 ml) olive oil

12 cloves garlic

12 thin slices coarse country bread, crusts removed

2 teaspoons sweet paprika

6 cups (48 fl oz/1.5 l) chicken stock or water

Salt and freshly ground pepper to taste

6 eggs

Chopped fresh flat-leaf (Italian) parsley

Serves 6

1 Preheat the oven to 350°F (180°C).

2 In a large saucepan over medium heat, warm the oil. Add the garlic cloves and sauté until golden and fragrant, 3–4 minutes. Using a slotted spoon, remove and discard the garlic. Working in batches, add the bread to the garlic-flavored oil and sauté, turning as needed, until pale gold and crisp, 4–5 minutes. Using the slotted spoon, transfer the bread to 6 ovenproof bowls or *cazuelas*, placing 2 slices in each bowl. Put the bowls on a baking sheet. Add the paprika to the pan over medium heat, stir once, and then add the stock or water and bring to a boil. Season with salt and pepper.

3 Break 1 egg into each bowl and ladle the boiling stock or water over the eggs, dividing it evenly. Slip the baking sheet into the oven and bake until the egg whites have set up but the yolks are still runny, about 10 minutes.

4 Garnish each bowl with parsley and serve at once.

EARTHENWARE COOKING VESSELS

Every cook in Spain and Portugal has at least one—and more likely several—earthenware cooking vessels on the kitchen shelf. In Spain, these invaluable dishes are called *cazuelas*, from the Arabic *qas'ah*, or bowl, while in Portugal they are known as *tachos de barro*. They come in all colors and sizes, from small enough to contain a tapa of *champiñones al ajillo* to large enough to handle a *caldeirada* served to a dozen friends. They retain heat magnificently and can be used in the oven and carefully over a direct flame.

New earthenware dishes must be seasoned before they are used, or you risk their cracking when they come in contact with direct heat.

A Spanish cook observes all the intricacies of the curing process. First, rub the unglazed base of the *cazuela* with three cloves of garlic, then allow it to stand for a bit until the garlic juices are absorbed. Finally, fill it with hot water and bring the water slowly to a boil. Once it boils, discard the water, and then the *cazuela*—or *tacho de barro*—is ready to use. To avoid future cracking, remember to never pour boiling liquid into a cold *cazuela*, nor put a hot *cazuela* onto a cold surface.

Spring Vegetable Stew

Menestra de Primavera • Navarre • Spain

The measurements don't have to be precise in this vegetable dish from Navarre, but the ingredients must be fresh and full of flavor. The abundant vegetable plots of the region's Ebro Valley contribute to the rich mix.

1 Preheat the broiler (grill). Cut the bell pepper or pimiento in half lengthwise and remove the stem, seeds, and ribs. Place, cut sides down, on a baking sheet. Broil (grill) until the skin blackens and blisters. Remove from the broiler, drape the pepper loosely with aluminum foil, and let cool for 10 minutes, then peel away the skin and chop the pepper. Set aside.

2 Bring a saucepan three-fourths full of water to a boil, add the fava beans, and boil for 30 seconds. Drain, rinse under cold water, and slip the beans from their tough skins. Refill the saucepan with salted water and bring to a boil. Add the fava beans and boil until tender but still firm, 5–10 minutes, depending upon their size. Drain and set aside.

3 Refill the same saucepan with salted water and bring to a boil. Add the peas and boil until tender but still firm, 3–7 minutes; again, the timing will depend upon their size. Drain and set aside.

4 Fill a large bowl with cold water. Cut the lemon in half and squeeze the juice into the water. Working with 1 artichoke at a time, remove all the leaves until you reach the pale green heart. Pare away the dark green area from the base. Cut the artichoke into quarters lengthwise and scoop out and discard the choke from each piece. Drop into the lemon water to prevent discoloration. When all the artichokes are trimmed, drain and place in a saucepan with salted water to cover. Bring to a boil and cook until tender, 15–20 minutes; the timing will depend on the size of the artichokes.

5 In a large frying pan over medium heat, warm the olive oil. Add the green onions and garlic and sauté briefly. Add the chopped pepper and the ham and sauté for 1–2 minutes longer. Add the peas, favas, and artichokes, and swirl them in the oil for 1–2 minutes. Then sprinkle with the flour, salt, pepper, and paprika and stir in the tomato sauce and water or stock. Bring to a simmer and cook over medium-low heat for about 10 minutes to thicken the pan juices.

6 Taste and adjust the seasoning. Transfer to a warmed platter, garnish with parsley or mint, and serve at once.

1 red bell or fresh pimiento pepper (capsicum)

3 lb (1.5 kg) fava (broad) beans, shelled (about ¾ lb/375 g shelled beans)

2 lb (1 kg) English peas, shelled (about 10 oz/ 315 g shelled peas)

1 lemon

6 small or medium artichokes

¼ cup (2 fl oz/60 ml) olive oil

4 green (spring) onions, including tender green tops, chopped

2 or 3 cloves garlic, minced

½ lb (250 g) ham, diced

1 tablespoon all-purpose (plain) flour

Salt and freshly ground pepper to taste

1 teaspoon sweet paprika

3 tablespoons tomato sauce

6 tablespoons (3 fl oz/90 ml) water or vegetable or chicken stock

Chopped fresh flat-leaf (Italian) parsley or mint

Serves 4–6

Fisherman's Soup

Caldeirada • Estremadura • Portugal

Caldeirada, the Portuguese fisherman's hearty soup, is prepared with an unchanging list of basic ingredients: onions, garlic, tomatoes, chiles, bell peppers, and, of course, white wine.

2 lb (1 kg) assorted white fish fillets such as cod, halibut, snapper, flounder, and sea bass, cut into 2-inch (5-cm) pieces

Kosher salt for sprinkling

3 tablespoons olive oil, plus more for frying bread

2 yellow onions, chopped

2 green bell peppers (capsicums), seeded and chopped

4 tomatoes, peeled, seeded, and chopped

3 large cloves garlic, minced

1 cup (8 fl oz/250 ml) dry white wine, plus about ¼ cup (2 fl oz/60 ml) if steaming clams separately

Freshly ground pepper to taste

2 lb (1 kg) clams, scrubbed

6 slices coarse country bread, crusts removed

6 tablespoons (3 oz/90 g) unsalted butter

Chopped fresh flat-leaf (Italian) parsley

Serves 6

1 Sprinkle the fish fillets with kosher salt, cover, and refrigerate for at least 1 hour or up to 2 hours.

2 In a large saucepan over medium heat, warm the 3 tablespoons olive oil. Add the onions and bell peppers and sauté until softened, about 10 minutes.

3 Add the tomatoes, garlic, and the 1 cup (8 fl oz/ 250 ml) wine and season with salt and pepper. Add the fish, raise the heat to high, and bring to a boil. Reduce the heat to low, cover, and simmer gently for about 10 minutes. If the pan is large enough, add the clams (discard any that fail to close to the touch), cover, and steam until they open, about 5 minutes. By then, the fish should test done. If the pan is too small to accommodate the clams, steam them in a separate pan with the ¼ cup (2 fl oz/60 ml) wine for about 5 minutes and then add them to the stew. Discard any clams that failed to open.

4 In a large sauté pan over medium heat, warm about 4 tablespoons (2 fl oz/60 ml) olive oil. In batches, add the bread and fry, turning as needed, until golden, 5–6 minutes. Using tongs, transfer to paper towels to drain. Add more oil to the pan for each batch. Cut each slice on the diagonal and place 2 triangles on the bottom of each of 6 large soup bowls.

5 When the soup is ready, add the butter and swirl the pan a few times to thicken the juices. Ladle the soup and the fish over the bread. Sprinkle with parsley and serve at once.

Stone Soup

Sopa de Pedra • Ribatejo • Portugal

This soup is based on the legend of a stranger who made "soup" from stones and water for a peasant couple whose larder was bare. The kidney beans here represent the stones.

1 rounded cup (8 oz/250 g) dried red kidney beans

3 tablespoons olive oil

2 yellow onions, chopped *and* 2 cloves garlic, minced

¼ lb (125 g) bacon, in one piece, *and* ¼ lb (125 g) *chouriço* or garlic sausage

4 boiling potatoes, 4 carrots, *and* 2 turnips, peeled and diced

1 small head savoy cabbage, shredded

2 cups (12 oz/375 g) diced canned plum (Roma) tomatoes

1 bay leaf

8 cups (64 fl oz/2 l) chicken stock

½ cup (¾ oz/20 g) chopped fresh cilantro (fresh coriander)

Serves 6

1 Pick over the beans and discard any stones or misshapen beans. Rinse well and place in a bowl with water to cover generously. Let soak overnight in the refrigerator.

2 The next day, drain the beans and place them in a saucepan with water to cover. Bring to a boil over hight heat, then reduce the heat to low, cover, and simmer until tender, about 1 hour. Drain.

3 Meanwhile, in a saucepan over medium heat, warm the olive oil. Add the onions and garlic and sauté until tender, about 10 minutes. Add the bacon, sausage, potatoes, carrots, turnips, cabbage, tomatoes, bay leaf, and stock. Raise the heat to high, bring to a boil, reduce the heat to very low, and simmer until the vegetables are tender, about 30 minutes.

4 Discard the bay leaf. Remove the meats and cut into ½-inch (12-mm) pieces. Return the meats and beans to the pan, add the cilantro, and simmer over medium heat for 5 minutes to warm through. Ladle into warmed bowls and serve at once.

Butternut Squash Soup

Sopa de Abóbora • Estremadura • Portugal

Squash soups are rich, but lemon juice adds a welcome lightness. For an extra flourish, garnish with toasted croutons. Once you add the egg yolks, you cannot reheat the soup.

¼ cup (2 oz/60 g) unsalted butter

2 yellow onions, chopped

1 butternut squash, about 1½ lb (750 g), halved, seeded, peeled, and cut into 1-inch (2.5-cm) pieces

5–7 cups (40–56 fl oz/1.25–1.75 l) chicken stock

Salt and freshly ground pepper to taste

2 egg yolks (see page 223)

½ cup (4 fl oz/125 ml) heavy (double) cream

2 tablespoons fresh lemon juice

2 tablespoons chopped fresh cilantro (fresh coriander)

Serves 6

1 In a heavy saucepan over medium heat, melt the butter. Add the onions and sauté until tender, 8–10 minutes. Add the squash pieces and 5 cups (40 fl oz/1.25 l) of the chicken stock. Raise the heat to high, bring to a boil, cover partially, reduce the heat to low, and simmer until the vegetables are very soft, about 30 minutes. Remove from the heat and let cool slightly.

2 Working in batches, ladle the soup into a food processor or blender and purée until smooth. Return the purée to the saucepan. If it is too thick, add as much of the remaining stock as needed to correct the consistency. Bring to a simmer over medium-low heat and season with salt and pepper.

3 In a small bowl, whisk together the egg yolks, cream, and lemon juice and swirl the mixture into the hot soup. Ladle immediately into warmed bowls. Garnish with the cilantro and serve at once.

PORTUGUESE BREADS

The breads of Portugal are generally dark-crusted beauties, and Portuguese cooks are reluctant to waste even a crumb. This has led to a trio of *escudo*-saving dishes made with the unfinished loaves left from family meals.

The best known of the three is the *açorda*, a soup in which bread and eggs are added to simmering broth. *Açorda de mariscos*, featuring the shrimp caught off Portugal's seacoast, is a specialty of Lisbon. *Açorda à alentejana*, served in farmhouses and *tascas* throughout the Alentejo, is a more frugal mixture of bread, water, eggs, olive oil, and garlic.

Migas are commonly thicker, meatier preparations. They are cooked and served in a *cazuela* or *tacho de barro*, with the moistened, seasoned bread cubes on the bottom and pork or other meats on top.

The last of the trio is the *sopa seca*, a specialty of northern Portugal. This hearty concoction is made by layering cooked meat or poultry and vegetables alternately with bread slices in an earthenware dish and topping it off with boiling stock—a perfect dish for the rugged, verdant north.

Shellfish and Bread Soup

Açorda de Mariscos • Estremadura • Portugal

Typical of Lisbon, this soup sometimes includes chunks of fish to stretch it when economy is a concern. Occasionally, it uses only shrimp and a stock made from the shells, with a bit of chopped tomato added, along with a garnish of chopped hard-boiled eggs. Be sure the bowls are piping hot so that the stock will not cool down too quickly. It needs to remain hot enough to cook the eggs partially.

12–18 slices coarse country bread, about 1 inch (2.5 cm) thick

1 clove garlic, plus 4 tablespoons (1½ oz/45 g) finely minced garlic

½ teaspoon salt

6 cups (48 fl oz/1.5 l) fish stock or a mixture of fish stock and shrimp stock

¾ cup (6 fl oz/180 ml) extra-virgin olive oil

2 yellow onions, chopped

1–2 teaspoons red pepper flakes

12 mussels, scrubbed and debearded

18 hard-shelled clams (more if tiny), scrubbed

⅓ cup (3 fl oz/80 ml) dry white wine

18 shrimp (prawns), peeled and deveined

¼ cup (⅓ oz/10 g) finely chopped fresh flat-leaf (Italian) parsley

½ cup (¾ oz/20 g) finely chopped fresh cilantro (fresh coriander)

6 eggs, at room temperature (see page 223)

Serves 6

1 Preheat the broiler (grill). Arrange the bread slices on a baking sheet and slip under the broiler. Toast, turning once, until golden. Remove from the broiler. While the slices are still warm, rub them on both sides with the whole garlic clove and then cut them into 1-inch (2.5-cm) cubes. Set aside.

2 In a mortar, combine 2 tablespoons of the minced garlic and the salt and mash to a paste with a pestle.

3 In a saucepan, bring the stock to a boil. Adjust the heat so that it remains at a simmer.

4 In another saucepan over low heat, warm 2 tablespoons of the olive oil. Add the onions and sauté until tender, 8–10 minutes. Add the remaining 2 tablespoons minced garlic and the red pepper flakes to taste and sauté until the garlic is fragrant, about 3 minutes. Add the hot stock and simmer for 3–5 minutes to allow the flavors to marry.

5 In a large sauté pan, combine the mussels and clams, discarding any mussels or clams that fail to close to the touch. Pour in the wine, place over high heat, cover, and cook until the shellfish open, 3–6 minutes. Using a slotted spoon, transfer the mussels and clams to a bowl, discarding any that failed to open; cover and keep warm. Strain the shellfish cooking liquid through a sieve and add to the stock.

6 Add the shrimp to the hot stock and poach until opaque throughout, about 3 minutes.

7 Divide the bread, parsley, cilantro, and garlic paste evenly among warmed soup bowls. Divide the remaining 10 tablespoons (5 fl oz/160 ml) olive oil evenly among the bowls. Now distribute the cooked shrimp, clams, and mussels among the bowls. Break 1 egg in each bowl. Bring the remaining stock to a boil and ladle into the bowls. Serve at once.

Leek and Potato Soup

Purrusalda · Basque Country · Spain

The name of this soup comes from *puerro*, meaning "leek." In the Basque provinces, leeks are highly regarded, and this popular soup is considered the classic way to begin a meal.

⅓ lb (5 oz/155 g) boneless salt cod (optional)

¼ cup (2 fl oz/60 ml) olive oil

2 cloves garlic

1½ lb (750 g) leeks (about 8 medium), including some tender green tops, halved lengthwise and sliced

1 lb (500 g) potatoes, peeled and diced

1 bay leaf

Salt and freshly ground pepper to taste

3¾ cups (30 fl oz/940 ml) water or fish stock

1 teaspoon sweet paprika

Serves 4–6

1 If using salt cod, in a bowl, combine the salt cod with cold water to cover generously. Cover and refrigerate for 24–36 hours, changing the water at least 4 times. Drain the cod and break into small pieces, removing any bits of skin and any small bones. Set aside.

2 In a saucepan over medium heat, warm the olive oil. Add the garlic and sauté until golden, 4–5 minutes. Using a slotted spoon, transfer the garlic to a mortar.

3 Add the leeks to the oil remaining in the pan and sauté slowly over low heat until wilted, about 5 minutes. Add the potatoes, bay leaf, salt, pepper, and the cod, if using. Pour in the water or stock. Add the paprika to the garlic and crush with a pestle. Add the mixture to the pan, bring to a boil over high heat, reduce the heat to low, and simmer until the leeks and the cod, if using, are tender and the potatoes fall apart, about 30 minutes.

4 Ladle into warmed bowls and serve at once.

Meatball Soup

Sopa de Albóndigas • Andalusia • Spain

This soup was probably of Jewish origin, initially made with beef. After the Inquisition, pork was added to demonstrate one's conversion to Christianity. Tomatoes, potatoes, chickpeas, saffron, and chopped hard-boiled eggs are added along with the tiny meatballs to a rich meat stock, making this soup almost hearty enough to be declared a stew.

MEATBALLS

¾ lb (375 g) ground (minced) beef, half beef and half pork, or lamb

⅓ cup (2 oz/60 g) grated yellow onion

½ cup (2 oz/60 g) dried bread crumbs

1 egg, lightly beaten

3 tablespoons chopped fresh flat-leaf (Italian) parsley

1 clove garlic, finely minced

½ teaspoon ground cinnamon (optional)

½ teaspoon ground cumin (optional)

1 teaspoon salt

½ teaspoon freshly ground pepper

2 tablespoons olive oil

1 yellow onion, chopped

¼ teaspoon saffron threads, crushed (optional)

1 cup (7 oz/220 g) drained cooked chickpeas (garbanzo beans)

1 cup (5 oz/155 g) peeled and diced boiling potatoes

6 cups (48 fl oz/1.5 l) flavorful meat stock

2 cups (12 oz/375 g) peeled, seeded, and diced tomatoes (fresh or canned)

Salt and freshly ground pepper to taste

¼ cup (⅓ oz/10 g) chopped fresh flat-leaf (Italian) parsley

2 hard-boiled eggs, peeled and chopped (optional)

Serves 6

1 To make the meatballs, in a bowl, combine the meat, onion, bread crumbs, egg, parsley, garlic, the cinnamon and cumin (if using), salt, and pepper. Knead with your hands until all the ingredients are fully incorporated and evenly distributed throughout the mixture. (If you have time, cover and refrigerate the mixture for 1 hour to make forming the meatballs easier.) Using your hands, shape the mixture into tiny meatballs and set aside.

2 In a large saucepan over medium heat, warm the olive oil. Add the onion and sauté until tender, about 10 minutes. Add the saffron (if using), the chickpeas, potatoes, stock, and tomatoes. Raise the heat to high and bring to a boil. Reduce the heat to low and simmer, uncovered, to blend the flavors and partially cook the potatoes, about 10 minutes.

3 Slip the uncooked meatballs into the broth and simmer gently until cooked through, about 20 minutes. Season with salt and pepper.

4 Using a slotted spoon, transfer the meatballs to warmed soup bowls, dividing them evenly. Ladle the hot soup stock and an equal amount of the vegetables over the meatballs. Sprinkle with the parsley and chopped eggs, if using, and serve at once.

Summer Vegetable Stew

Pisto Manchego • New Castile • Spain

Pisto evolved from an ancient stew called *alboronia*, Moorish for "eggplant." The original *alboronia* is thought to have included Arabic seasonings such as cumin, saffron, and cilantro. Over time, vegetables from the New World were also introduced into the mix, as the ingredients used in this delicious recipe illustrate.

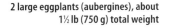

2 large eggplants (aubergines), about 1½ lb (750 g) total weight

Salt and freshly ground pepper to taste

¾ cup (6 fl oz/180 ml) olive oil

2 large yellow onions, chopped

1 lb (500 g) bell peppers (capsicums), a mixture of red and green, seeded and chopped

½ cup (2½ oz/75 g) all-purpose (plain) flour

2 lb (1 kg) tomatoes, peeled, seeded, and diced

1 teaspoon dried oregano

2 tablespoons pine nuts, toasted

Serves 6

1 Peel the eggplants and cut into 1½-inch (4-cm) pieces. Place in a colander, sprinkling salt between the layers, and let drain for 1 hour.

2 In a large frying pan over medium heat, warm ¼ cup (2 fl oz/60 ml) of the olive oil. Add the onions and sauté until tender, 8–10 minutes. Add the peppers and sauté until softened, about 5 minutes longer.

3 Meanwhile, rinse the eggplant pieces and pat dry. Place the flour in a shallow bowl. In another large frying pan over high heat, warm the remaining ½ cup (4 fl oz/120 ml) oil. Dip the eggplant in the flour, tapping off the excess. In batches, add to the hot oil and fry, turning as needed, until golden, 5–8 minutes. Using a slotted spoon, transfer to a plate.

4 When all of the eggplant pieces have been fried, add them to the onion-pepper mixture along with the tomatoes, oregano, salt, and pepper. Reduce the heat to low and simmer until the flavors are well blended and the tomatoes have broken down into a saucelike consistency, about 20 minutes. Spoon into a warmed serving bowl and garnish with the pine nuts. Serve warm or at room temperature.

PEPPERS

Today, it is difficult to imagine Spanish and Portuguese food without its sweet peppers. But these contemporary staples of the Iberian table did not arrive until the fifteenth and sixteenth centuries, when great Portuguese explorers and Spanish conquistadores carried them back to the Old World from the New. The chile made the same voyage, but the Portuguese took to its fiery taste with far more enthusiasm than the Spanish, introducing it with great success both at home and in their overseas colonies.

Red and green bell peppers are known as *pimentos* in Portugal and *pimientos* in Spain. *Chilindrón*, a popular sauce in Aragon and Navarre, is but one of the many Spanish recipes in which peppers play a central role. In Portugal, cooks assemble platters of roasted peppers in oil and vinegar or make *massa pimentão*, a dry rub for roasting meats.

Spain's most prized peppers are the slightly spicy *piquillo* and the mildly hot *romesco*. The best *piquillos* come from Navarre, where they are cultivated in the valley that lines the Ebro River. Much of the crop is roasted over wood fires, peeled, and packed into jars, for stuffing with squid, salt cod, eggs, and mushrooms, or other fillings. The *romesco* pepper, smaller and usually dried, is the basis of the famed Catalan *salsa romesco*.

Shellfish Stew

Zarzuela de Mariscos • Catalonia • Spain

Zarzuela is both the name for this stew and Spanish for "operetta." This little shellfish mélange is so festive it resembles a lighthearted musical. Keeping the lobster in the shell and the tails on the shrimp makes for mildly messy eating, but the shells contribute additional flavor to the dish and create a more dramatic presentation. Some versions of this recipe include crushed toasted almonds, and others a hint of chile. Some cooks add both.

2 small to medium live lobsters

¼ cup (2 fl oz/60 ml) olive oil

1½ cups (7½ oz/235 g) chopped yellow onions

1–2 tablespoons finely minced garlic

1 red bell pepper (capsicum), seeded and finely diced

1 green bell pepper (capsicum), seeded and finely diced

3 cups (18 oz/560 g) peeled, seeded, and diced tomatoes (fresh or canned)

½ cup (2½ oz/75 g) almonds, toasted and ground (optional)

¼ teaspoon saffron threads, steeped in ¼ cup (2 fl oz/60 ml) dry white wine

1 bay leaf, torn into pieces

Salt and freshly ground black pepper to taste

Pinch of red pepper flakes (optional)

1½ cups (12 fl oz/375 ml) dry white wine

12–18 mussels, scrubbed and debearded

12–18 clams, scrubbed

12–18 large shrimp (prawns), peeled and deveined with tail fin shell intact

½–¾ lb (250–375 g) sea scallops, halved if large

1–2 tablespoons fresh lemon juice (optional)

Romesco sauce (optional; page 140)

Serves 6–8

1 Bring a large saucepan three-fourths full of salted water to a boil. Add the lobsters, immersing completely, and boil until the shells turn red, about 5 minutes. Using tongs, remove the lobsters and place under running cold water to cool. Working with 1 lobster at a time, and holding it over a sink, twist off the head and discard. Remove the claws and separate at the knuckles. Lay the lobster, underside down, on a cutting board. Using a knife, cut the tail crosswise into 2-inch (5-cm) pieces. Crack the claws to expose the meat. Set the spindly legs aside for garnish. Repeat with the other lobster.

2 In a large, heavy pot over medium heat, warm the olive oil. Add the onions and sauté until softened, about 5 minutes. Add the garlic and bell peppers and sauté until the vegetables are soft but not browned, about 5 minutes longer.

3 Add the tomatoes, almonds (if using), saffron and wine, bay leaf, salt, black pepper, and the red pepper flakes, if desired. Raise the heat to high and bring to a boil. Cook until thickened, about 10 minutes.

4 Add the wine, return to a boil, and add the lobsters, mussels, and clams, discarding any mussels or clams that fail to close to the touch. Cover and cook for about 5 minutes. Add the shrimp and scallops, re-cover, and cook until the lobsters, shrimp, and scallops are cooked and the clams and mussels have opened, 3–5 minutes more. Discard any clams or mussels that failed to open. Taste and adjust the seasoning as needed. Add the lemon juice, if desired, to balance the flavor.

5 Ladle the stew into warmed bowls and serve at once.

NUTS

Nuts are Iberian pantry staples. They are at the heart of many sweets, particularly those made for centuries in convents and now sold in elegant shops such as Madrid's venerable Casa Mira. But nuts also turn up in the form of fried almonds sprinkled with salt and cayenne, in sauces such as *romesco*, and in soups such as *gazpacho blanco*.

Many historians—although not all—believe the Romans planted the first walnut trees in northern Spain and Portugal. Today the harvest is modest, but residents of the Douro are quick to extol the virtues of pairing a handful of freshly cracked walnuts with a glass of tawny port. This same area harbors the peninsula's primary chestnut orchards, the yield of which goes into such dishes as Galicia's *sopa de castañas* and the olive oil–dressed boiled dried chestnuts of Minho and Trás-os-Montes. The Greeks—or perhaps the Romans—may be responsible for the numerous hazelnut orchards around the rampart-rimmed city of Tarragona, where many of the rich, spherical nuts go into the region's celebrated romesco sauces. Pine nuts still in the shell are sold as snacks; once shelled, they turn up in exquisite desserts.

The nut most closely associated with Iberia is the almond. Introduced and popularized in cooking by the Moors, it is widely grown in Andalusia, Alentejo, Algarve, and on the island of Majorca, where trees covered with thick, snowy blossoms carpet the countryside in spring. Almonds are used whole, chopped, or ground in many different soups and stews.

Cold Almond Soup with Grapes

Gazpacho Blanco · Andalusia · Spain

The texture of this chilled soup may seem a bit unusual at first, but it quickly becomes appealing. This gazpacho, as opposed to the more familiar tomato-based one laced with vegetables, is probably closest to the original version, which was nothing more than bread, water, oil, and vinegar. In bustling Málaga, where the harvest from nearby hillside vineyards is turned into a full-bodied, very sweet aperitif or dessert wine and sugary plump raisins, the soup is given an elegant and refreshing finish with the addition of peeled grapes.

1 cup (5½ oz/170 g) blanched almonds

4 small slices day-old coarse country bread, crusts removed, soaked in water to cover, and squeezed dry

2 cloves garlic

1 teaspoon salt, plus salt to taste

6 tablespoons (3 fl oz/90 ml) olive oil

3 tablespoons white wine vinegar

3 cups (24 fl oz/750 ml) ice water, or as needed

Freshly ground pepper to taste

36 green seedless grapes, peeled and cut in half

Serves 4

1 In a food processor or blender, combine the almonds, bread, garlic, and the 1 teaspoon salt and pulse until the almonds are very finely ground. With the motor running, slowly add the olive oil, vinegar, and 1 cup (8 fl oz/250 ml) of the ice water and process until you have a creamy white liquid. Transfer to a bowl.

2 Stir in as much of the remaining 2 cups (16 fl oz/ 500 ml) ice water as needed to achieve the soup consistency you prefer. Season with salt and pepper. Cover and refrigerate until well chilled.

3 Just before serving, stir in the grapes. Ladle the soup into chilled bowls and serve.

GLOSSARY

ACHIOTE PASTE This Mexican seasoning paste, made from the tough, brick red seeds of the annatto tree, contributes a mild flowery flavor and a deep yellow-orange color to foods.

AMARANTH SEEDS These nutritious, protein-rich seeds, native to Mexico and used in rituals since Aztec times, are occasionally featured in contemporary Mexican salad recipes.

ANCHOVIES These shimmering blue-green fish measure no more than 6 inches (15 cm) long. When freshly caught, they may be fried and eaten whole; they are sometimes pickled with vinegar. The bulk of the catch is preserved by layering the fish with salt. Whole salted anchovies are packed in cans, to be filleted at home before use. They can be found in some delicatessens. Salted anchovy fillets immersed in olive oil in small, flat tins or in glass jars are more commonly available. Jars of anchovy fillets are generally preferred.

ARTICHOKES Prickly on the outside but tender within, artichokes are one of nature's more peculiar vegetables. They are actually the flower bud of a large-leaved perennial in the sunflower family. If left on the plant, the buds would gradually open to reveal glorious purple blossoms, but harvesters cut them when they are tightly closed.

To trim artichokes, cut the stem flush with the bottom. Using a serrated knife, cut about 1½ inches (4 cm) off the top of the artichoke. Using scissors, snip off the pointed tips of each leaf. Rub the artichoke with a lemon half to preserve its color while you prepare it.

ARUGULA Throughout Italy, this slender, green leaf vegetable can be found growing wild in the countryside and is valued in both salads and quickly cooked dishes. The finest, most tender young arugula (rocket) leaves have a pleasing delicacy, while the older specimens have a more peppery, slightly bitter taste.

ASAFETIDA Asafetida, a resinous substance of the giant fennel, is best known for its foul smell. The odor is released when the spice is ground but mellows when it is cooked. Asafetida is always used in small amounts of ¼–½ teaspoon. It can be replaced with about 1 teaspoon of minced garlic, or to taste.

BAMBOO SHOOTS The edible shoots of certain types of bamboo are known as *qingsun*. Fresh, untreated shoots have tough outer leaves over a golden-colored, horn-shaped, tender shoot of layered construction. Ready-to-use shoots are sold fresh, frozen, or canned in whole pieces, slices, or shreds, and what is not used can be kept fresh in the refrigerator in lightly salted water for up to one week. Winter bamboo shoots (*dongsun*) are small and tender. Salted dried bamboo shoots should be soaked and rinsed thoroughly before use.

BEAN CURD Protein-rich bean curd is a bland-tasting, jelly-like substance produced by adding a coagulating ingredient to a liquid of crushed and boiled dried yellow soybeans and water. Soft or "silk" fresh bean curd has a smooth and fragile texture, suited to soups. Firm fresh bean curd has been compressed to extract water, giving it a firmer texture and slightly stronger taste, suited to deep-frying. Fresh bean curd is packed in water and sold in blocks, packs, or squares, and should be used within 2 to 3 days of opening. The water should be changed frequently. Fried bean curd is the fresh product first cut into blocks, strips, and slices and then deep-fried to crisp the surface. It should be rinsed before use. Bean curd sheets are made by drying the firm, thin skin that coagulates on the top of heated soybean milk, and is also available folded into sticks. They last indefinitely, but both varieties must be soaked to soften them before use in any recipe.

BEANS Whether beans are enjoyed fresh in spring or dried for use throughout the year, enthusiastic bean eaters value such favorites as speckled, pale pink borlotti, similar to cranberry beans; cannellini, ivory-colored kidney beans of moderate size; and large, pale green fava (broad) beans. Beans also play a central part in the Indian diet. When black gram beans are skinned and split, they are known as white gram beans, or *urad dal*. Green mung beans, also known as green gram beans, are whole seeds of a plant and should always be soaked before they are cooked. Skinned and split, they are known as yellow mung beans and do not need to be soaked before use.

To cook dried beans, first sort through them to discard any stones or misshapen specimens. Presoak in cold water to cover overnight in the refrigerator, or quick-soak in a large pot by covering well with cold water, bringing to a boil, then letting stand for 1–2 hours. After soaking, drain the beans, put in a pot with fresh water to cover, bring to a rolling boil, then simmer until tender, 1–2 hours, depending on the type of bean. In some recipes that don't require long cooking, you can substitute canned beans. A 15-ounce (470-g) can, rinsed and drained, yields about 2 cups beans, which is equivalent to the yield of 3 ounces (90 g) dried beans.

BEAN SPROUTS Mung bean sprouts are slender, silver-cream shoots about 2 inches (5 cm) long with a seedpod at one end and a tapering root at the other. Fresh sprouts are readily available and are a superior choice to canned sprouts. Both should be blanched in boiling water and then crisped in ice water before use. Keep fresh sprouts in an airtight container in the refrigerator for 3–5 days. Longer sprouts can be used in the same way.

BEANS, YARD-LONG As their name suggests, yard-long beans can grow up to 3 feet (1 m) in length. Also known as snake beans or long beans, the species is native to Asia. Dark green varieties are more tender than the pale green, slightly thicker beans. Substitute green beans if alternatives are not available. They should be stored in a plastic bag in the refrigerator and used within 4 days.

BELL PEPPERS Also called capsicums and sweet peppers, large and meaty green bell peppers turn red and become sweeter when fully ripened. As attractive as they are versatile, red bell peppers add crunch when used raw in salads; take on a silky sweetness when cooked slowly in soups or stews; and contribute a distinctive smokiness when roasted over an open flame.

To roast bell peppers, using tongs or a large fork, hold a whole pepper over the flame of a gas burner for 10–15 minutes, turning it to char and blister the skin evenly. Place in a bowl, cover, and leave for 10 minutes. The steam will loosen the skin and allow for easier peeling. When the pepper is cool, peel off the blackened skin, then slit the pepper lengthwise and remove the stem, seeds, and membranes. If you have a large number of peppers to roast or if you have an electric range, broil (grill) the peppers, turning as needed, until charred on all sides.

BLACK SALT Not a true sodium salt, but a sulfur compound or deposit, black salt has the taste and smell of boiled eggs with onions. The salt is mined from underground deposits in central India, Pakistan, and Afghanistan, where it is known as *kala namak*. It is brownish black in its natural form, hence the name. When ground, however—the form in which the salt is commonly sold—the crystals become light pink. It acts as both a flavor enhancer and appetite stimulant.

BOUQUET GARNI The classic bouquet garni includes only three herbs: fresh flat-leaf (Italian) parsley sprigs, fresh thyme sprigs, and bay leaves. When a recipe calls for a bouquet garni, use 3 large parsley sprigs, 2 large thyme sprigs, and 1 bay leaf. Lay the thyme and bay leaf on the parsley sprigs, "pleat" the parsley sprigs to hold the other herbs firmly in the center, tightly wind kitchen string around the whole packet, and then tie securely, leaving a tail of string to permit easy removal of the bundle from the dish. The sprigs must be fresh, as any mustiness will diminish the flavor.

BREAD, COARSE COUNTRY European-style country bread has a thick and chewy crust enveloping a tender and moist crumb. The classic loaf is white, but darker whole-wheat (wholemeal) versions are also sold. Seek out similar loaves at boutique bakeries, which usually label them country or peasant breads.

CAPERS Growing wild throughout the Mediterranean, the caper bush yields tiny gray-green buds that are preserved in salt or pickled in vinegar for a piquant seasoning.

CARDAMOM These pale green oval pods are about ½ inch (12 mm) long and contain up to 20 black seeds. When ground, they give off an intense camphorlike aroma and a sweet, lemony taste. The seeds lose flavor quickly, so buy them whole and remove, toast (see page 229), and grind as needed.

CASSIA LEAVES The leaves of the cassia tree, also known as Indian bay leaves, have a slightly clovelike aroma and flavor and are

available dried from Indian grocers. Despite their alternative name, they are not related to European bay leaves (*Laurus nobilis*). If cassia leaves are unavailable, the same quantity of European bay leaves may be used, although they will give a somewhat different taste.

CHAT MASALA In India, various saladlike snacks are known by the generic name *chat*, and *chat masala* (*masala* simply means "blend") is the tart and salty spice mixture commonly used. Every Indian cook has a favorite recipe, but *chat masala* typically contains cumin seeds, red pepper, black pepper, black salt, coarse salt, asafetida, and mango powder; the last gives the blend its sharp, tart flavor.

CHAYOTE A pear-shaped member of the squash family, the chayote, also known as the vegetable pear, mirliton, or christophene, has a mild, cucumber-like flavor. It comes in varieties with skin color ranging from a smooth-textured ivory to a prickly dark green.

CHICHARRONES Known in English as fried pork rinds, these are the crisp cracklings made from sheets of air-dried pork skin with just a paper-thin layer of fat. In Mexican markets, they are sold in huge sheets. The more widely available snack variety, sold as bite-sized pieces, may be used in most recipes.

CHILE OIL Chile oil is an infusion of fresh or dried hot red chiles in vegetable oil or sesame oil. The hot, flavored red oil is used sparingly as a condiment and seasoning and can be purchased from well-stocked markets.

CHILE PASTE, ROASTED This paste is made from red chiles, garlic, shallots, dried shrimp, dried shrimp paste, tamarind, brown sugar, salt, and vegetable oil. A variety of commercial pastes are available in Asian markets.

CHILES, DRIED Buy dried chiles with skins that are flexible rather than brittle in texture, and store them in airtight containers, away from both light and moisture.

ANCHO A dried form of the poblano, anchos measure 4½ inches (11.5 cm) long, with wide shoulders and wrinkled, deep reddish brown skin, and have a mild bittersweet chocolate flavor and a slight aroma of prunes.

ÁRBOL Smooth-skinned, bright reddish orange chile about 3 inches (7.5 cm) long, narrow in shape and fiery hot

CHIPOTLE The smoke-dried form of the ripened jalapeño, rich in flavor and very hot. Sold in its dried form, it is typically a leathery tan, although some varieties are a deep burgundy. It is available packed in a vinegar-tomato sauce (*chiles chipotles en adobo*) as well as lightly pickled (*en escabeche*)

PASILLA Skinny, wrinkled, raisin-black pasillas are about 6 inches (15 cm) long, with a sharp, fairly hot flavor.

To seed dried chiles, clean them with a damp cloth, then slit them lengthwise and use a small, sharp knife to remove the seeds.

To toast dried chiles, clean them with a damp cloth, then heat a heavy frying pan over medium heat. Add the whole or seeded chiles, press down firmly with a spatula, turn the chiles, and press down once more before removing. The chiles will change color only slightly and start to give off their aroma.

Caution The oils naturally present in chiles can cause a painful burning sensation when they come in contact with your eyes or other sensitive areas. After handling them, wash your hands thoroughly with warm, soapy water. If you have particularly sensitive skin, wear latex kitchen gloves or slip plastic bags over your hands before working with chiles.

CHILES, FRESH Choose firm, bright fresh chiles. Smaller chiles are usually hotter. Store them in the refrigerator for 1 week.

ANAHEIM This long, green, mild to moderately spicy chile is found in most markets. It is similar to the New Mexican chile variety.

GÜERO A pale yellow to light green chile. Several varieties may be used, including the Fresno, yellow banana, and Hungarian wax, which vary in degree of heat. Most are rather sweet with a pungent punch.

JALAPEÑO This popular chile, measuring 2–3 inches (5–7.5 cm) in length, has thick flesh and varies in degree of hotness. It is found in green and sweeter ripened red forms.

POBLANO Named for the Mexican state of Puebla, this moderately hot chile is usually about 5 inches (13 cm) long and is known for its polished deep green skin.

SERRANO Slender chiles measuring 1–2 inches (2.5–5 cm) long that are very hot, with a brightly acidic flavor. Available in both green and ripened red forms at most markets.

To roast, peel, and seed fresh chiles, using tongs, hold a whole chile over the flame of a gas burner for 10–15 minutes (5–8 minutes for smaller chiles), turning it to char the skin evenly. Place in a bowl, cover, and leave for 10 minutes. The steam will loosen the skin and allow for easier peeling. When the chile is cool, peel off the blackened skin, then slit the chile lengthwise and remove the stem, seeds, and membranes. If you have a large number of chiles to roast or if you have an electric range, broil (grill) the chiles, turning as needed, until charred on all sides.

CINNAMON BARK, TRUE *Canela,* the flaky, aromatic bark of a laurel tree native to Sri Lanka, is true cinnamon. The paper-thin inner layer of the bark is stripped from the trees and then rolled into cylinders about ½ inch (12 mm) in diameter. The cinnamon sticks commonly found in stores and called for in recipes are about 3 inches (7.5 cm) long. Cassia, a close relative of cinnamon, has a coarser texture and comes from the bark of a variety of Asian laurel tree. Its flavor is similar, but stronger and more astringent. Products labeled "cinnamon" in the United States and Europe are usually cassia, but in many countries, the two are interchangeable.

COCONUT CREAM AND COCONUT MILK Coconut cream and coconut milk are both derived from an infusion of grated coconut flesh in water or, less commonly, milk. (They are not to be confused with the clear juice inside the whole nut.) The first infusion yields coconut cream, a thick liquid with a high fat content. If the same batch of coconut is steeped again, the resulting liquid is called coconut milk. A third steeping produces thin coconut milk. Freshly grated coconut gives the best results, but commercially packaged, unsweetened coconut can also be used. Good-quality unsweetened canned coconut milk is a welcome shortcut when time is at a premium. Do not shake the can before opening. Once it is open, first scrape off the thick mass on top, which is the cream. The next layer is opaque white coconut milk, and finally there is a clear liquid, which is thin coconut milk. It can be found in well-stocked grocery stores.

CRAB, FRESH To clean a freshly cooked crab, hold the top shell of the crab in one hand while grasping the legs and claws with the other hand. Gently twist and pull away the shell. Turn the crab's body over and twist off and discard the triangular apron. Pull off and discard the feathery gills, then cut out the mandibles at the face end. Gently bend each leg and claw backward and twist them free from the body. Spoon out the creamy yellow tomalley and reserve it for another use, if desired. Rinse the body and pat dry with paper towels. Using a cleaver, chop the body into quarters. Crack each leg and claw at the joint with a mallet. To extract the crabmeat, pick it out from the body and legs.

CREMA Although *crema* translates simply as "cream," Mexican *crema* is a thick, rich, slightly soured product that can be found in jars in grocery stores specializing in Latin American products. In its place, you can use the more widely available French *crème fraîche,* which is similar in consistency. An adequate substitute may be made by thinning commercial sour cream slightly with whole milk or half-and-half (half cream).

To make crema, in a small nonaluminum bowl, stir together 1 cup (8 fl oz/250 ml) heavy (double) cream (do not use an ultrapasteurized product) and 1 tablespoon buttermilk or good-quality plain yogurt with active cultures. Cover with plastic wrap, poke a few holes in the plastic, and leave at warm room temperature (about 85°F/30°C) until well thickened, 8–24 hours. Stir, cover with fresh plastic wrap, and refrigerate until firm and well chilled, about 6 hours. If the *crema* becomes too thick, thin with a little whole milk or half-and-half (half cream).

CRÈME FRAÎCHE Thick enough to spread when chilled, but fluid enough to pour at room temperature, this tangy, fresh cream is a popular enrichment for sauces and soups.

CURRY LEAVES These small leaves of a tropical shrub are used whole, fresh or dried, to add aromatic flavor. They are also sometimes pounded to a powder. Bay leaves may be substituted, although their perfume differs.

CURRY POWDER Contrary to popular belief, it is not a single spice but a mixture of spices that

make up curry powder. The Western-style curry powder that is stocked on supermarket shelves bears little resemblance to the carefully blended, personalized mixtures that Indian cooks favor. The ingredients and their proportions vary between dishes, region, and individual cooks, but usually include a mixture of coriander seeds, brown mustard seeds, fenugreek seeds, black peppercorns, cumin seeds, whole cloves, dried red chiles, roasted chickpeas (garbanzo beans), and turmeric.

EGG, RAW Eggs are sometimes used raw or partially cooked in sauces, dressings, soups and preparations such as aioli. These eggs run the risk of being infected with salmonella or other bacteria, which can lead to food poisoning. This risk is of most concern to small children, older people, pregnant women, and anyone with a compromised immune system. If you have health or safety concerns, do not consume raw or partially cooked eggs.

FAVA BEANS Slipped from their large, puffy green pods, fresh fava beans, also known as broad beans, have a nutty, slightly bitter flavor and a dense texture. Fresh and dried fava beans are markedly different in flavor and should not be substituted for each other. With the exception of the first of the spring crop, favas require peeling, as the thin skin covering each bean can be tough and bitter.

To prepare fresh fava beans, split the pods with your fingers and remove the beans. To peel them easily, blanch the shelled beans in boiling water for about 30 seconds. Drain, cool slightly under cold water, and then simply pinch each bean to slip it from its skin.

FENUGREEK Both the leaves and the seeds of the fenugreek are used for cooking. They have different flavors and aromas, however, so are not interchangeable. The golden-brown, small, nuggety seeds have a maple syrup–like aroma and a bitter flavor, both of which are intensified by roasting. If the seeds are over-roasted, or added with too generous a hand, they can become unpleasantly bitter and overpower other flavors. The leaves, either fresh or dried, are used in pickles, breads, and especially vegetarian dishes.

FISH SAUCE In many Southeast Asian kitchens, fish sauce assumes the same seasoning role played by soy sauce throughout Chinese and

Japanese cuisine. Made by layering anchovies or other tiny fish with salt in barrels or jars and leaving them to ferment, the dark amber liquid adds a pungent, salty flavor. Two common types are Vietnamese *nuoc mam* and Thai *nam pla*; the latter has a milder flavor.

FUNGI, DRIED BLACK Sold fresh or dried in Asian stores, black fungi are also known as wood ear fungi (larger, thicker tree fungi) and cloud ear fungi (smaller, dark, curled fungi). Dried black fungus is sold whole, in pieces of approximately 2 inches (5 cm) square, or shredded. It must be soaked to soften, and any woody root sections should be trimmed off before use. Store in an airtight container for many months. Fresh fungus should be used within 3 to 4 days of purchase.

GALANGAL Similar in appearance to ginger, to which it is related, this gnarled rhizome has a mustardlike flavor. It is available fresh and frozen whole and as dried slices. If only the dried form can be found, use half the quantity you would for fresh. Reconstitute dried galangal by soaking it in warm water for 30 minutes until pliable.

GARAM MASALA This keynote spice mixture of northern India also turns up in Southeast Asian kitchens. The blend—sold commercially or made at home—almost always features coriander seeds, cumin, cardamom, cloves, black pepper, cinnamon, nutmeg, and mace. It is typically used to season dishes at the beginning of cooking and is sometimes sprinkled over finished dishes.

GHEE Used throughout Indian cooking, *ghee* literally means "fat." There are two types: *usli ghee* (clarified butter) and *vanaspati ghee* (vegetable shortening). A recipe that calls simply for ghee is understood to mean *usli ghee*. Indian clarified butter differs from the European equivalent in having been simmered until all the moisture is removed from the milk solids and the fat is amber colored. This gives *usli ghee* its unique nutty taste. Clarification also increases the butter's storage life. *Vanaspati ghee* is a pale yellow, hydrogenated blend of various vegetable oils that is processed to look, smell, and taste very similar to *usli ghee*. Both are readily available; *usli ghee* can also be easily made at home.

To make *usli ghee*, heat ½ lb (250 g) butter in a pan over medium-low heat, uncovered, until it melts. Increase the heat to medium and simmer the butter, stirring often, until the clear fat separates from the milk solids, about 15 minutes. During this process a layer of foam will rise to the top of the butter and the butter will crackle as its milk solids lose moisture. When the milk solids lose all moisture, the fat as well as the milk residue will turn amber colored. When this occurs, remove the pan from the heat and let the residue settle on the bottom. When cool enough to handle, pour the clear fat, which is the *usli ghee*, into a jar, ensuring that no residue gets in. Alternatively, strain it through two layers of cheesecloth (muslin). Discard the residue. *Usli ghee* may be refrigerated, covered, for up to 6 months or frozen for up to 12 months. Allow to thaw before use. Makes ¾ cup (6 fl oz/180 ml) *usli ghee*.

GINGER The edible root or rhizome of ginger is buff colored and smooth when young, and sometimes comes with slender, pink-tipped green shoots attached. When older, root ginger becomes a dull, deep buff color with slightly wrinkled skin; its flavor intensifies and the flesh becomes fibrous. It is peeled and grated, minced, sliced, or chopped for use as a flavoring of unique taste and appealing spiciness. Dried powdered ginger is not a suitable substitute; however, processed ginger products packed in brine or vinegar may be appropriate substitutes, if rinsed first.

To make ginger juice, peel and finely grate fresh root ginger onto a piece of fine cloth, gather up into a ball, and squeeze to extract the juice. The pulp can be discarded or used in a soup or stir-fry. One tablespoon of grated ginger will produce about 1½ teaspoons of ginger juice. Ginger wine is a seasoning and marinade made by combining 1 part ginger juice with 2–3 parts rice wine.

HERBS

BASIL This sweet and spicy fresh herb is especially popular in the cooking of Italy and the south of France. It pairs perfectly with sun-ripened tomatoes.

BASIL, THAI Three types of basil are used in Thailand: *kraprow*, *maenglak*, and *horapa*. *Kraprow* has serrated green leaves with a tint of purple and a hint of anise flavor overlaying the familiar basil scent. *Maenglak*, also known as lemon basil, has smaller leaves and a lemony scent. *Horapa* has purple stems, shiny leaves, and an anise aroma. All three can be used interchangeably, or European sweet basil can be substituted.

CHIVE This thin green shoot of a member of the onion family is used fresh to add a hint of onion flavor to salads and mild-tasting ingredients such as eggs, cheeses, seafood, and poultry.

CILANTRO This lacy-leafed annual herb, also known as fresh coriander, has a fresh, assertive scent and bright, astringent flavor—an acquired taste for some. Cilantro leaves should be added at the end of the cooking time or used raw, as long cooking destroys their delicate flavor.

DILL This feathery, grassy-tasting herb is often used to season vinegars and pickling brines. It is often used to flavor cucumber salads.

EPAZOTE This distinctly flavored, pungent herb is used frequently in Mexican dishes, especially with black beans. It can be hard to find outside Mexico, but fresh bunches can be found in Latin American markets.

KAFFIR LIME LEAVES The kaffir lime contributes its rich, citrusy flavor to curry pastes and other savory and sweet dishes through its dried, fresh, or frozen leaves and its gnarled rind. Its juice, however, is not used. Pesticide-free lemon or lime leaves may be substituted.

MINT More than 600 different types of mint exist, although peppermint and spearmint are the most common. Mint is typically used as an accompaniment to lamb and as a salad-like garnish (often in combination with Thai basil and cilantro) to many Thai and Vietnamese dishes. Fresh mint leaves are also infused in hot water to make an herbal tea.

OREGANO Related to mint and thyme, this strongly scented herb actually gains in flavor from drying, unlike most herbs. It is added to many sauces and marinades.

OREGANO, MEXICAN Although similar in flavor to the more familiar Mediterranean oregano, Mexican oregano is more pungent and less sweet than its Mediterranean kin, making it a perfect match for spicy, cumin-laden dishes. Add it at the beginning of cooking to allow time for its complex flavor to emerge and meld with others. Purchase small packets of the dried herb in Latin American markets.

PARSLEY Southern European in origin, this widely versatile herb adds its bright, fresh flavor to many different kinds of savory foods. The flat-leaf variety, also known as Italian parsley, has a more pronounced flavor than the curly type, which is used predominantly as a garnish.

POLYGONUM LEAVES Known also as Vietnamese mint and in Malaysia as *laksa leaves* or *daun kesom*, these slender green-and-purple leaves have an exotic, herbaceous flavor. They are added fresh to noodle dishes in Malaysia and to salads in Laos, Thailand, and Vietnam, where they are called *rau ram*.

ROSEMARY Taking its name from the Latin for "rose of the sea," this spiky evergreen shrub thrives in Mediterranean climates. Its highly aromatic, piney flavor goes well with lamb and poultry, as well as with tomatoes and other vegetables.

SAGE Sharply fragrant, with traces of both bitterness and sweetness, this gray-green herb is often used to season pork and veal.

TARRAGON Native to Siberia, this heady, anise-flavored herb can perfume wine vinegar and Dijon mustards, flavor sauces and dressings, and season seafood, poultry, and eggs.

THYME This low-growing, aromatic herb grows wild throughout the Mediterranean, and often flavors food without the cook's help, as game birds and wild rabbits like to feed upon it. A key element of many slow-cooked savory dishes, it is considered a digestive aid and is often used to season rich meats such as mutton, pork, duck, and goose.

JICAMA Sold year-round in most markets, this large, brown-skinned tuber, also called a yam bean, has a refreshingly crisp, mild white flesh that is most often eaten raw, usually in salads. Before serving or using in a recipe, carefully peel away the thick layer of skin and the fibrous layer beneath it.

KARI LEAVES These small, shiny, highly aromatic leaves come from the kari tree, native to southern India and Sri Lanka. Although sometimes called curry leaves and used in curries, they bear no relation to curry powder and are not interchangeable with it. Rather, both their flavor and aroma are citrusy, as befits a member of the citrus family. Kari leaves are available in Indian grocery stores.

Fresh leaves have the best flavor, but dried are usually more easily found and may be substituted: Use double the quantity of dried leaves as for fresh. If kari leaves are not available, substitute 2 teaspoons minced fresh flat-leaf (Italian) parsley and 1 teaspoon grated lemon zest for every 20 kari leaves.

LEMONGRASS This stiff, reedlike grass has an intensely aromatic, citrusy flavor that is one of the signatures of Southeast Asian cooking. Use only fresh lemongrass, as it lacks good flavor when dried. Lemon zest, often mentioned as a substitute, can play its role but in no way equals its impact.

To prepare lemongrass, if a recipe calls for the tender midsection of a stalk, use only its bottom 4–6 inches (10–15 cm). Peel off any tough outer layers of the stalk to reveal the inner purple ring. To release the aromatic oils, smash or chop the stalk before use.

MANGO Native to India, the mango thrives in tropical climates, and its many varieties are enjoyed as a refreshing breakfast food, dessert, or snack. Canned mango is a popular flavoring for ice creams and other sweets. To avoid any mess when preparing the fresh fruit for use in a recipe, cut and peel it in the following manner.

To prepare a mango, place it horizontally on a cutting board and make a slice that is slightly off-center, cutting off the flesh from one side of the flat pit in a single piece. Repeat on the other side. Hold each slice, cut side up, and score the flesh lengthwise to make slices. Then, if desired, score crosswise in a lattice pattern, creating cubes of the dimension called for in a particular recipe. Do not cut through the peel. Press against the skin side of the peel to invert the slice, then carefully slice the flesh from the peel. Place the fruit in a nonreactive bowl. Cut the remaining skin from around the pit, cut away any flesh, and use as directed in the recipe.

NUOC CHAM Every Vietnamese cook has his or her recipe for *nuoc cham*, a sauce eaten with nearly every meal and snack. Adjust the ingredient amounts to suit your taste.

To make *nuoc cham*, in a mortar, using a pestle, pound together 1 large clove garlic and 1 fresh, seeded red chile until the mixture is puréed (or pass the garlic clove through a garlic press). Stir in ¼ cup (2 fl oz/60 ml) fresh

lime juice, 5 tablespoons (2⅓ fl oz/75 ml) fish sauce, 6 tablespoons (3 fl oz/90 ml) water, and 3 tablespoons sugar. Pour into a dipping saucer, add 2 tablespoons grated carrot, and serve as directed. Any leftover sauce should be refrigerated in a tightly covered container.

NUTS When purchasing nuts, seek out only those that are free of cracks, holes, and discoloration. To make sure the nutmeat is not dried out inside, shake the shells.

ALMONDS These oval nuts are the meat found inside the pit of a dried fruit related to the peach—which is why almonds pair so well with peaches and other stone fruits like cherries and plums. Almonds are delicate and fragrant and have a smooth texture. They are sold unblanched, with their natural brown skins intact, and blanched, with the skins removed to reveal their light ivory color.

To blanch and peel almonds, put the shelled nuts in a heatproof bowl and pour boiling water over them. Let stand for about 1 minute, then drain the nuts in a colander and rinse with cold running water to cool. Pinch each almond to slip off its bitter skin.

CASHEWS Cashew trees measure up to 40 feet (12 m) in height and produce fruits called cashew apples (although actually pear shaped), inside of which the nut grows. When the fruits ripen, the nuts protrude from the end of them. The shells of the nuts contain an acidic, oily substance that can burn and blister the skin but which is neutralized by heating.

HAZELNUTS Also known as filberts, grape-sized hazelnuts have very hard shells that come to a point and resemble an acorn, cream-colored flesh, and a sweet, rich, buttery flavor. They can be difficult to crack, so they are usually sold already shelled.

To remove the skin from hazelnuts, while they are still warm from toasting, transfer the nuts to a thick, clean kitchen towel. Wrap the towel around them and rub them briskly to remove their skin. Gather the hazelnuts up carefully with your hands, leaving behind as much of the loose skin as you can.

PEANUTS Not really a nut at all, but rather a type of legume that grows underground, peanuts are seeds nestled inside pods that become thin and brittle when dried.

PECANS Native to North America, the pecan has two deeply crinkled lobes of nutmeat, much like its relative the walnut. The nuts have smooth, brown, oval shells that break easily. Their flavor is sweeter and more delicate than that of walnuts.

PINE NUTS Umbrella-shaped stone pines grow throughout the Mediterranean, and their long, slender seeds (also called pignoli) are high in oil and delicately flavored. As with all nuts, a gentle toasting enhances their flavor.

PISTACHIOS Pistachios have thin, very hard, rounded outer shells that are naturally creamy tan in color but are sometimes dyed bright red. As the nuts ripen, their shells crack to reveal light green kernels.

WALNUTS The furrowed, double-lobed nutmeat of the walnut has an assertive, rich flavor. The most common type is the English walnut, also known as the Persian walnut, which has a light brown shell that cracks easily. Black walnuts have a stronger flavor and tougher shells but can be hard to find.

To toast nuts, spread them on a baking sheet and toast in a 325°F (165°C) oven until they are fragrant and take on a golden color, 10–20 minutes; the timing depends on the type of nut and the size of the nut or nut pieces. Stir once or twice to cook evenly. Remove from the oven and immediately pour onto a plate, as they will continue to darken if left on the hot pan. Toast small amounts of nuts in a frying pan over medium-low heat, stirring frequently, until fragrant and golden.

ORANGE JUICE, FRESH BITTER The aromatic bitter oranges of Mexico's Yucatán province are seldom found outside their native region. When a recipe calls for their juice, look for Seville oranges, which also have a thick, wrinkled peel, or approximate the taste with a mixture of 1 part regular orange juice, 2 parts lime juice, and 1 part grapefruit juice. To intensify the flavor, add a bit of finely grated grapefruit zest.

PANCETTA A form of unsmoked Italian bacon, this long, flat cut of fatty pork belly is first seasoned with black pepper and sometimes garlic, cinnamon, and nutmeg, then rolled up tightly and salt-cured.

PARMESAN The king of cheese, Parmesan is fashioned into large wheels and aged for 1 to 3 years to develop a complex, nutty flavor and dry, granular texture. "Parmigiano-Reggiano" stenciled on the rind ensures that the cheese is a true Parmesan made in Emilia-Romagna. Grana padano, a hard grating cheese,

resembles Parmigiano-Reggiano and is often used in its place.

PLANTAIN Closely related to the banana, the large plantain, or *plátano,* is starchier and firmer. It is always cooked before eating. Fresh plantains have almost uniformly black skins when they are ripe.

POLENTA Both cornmeal and the thick, porridgelike dish made from it, polenta is endlessly versatile. Soft polenta serves as a base for a hearty sauce, an accompaniment to roast meat or poultry, or a simple meal on its own with a swirl of Gorgonzola cheese. It can be used as a thickening agent in soups.

POZOLE The Mexican term for hominy, *pozole* (posole in English) is commercially made by first boiling dried field corn with calcium hydroxide (powdered lime) to dissolve its tough hull. The resulting grain is simmered until tender to make a foundation for robust soups of the same name, usually containing pork and chile, or to add to the tripe stew known as *menudo.* In Mexican markets, *pozole* is also sold freshly cooked or frozen. Canned white hominy may be used, although it lacks the rich aroma and chewier texture of the other forms.

PRAHOK A popular Camobodian seasoning sold in jars, this fish paste is more easily used if an extract is made from it.

To prepare prahok juice, put ¼ cup (2 fl oz/60 ml) of the fermented fish (including the fish meat) into a saucepan with 1 cup (8 fl oz/250 ml) water and bring to a boil over high heat. Reduce the heat and simmer uncovered, stirring once or twice, for 20 mintues. Pour through a sieve placed over a bowl, pressing against the solids to extract as much liquid as possible. Discard the solids. Refrigerate the liquid in a covered jar for up to 2 weeks. Makes about 1 cup (8 fl oz/250 ml).

PUMPKIN SEEDS Mexican cooks have long ground the hulled seeds of various pumpkins and other hard-shelled winter squashes for use as thickening agents in sauces. Whole hulled seeds may also be eaten as a snack or used as an ingredient.

To toast pumpkin seeds, spread them in a dry frying pan over medium heat and cook, stirring constantly, until they just begin to

darken. Transfer to a heat-resistant dish to cool; the seeds will continue to darken slightly from the residual heat. Use as directed.

QUESO FRESCO Fresh Mexican cheeses, or *quesos frescos,* are soft, tangy, lightly salted cow's milk cheeses that are crumbled or sliced to add richness and piquant creaminess. When aged, it becomes *queso añejo,* a tangy, dry cheese that is usually grated before use.

RADICCHIO Pleasantly astringent, bitter, and crisp, this member of the chicory family may be found in various forms. The most familiar type is a compact, round head of white-ribbed burgundy leaves. In late autumn, markets offer the less bitter Treviso variety, which has spearlike purple leaves the shape of romaine (cos) lettuce leaves.

RICE WINE Rice wine (*liaojiu*) adds flavor in Chinese cooking, and works as a tenderizer and seasoning in marinades. Rice wine can be purchased at most Asian food stores. Those labeled "cooking wine" may contain 5 percent added salt, so check labels before seasoning a dish. Dry sherry is a substitute in most recipes, while Japanese mirin is the alternative choice when a mild, aromatic wine is required.

SAFFRON Taking its name from the Arabic for "yellow," this rare and costly spice is the dried stigmas of a purple crocus flower, *Crocus sativa.* The best form to buy is saffron threads, the actual whole dried stigmas. Before the threads are added to a dish, they are generally treated in one of two ways to release their maximum flavor and aroma: slowly toasted in a dry pan over low heat, or lightly crushed and then steeped for a few minutes in a warm liquid such as wine, stock, milk, or water.

SALT Some cooks contend that the iodine added to common table salt clouds stocks and clear sauces, and that the salt's fine grains lack the texture and depth of flavor of sea salt or kosher salt. Sea salt, gathered from evaporated seawater, retains small amounts of naturally occurring minerals, and it often carries a slight tint of gray or pink from these minerals. Available in both fine and coarse crystals, sea salt is excellent used in cooking. Sprinkling it over dishes just before serving allows diners to appreciate its complex flavor. Kosher salt was originally developed for the preparation of kosher meats, but its flat, coarse grains dissolve quickly, an often-desirable quality.

SALT COD, BONELESS This strong, briny-tasting, tender fish must be soaked in cold water to reduce its saltiness before use. Be sure to use filleted salt cod.

To rehydrate salt cod, immerse the fish in a bowl of cold water. Cover and refrigerate, changing the water 4–6 times, for 24–36 hours. The soaking time will depend upon how heavily salted and how thick the cod is. When ready, the fish will be puffy and lighter in color. Drain and proceed as directed in the recipe.

SAUSAGES, FRESH ITALIAN A variety of fresh pork sausages are made throughout Italy, ranging from the sweet sausages of Emilia-Romagna, to the coriander-spiked links from Lazio, to Calabria's fiery-hot *peperoncini*-seasoned type, to Mantua's simple *luganega*, seasoned merely with salt and pepper.

SHALLOTS AND PICKLED SHALLOTS Covered in amber-colored, papery skins, small, mild-flavored shallots are used as a flavoring base for dishes in many different cuisines. Asian markets also carry jarred pickled shallots, which have been packed in a vinegar brine.

SOY SAUCE Typically made by fermenting and aging soybeans along with wheat, salt, and water, soy sauce is an indispensable seasoning in kitchens in China and, to a far lesser degree, in Southeast Asia. Dark soy sauce gains its dark color, thicker consistency, and edge of sweetness from the addition of caramel. Light soy sauce has a thinner consistency and a lighter flavor. Japanese soy sauces tend to be milder tasting, slightly sweeter, and less salty than Chinese varieties.

SPICES, TOASTING To toast whole spices, use a dry (ungreased) cast-iron frying pan over medium low heat. Add the spice and toast it, stirring frequently, until it exudes a heady bouquet and turns a shade or two darker. Depending upon the spice, this may take anywhere from 1–5 minutes. While the spice is still warm, transfer it to a mortar or spice grinder and pound or grind to a fine powder.

SQUASH BLOSSOMS With their delicate flavor and vivid color, the yellow blossoms of native Mexican squashes may be stuffed or rolled or chopped and used as fillings. Harvest them from your own garden or buy them at farmers' markets. The blossoms should be freshly picked early in the morning, just before they open. Most gardeners take only the male flowers, leaving the rest to develop into mature squash.

SQUID Many seafood merchants sell squid already cleaned and ready to cook. If you need to clean squid yourself, begin by cutting off the tentacles just above the eyes. Grab the tentacles at their base and squeeze to pop out the squid's beak, discarding it. Rinse the tentacles well under running cold water. With your finger, pull out and discard the clear quill (rudimentary shell) from the body, then rinse the body well, discarding all the entrails. Cut as directed in the recipe.

SRIRACHA Named for the seaside Thai town in which it originated, this bottled, hot or mild, sweet-tart, all-purpose sauce is made from red chiles and resembles a light-colored ketchup. Keep in mind that even the so-called mild version is still quite hot.

TAMARIND AND TAMARIND WATER The sweet-sour pulp from the seedpods of this tree native to India is a popular flavoring. Tamarinds are also known as Indian dates. The brown seedpods resemble fava (broad) bean pods. Tamarind paste and concentrate are also available. Tamarind pulp is sold in block form in most well-stocked Asian markets.

To make tamarind water, cut up ¾ pound (375 g) tamarind pulp into small pieces, place in a bowl, and add 2 cups (24 fl oz/750 ml) boiling water. Mash the pulp to separate the fibers and seeds, then let stand for 15 minutes, stirring 2 or 3 times. Pour the liquid through a fine-mesh sieve placed over a bowl, pushing against the pulp with the back of a spoon and scraping the underside of the sieve to dislodge the clinging purée. Use as directed or transfer to a jar and refrigerate for up to 4 days or freeze in an ice-cube tray for up to 1 month. Tamarind concentrate dissolved in hot water can be subsitituted.

TOMATILLOS Resembling small, unripened green tomatoes, these fruits are actually members of the gooseberry family. They have a bracing, stringent flavor and tomatolike texture that is often featured in fresh and cooked salsas as well as in stews. The fruits are found fresh and are also available canned. Fresh tomatillos come encased in their parchmentlike calyx, which must be removed before using.

VINEGAR, BALSAMIC While vinegar is most commonly made from red or white wine, Italy's most renowned vinegar, *aceto balsamico*, or "balsamic vinegar," is based on white grape juice that is reduced by boiling it down to a thick syrup, or must, then aged for many years in a succession of ever-smaller barrels made of different woods, each of which contributes its own taste to the final syrupy, sharp-and-sweet product. Rare and expensive, true *aceto balsamico* is used sparely as a condiment, a few drops at a time, often over Parmesan cheese or ripe strawberries. More commonly available balsamic vinegar, appropriate for cooking or salad dressings, is made from a mixture of wine vinegar, must, and caramel coloring.

VINEGAR, BLACK Black (also labeled brown) vinegar, dark colored and subtly flavored, is distilled from rice. Balsamic vinegar can be used to replace black vinegar.

VINEGAR, PINEAPPLE Pineapple is a common source for a mild commercial vinegar favored in Mexico. If you cannot find it, use equal amounts of apple cider vinegar, water, and rice vinegar.

INDEX

ACKNOWLEDGMENTS

Weldon Owen wishes to thank the following people for their generous support in producing this book: Desne Ahlers, Heather Belt, Ken DellaPenta, Lucie Parker, and Sharron Wood.

CREDITS

Recipe photography by Noel Barnhurst, except for the following by Andre Martin: Pages 70, 72, 78, 80, 81, 87, 91, 96, 102, 104, 107, 109.

Travel photography by Maren Caruso: ©Page 13; Robin Bachtler Cushman: ©Page 12 (bottom); Michael Freeman: Pages 6 (bottom), 66 (top and bottom), 67; R. Ian Lloyd: ©Page 68; Jason Lowe: Pages 6 (top), 9 (left and right), 64–65, 69 (left and right), 114 (top and bottom), 115, 116, 117 (left and right), 148–149, 151, 152; Stephen Rothfeld: Pages 4 (right), 7, 15 (right), 112–113, 150 (top and bottom), 153 (left and right), 184–185, 186 (top and bottom), 187, 188, 189 (left and right); Ignacio Urquiza: Pages 5 (left), 8, 12 (top), 14, 15 (left), 220; Rachel Weill: ©Pages 10–11.

Recipes and sidebars by Georgeanne Brennan: Pages 118, 120, 122, 127, 129, 138, 139, 142, 143; Kerri Conan: Pages 31, 33; Lori de Mori: Pages 155, 157, 163, 165, 166, 168, 169, 174, 175, 178, 180, 181, 182, 183; Abigail Johnson Dodge: Pages 27, 48, 62; Janet Fletcher: Pages 17, 26, 49; Joyce Goldstein: Pages 191, 192, 193, 194, 196, 197, 198, 200, 201, 203, 204, 206, 207, 208, 210, 211, 212, 213, 214, 217, 218, 219; Diane Holuigue: Pages 121, 124, 125, 126, 130, 131, 132, 133, 135, 136, 137, 140, 145, 146; Joyce Jue: Pages 73, 74, 77, 82, 85, 88, 90, 92, 93, 95, 98, 99, 100, 103, 108, 111; Michael McLaughlin: Pages 32, 42, 43; Cynthia Nims: Page 59; Ray Overton: Pages 38, 39; Jacki Passmore: Pages 71, 72, 106, 109; Julie Sahni: Pages 78, 79, 80, 81, 86, 87, 91, 96, 97, 102, 105; Michele Scicolone: Pages 156, 158, 159, 161, 162, 167, 170, 172, 173, 176, 179; Marilyn Tausend: Pages 18, 19, 20, 21, 22, 24, 25, 28, 29, 34, 36, 37, 41, 44, 45, 46, 47, 50, 51, 52, 54, 55, 56, 57, 60, 61.

Page 4 (right): The Trevi Fountain, Rome's largest, depicts Neptune flanked on either side by Tritons, one attempting to control a bucking seahorse and the other leading a more placid animal. Page 5 (left): A waiter at the Morelia's Villa Montaña Hotel in Mexico, prepares for dinner service. Page 220: A Porfidio tequila plant in Puerto Vallarta exports its 100 percent blue agave tequila in bottles containing miniature glass cacti.

Cover: Onion Soup with Maytag Croutons, page 31

Oxmoor
House.

OXMOOR HOUSE INC.

Oxmoor House books are distributed by Sunset Books
80 Willow Road, Menlo Park, CA 94025
Telephone: 650-321-3600 Fax: 650-324-1532
Vice President/General Manager Rich Smeby
National Accounts Manager/Special Sales Brad Moses
Oxmoor House and Sunset Books are divisions of
Southern Progress Corporation

WILLIAMS-SONOMA

Founder and Vice-Chairman Chuck Williams

THE SAVORING SERIES

Conceived and produced by Weldon Owen Inc.
814 Montgomery Street, San Francisco, CA 94133
Telephone: 415 291 0100 Fax: 415 291 8841

In collaboration with Williams-Sonoma, Inc.
3250 Van Ness Avenue, San Francisco, CA 94109

A WELDON OWEN PRODUCTION

Copyright © 2006 by Weldon Owen Inc. and Williams-Sonoma Inc.
All rights reserved, including the right of reproduction in whole or in
part in any form.

Set in Minion and Myriad.
Color separations by Bright Arts in Singapore.
Printed and bound by Tien Wah Press in Singapore.

First printed in 2006.
10 9 8 7 6 5 4 3 2 1

Library of Congress Cataloging-in-Publication data is available.
ISBN: 0-8487-3127-1

First published in the USA by Time-Life Custom Publishing
Originally published as Williams-Sonoma Savoring:
Savoring France (© 1999 Weldon Owen Inc.)
Savoring Italy (© 1999 Weldon Owen Inc.)
Savoring Southeast Asia (© 2000 Weldon Owen Inc.)
Savoring Spain & Portugal (© 2000 Weldon Owen Inc.)
Savoring India (© 2001 Weldon Owen Inc.)
Savoring Mexico (© 2001 Weldon Owen Inc.)
Savoring Tuscany (© 2001 Weldon Owen Inc.)
Savoring America (© 2002 Weldon Owen Inc.)
Savoring Provence (© 2002 Weldon Owen Inc.)
Savoring China (© 2003 Weldon Owen Inc.)

WELDON OWEN INC.

Chief Executive Officer John Owen
President and Chief Operating Officer Terry Newell
Chief Financial Officer Christine E. Munson
Vice President International Sales Stuart Laurence
Creative Director Gaye Allen
Publisher Hannah Rahill

Senior Editor Kim Goodfriend
Assistant Editor Juli Vendzules

Designer Rachel Lopez

Production Director Chris Hemesath
Color Manager Teri Bell
Production and Reprint Coordinator Todd Rechner

Food Stylists George Dolese, Sally Parker
Illustrations Marlene McLoughlin
Text Stephanie Rosenbaum

A NOTE ON WEIGHTS AND MEASURES

All recipes include customary U.S. and metric measurements. Metric
conversions are based on a standard developed for these books and
have been rounded off. Actual weights may vary.